AF412047

NON-STATE ACTORS IN INTERNATIONAL RELATIONS

Manchester University Press

SERIES EDITORS: THOMAS CHRISTIANSEN AND EMIL KIRCHNER

Anne-Marie Le Gloannec
EDITOR

NON-STATE ACTORS IN INTERNATIONAL RELATIONS

The Case of Germany

MANCHESTER UNIVERSITY PRESS
Manchester and New York

distributed exclusively in the USA by Palgrave

Published by Manchester University Press
Oxford Road, Manchester M13 9NR, UK
and Room 400, 175 Fifth Avenue, New York, NY 10010, USA
www.manchesteruniversitypress.co.uk

Distributed exclusively in the USA by
Palgrave, 175 Fifth Avenue, New York,
NY 10010, USA

Distributed exclusively in Canada by
UBC Press, University of British Columbia, 2029 West Mall,
Vancouver, BC, Canada V6T 1Z2

British Library Cataloguing-in-Publication Data
A catalogue record for this book is available from the British Library

Library of Congress Cataloging-in-Publication Data applied for

ISBN 0 7190 7416 9 *hardback*
EAN 978 0 7190 7416 5

First published 2007

16 15 14 13 12 11 10 09 08 07   10 9 8 7 6 5 4 3 2 1

Typeset in Minion
by Servis Filmsetting Limited, Manchester
Printed in Great Britain
by Bell & Bain Ltd, Glasgow

CONTENTS

Katharina Bluhm is Assistant Professor at the Friedrich-Schiller Universität, Institut für Soziologie, Jena. Her research fields include economic and organizational sociology, transition in CEE, MNCs, institutional change, and labor politics.

Tanja A. Börzel is Professor of Political Science and holds the Chair of European Integration at the Free University of Berlin. Her current research projects are on compliance with EU norms and rules in member states, accession countries, and neighborhood countries.

Fabienne Boudier-Bensebaa is Assistant Professor at the University of Paris XII – Val de Marne. Her research fields include international economics and the economics of transitions with Germany and CEECs.

Dorota Dakowska is Lecturer in Political Science at the Robert Schuman University in Strasburg. She is working on political foundations and think tanks in Europe, on the EU enlargement and dealing with the Communist past in Poland.

Lily Gardner Feldman is Senior Fellow at the American Institute for Contemporary German Studies, The Johns Hopkins University, where she works on German foreign policy, on international reconciliation, and on German–Jewish relations.

Charlie Jeffery is Professor of Politics at the School of Social and Political Studies, University of Edinburgh, UK, and directs the UK ESRC research program on Devolution and Constitutional Change. He works on comparative regional politics and multi-level governance in the EU.

Anne-Marie Le Gloannec is a Senior Research Fellow with CERI, Fondation Nationale des Sciences Politiques, Paris. She has written extensively on Germany, the German state and German foreign policy. She is currently working on a book on European foreign policy.

Gilles Lepesant is a Research Fellow at CNRS, TIDE, Maison des Sciences de l'Homme de l'Aquitaine, Bordeaux. His research area focuses on the economic and political geography of CEE.

Soledad Loaeza is a Research Professor at El Colegio de México, Mexico DF. She has extensively written on political institutions and processes in Mexico.

Sabine Saurugger is Professor of Politics at the Institut d'Etudes Politiques, Grenoble, and is editor of *Politique européenne*. Her current work concentrates on interest group participation in democratic political systems and associative democracy.

Elsa Tulmets is a Research Fellow with the Institute of International Relations (IIR), and lecturer at Charles University, Prague.

Acknowledgments

My thanks go to Gunther Hellmann, Peter J. Katzenstein, Michael Kreile, and Thomas Risse who commented on the project, to the Deutsche Forschungsgemeinschaft (DFG), and the French CNRS for financing the undertaking, as well as to the Centre Marc Bloch (Berlin) and the CERI (Paris) for their intellectual support. A particular thank you goes to Emil Kirchner, who gave this project the ultimate push.

AA   Auswärtiges Amt (Foreign Office)
AGEG   Arbeitsgemeinschaft Europäischer Grenzregionen
AER   Assembly of European Regions
ARPEJE   Association pour le renouveau et la promotion des échanges juridiques avec l'Europe centrale et orientale
ASEAN   Association of South East Asian Nations
ASEM   Asia-Europe Meetings
BDI   Bund der deutschen Industrie
BdV   Bund der Vertriebenen
BMA   Bundesministerium für Arbeit und Sozialordnung (Federal Ministry)
BMJ   Bundesministerium der Justiz (Federal Ministry of Justice)
BML   Bundesministerium für Ernährung, Landwirtschaft und Forsten (Federal Ministry of Food, Agriculture and Forest)
BMU   Bundesministerium für Umwelt, Naturschutz und Reaktorsicherheit (Federal Ministry of Environment, Nature protection and Atomic Security)
BMWi   Bundesministerium für Wirtschaft und Technologie (Federal Ministry of Economics and Technology)
BMZ   Bundesministerium für wirtschaftliche Zusammenarbeit und Entwicklung (Federal Ministry for Economic Cooperation and Development)
CAP   Common Agricultural Policy
CASE   Council for Advancement and Support of Education
CBC   cross-border cooperation
CDG   Carl Duisberg Gesellschaft
CDU   Christlich-Demokratische Union Deutschlands (Christian Democrat Party Germany)
CEE   Central and Eastern Europe
CEEC   Central and Eastern European countries (or ECE – East Central Europe)
CFSP   Common foreign and security policy
CIC   Centre for International Cooperation
CIS   Commonwealth of Independent States
CMEA   Council for Mutual Economic Assistance
CONCERT   Concertation on European Regulatory Tasks
CSU   Christlich-Soziale Union
CWC   Central Works Council
DAAD   Deutscher Akademischer Austauschdienst

DFI	Deutsch-Französisches Institut
DG	Directorate-general
DGAP	Deutsche Gesellschaft für Auswärtige Politik
DIG	Deutsch-Israelische Gesellschaft
DIHT	Deutscher Industrie- und Handelstag (German Federation of Industry and Commerce)
DPJW	Deutsch-Polnisches Jugendwerk
EBRD	European Bank for Reconstruction and Development
EC	European Community
ECB	European Central Bank
ECE	East Central Europe (CEEC – Central and Eastern European countries)
ECJ	European Court of Justice
EDF	Electricité de France
EIB	European Investment Bank
EMU	European Monetary Union
EP	European Parliament
EU	European Union
EUCOM	European Consortium Mochovce
EWC	Euro Works Council
FDI	foreign direct investment
FDP	Freie Demokratische Partei
FES	Friedrich Ebert Stiftung
FIDESZ	Alliance of Young Democrats
FNS	Friedrich Naumann Stiftung
FORATOM	Forum Atomique Européen
FRG	Federal Republic of Germany
FTA	free-trade area
GDP	gross domestic product
GDR	German Democratic Republic
GNP	gross national product
GRS	Gesellschaft für Anlagen und Reaktorsicherheit
GTZ	Gesellschaft für technische Zusammenarbeit
HBS	Heinrich Böll Stiftung
HRM	human relations management
HSS	Hanns Seidel Stiftung
IAEA	International Atomic Energy Agency
IGC	intergovernmental conference
IMF	International Monetary Fund
IPSN	Institut de Protection et de Sûreté Nucléaire
IRZ	Institut für rechtliche Zusammenarbeit
ISPA	Instrument for Structural Policies for Pre-Accession
JV	joint-venture
KAS	Konrad Adenauer Stiftung

KDU-CSL	Krestanské a Demokratické Unie (Christian-Democratic Union) – Cs Strany Lidové (Czech People's Party)
KfW	Kreditanstalt für Wiederaufbau
KWU	Kraftwerkunion
LDC	less-developed country
MBO	management by objectives
MdEP	Members of the EP
MDF	Magyar Demokrata Forum (Hungarian Democratic Forum)
MNC	multinational corporation
MNE	multinational enterprise
NAFTA	North American Free Trade Agreement
NATO	North Atlantic Treaty Organization
NIS	Newly Independent States
NGO	non-governmental organization
NTB	non-tariff barrier
ODA	overseas development assistance
OECD	Organization for Economic Cooperation and Development
OPT	outward processing trade
PAN	Partido Accion Nacional
PDS	Party of Democratic Socialism
PHARE	Poland–Hungary Assistance for Economic Reconstruction
PPP	private–public partnership
PRI	Partido Revolucionario Institucional
PSL	Polskie Stronnictwo Ludowe (Polish Peasant Party)
QMV	qualified majority voting
RAMG	Regulatory Assistance Management Group
RIA	Regional Integration Agreement
RLS	Rosa Luxemburg Stiftung
RSK	Reaktorsicherheitskommission
RWE	Rheinisch-Westfälische Elektrizitätswerke
SAPARD	Special Accession Program for Agriculture and Rural Development
SEA	Single European Act
SI	Socialist International
SKL	Stowarzyszenie Konserwatywno Ludowe (Conservative People's Party)
SLD	Sojusz Lewicy Demokratycznej (Democratic Left Alliance)
SME	small- and medium-sized enterprise
SOE	state-owned enterprise
SPD	Sozialdemokratische Partei Deutschlands
SSK	Strahlenschutzsicherheitskommission
TACIS	Technical Assistance for the CIS
TNA	transnational actor
TNC	transnational corporation
TOB	Treuhandanstalt Osteuropa Beratungsgesellschaft
TPEG	Twinning Program Engineering Group

TQM	total quality management
TSOG	Technical Safety Organization Group
UN	United Nations
UNCTAD	United Conference on Trade and Development
US	Unie Svobody (Union of Freedom, Czech Republic)
UW	Union of Freedom (Poland)
WANO	World Association of Nuclear Operators
WC	Work Council
WMD	weapons of mass destruction

A̶nne-M̶arie Le Gloannec

Non-state actors and 'their' state: an introduction

Diversity of non-state actors

Non-state actors have been increasingly recognized as major actors in international politics for the last three decades, arousing considerable interest – on the part of practioners of global politics, on the part of those who want to profit from the loopholes of national authorities and international regulations, or from those political scientists, sociologists, and philosophers who devote their time to the study of international relations. They also have aroused enthusiasm on the part of those who hold them as forerunners of an emerging, more ethical, and more democratic, world civil society; they have led some to question if not their ethics at least their lack of democracy; and they have caused concern among those, governments in particular, who worry about the possible havoc they can create – be it in the financial sphere, in the virtual world of computer networks, or in the very real world of weapons of mass destruction (WMD) and other illicit traffics. This should suffice to point to the diversity of non-state actors. Militants, migrants, multinational corporations (MNCs) or mafias, advocacy coalitions, diasporas, licit and illicit producers and traders: the list is quite long, especially if those non-state actors are included which pre-date the Westphalian state, such as churches, trading companies, or mercenaries. 'Diversity' here refers not only to the diversity of their nature and function, but also to the diversity in the ways they are integrated in national frameworks and in international networks, and in the way they interact with other non-state and state actors. All these elements are, of course, intertwined: depending on the nature of non-state actors, relations with states will be close or not and, depending on the nature of these non-state actors, their main aim will be to influence other governments and/or governments of the country they are located in.

This points to some shortcomings in the bulk of previous studies pertaining to non-state actors in transnational relations. Certainly most authors would now agree on one definition of non-state actors, such as Daphné Josselin's and William Wallace's, which refers to non-state actors as organizations 'largely or entirely autonomous from central government funding and control . . ., operating as or participating in networks which extend across the boundaries of two or more states, thus engaging in 'transnational' relations . . . [and] acting in ways which affect political outcomes, either within one or more states or within international institutions' (2001, pp. 3–4). However some non-state actors have been ignored: not all the diversity of non-state actors has been taken into account by theorists, let alone because the diversity of cases and situations may be at odds with the necessary simplicity of theories. First, a distinction may be drawn between 'heroes' and 'villains,' to borrow the expression from Josselin and Wallace (2001), and studies of militias and mercenaries, of traffickers and terrorists are often ignored by those who have a theoretical approach to non-state actors – while conversely most of those who write on such non-state actors do not take heed of more theoretical approaches or of works on advocacy coalitions and the like: Susan Strange (1996) as well as Josselin and Wallace (2001) are among welcome exceptions.

Second, and this is more relevant to our purpose here, some particular non-state actors and some particular patterns of relations between non-state and state actors have been looked at more than others: as Lily Gardner Feldman underlines in chapter 1 in this volume, most authors 'underscore the role of contestation in transnational relations and therefore of challenges to governments, echoing some of the initial views of the consequences of non-state behavior' (pp. 16–17), i.e. that non-state actors undermine the statist world. Certainly the dichotomy which was previously thought to exist between a non-state world and a statist one has been discarded and most authors insist, as Thomas Risse does, that 'the more interesting question [is] how inter-state and transnational relations interact. One does not have to do away with the 'state' to establish the influence of transnational relations in world politics' (1995, p. 15). In other words, transnational relations and inter-state relations are not to be framed within a zero-sum game. Yet even if one does not do so, to interpret them almost entirely under the sole angle of challenge – i.e. non-state actors challenging states – ignores a wide variety of models of actors and patterns of relations: for instance, cooperation instead of circumvention, which Tanja Börzel and Sabine Saurugger both look at in chapter 5 and 7, respectively, though from different angles; or again, as Lily Gardner Feldman suggests in chapter 1, roles of catalysts, complements, and conduits, besides the challenge they may represent. Lily Gardner Feldman's typology is very useful as it subsumes a number of policies: the four types that she puts in evidence – i.e. non-state actors as competitors, as complements, as catalysts, and as conduits – also encompass the distinction between circumvention and cooperation. In other words, non-state actors may in one way or another reinforce state policies.

The question, however, is relevant only when considering certain types of actors. And leaving aside others. While not doing away with the state, certain

networks and certain actors are engaged in a particular type of relation –
primarily of challenge – with states, which may or may not necessarily be states
they originate from. They aim at promoting a particular kind of policy, be it the
abolition of apartheid, of slavery, or of war against the civilian population, an
end to the arms race, or the conservation of natural resources, or again one
aimed at fostering ties between their country and another – i.e. they aim at prop-
agating certain values and norms and at creating and enforcing particular
regimes world-wide. Some of these actors are engaged in politics and policies
which are global from the start. Related to that, these non-state actors are, more
or less from the start, embedded in a transnational world, and the country they
originate from does not matter so much. This certainly is the case for advocacy
coalitions or for certain epistemic communities. This might also be the (reverse)
case of networks supporting illegal traffics and actions, in which case their aim
is to use the loopholes of national authorities and international regimes, or the
absence thereof, embedded as they are in a global world of opportunities. Yet
even in these particular cases, one should qualify the notion of extra-territorial-
ity lingering behind these two categories. In the first case, there may be some
connection between the country (or countries) that the advocacy coalitions
originate from and the values these coalitions propagate, be it that they thrive in
a particularly congenial environment, or that those who oppose the spreading
of values and norms equate liberalism and western values. In the latter case,
illicit traffics and actions may be detrimental to ''supportive' states', as they
thrive on the ground of failed states and entertain these failures, as examples
such as the Taliban's Afghanistan or Medellín's Columbia demonstrate.

Non-state actors and 'their' state

However, not all non-state actors are engaged primarily in a world-wide dimension which transcends all borders. Some non-state actors are originally embedded in a country, in a state with whose culture they entertain particular relations.
Susan Strange (1996) has underlined that MNCs are themselves embedded in a
particular culture, the culture of the country they originate from, and they have
particular connections to the state of this country: in chapter 9 in this volume,
Katharina Bluhm looks at the 'German model,' or bits and pieces of a 'German
model,' that German companies transfer to the countries where they have set up
branches, bolstering their production and exporting part of a particular culture
but also acting pretty much in the same way world-embedded actors do. Others
act in a different way and complement or support their government's policy, or
entice it to act. This question concerning the particular ties that link a non-state
actor to its state of origin applies to all sorts of non-state actors, enterprises,
lobbies, political foundations, Länder, or associations of ethnic minorities . . .
In this volume, we shall be looking at non-governmental organizations (NGOs),
mainly at political foundations (Lily Gardner Feldman (chapter 1), Soledad

Loaeza (chapter 2), as well as Dorota Dakowska and Elsa Tulmets (chapter 3)), at ethnic minorities and churches (Gilles Lepesant (chapter 4)), at Länder and regions (Gilles Lepesant (chapter 4), Charlie Jeffery (chapter 5), and Tanja Börzel (chapter 5)), at industrial lobbies and enterprises, both multinational and small- and medium-sized enterprises (SMEs) (Sabine Saurugger (chapter 7), Fabienne Boudier-Bensebaa (chapter 8), and Katharina Bluhm (chapter 9)), all of them embedded in *their* state.

Here one may very well interject that neither Länder nor political foundations constitute non-state actors, the first because they are states, defined as such by the German constitution, the latter because they are partly funded by the federal budget and as such defy Josselin's and Wallace's definition. Yet Fred Halliday calls into question the so-called independence of a number of non-state actors which, according to the previous definition, would qualify as such. Drawing on an old example, that of Christopher Columbus who might have been considered as a Genoese non-state actor *and* as an agent of the Spanish state, Halliday argues that non-state actors come 'to be closely associated with the state . . . Many NGOs are, in effect, contractors for states' (2001, p. 26). There are indeed very many institutional, financial, practical, or personal interconnections between non-state actors and states. This applies to political foundations in Germany which some researchers dub NGOs while others describe them as instruments or mailboxes of political parties, or again as agents of the German government. As Josselin and Wallace put it, 'defining non-state actors chiefly by their independence from states and state authority would be misleading.' Evoking relations between banks, MNCs, think tanks or elite networks with governments, they go to underline that 'The universe of non-state actors is . . . necessarily diverse. Private actors shade into public: degrees of autonomy from state authority and control vary' (2001, p. 2). Or, as Richard Higgott frames it: 'It is . . . difficult . . . to view NGOs, INGOs or other categories of non-state actors as genuinely distinct from state and state policy processes' (Higgott, Underhill, and Bieler, 2000, p. 6).

At this point, it is not necessary to enter the debate on the nature of the state, whether it is a structure, or an agent, or both. Let us only underline the fact that the opposition between state and non-state actors, between public and private, is merely an abstraction while reality is much more complex and subtle and many actors participate in state policy processes. To that extent, the name 'non-state actors' might be a misnomer from the start: as Charlie Jeffery suggests in chapter 6, it might be wiser to speak of, in order to include Länder, 'actors outside central government.' Including Länder in our analysis of non-state actors might however be, for the sake of purity, difficult to sustain. Länder are states according to the letter of the German constitution and to the practice of administrative and political life. However they may engage in cross-borders practices and policies with other actors outside central government: in Charlie Jeffery's case, Bavaria is seen as exporting its policing standards and engaging in an 'extraordinary level of networking with police forces . . . in ECE.' Moreover – and this is one of the main focus points of this volume – together with other non-state actors, the Länder raise the question of what happens to the state and to central governmental policies: here, in the case of Germany, they may circumvent the central state or again cooperate with it – or again the state may choose to cooperate or not with them. This tells us something on the particular fabric of the German state, which we will touch upon below.

By focusing on those non-state actors which reinforce their state, while cooperating with it, complementing, or again supplementing its actions, we intend here to understand the functioning of state–non-state actors' relations, some rules of which will be put in evidence, and we also aim to grasp the institutional make-up in which these actors are embedded. Last, but not least, we want to shed some light on the functions these non-state actors perform or not, intentionally or not, in their relationship with the state: do they eventually serve the state, or hamper its action? Some of these actors, such as ethnic minorities, may be challenging their state; others may not. To re-formulate a now old question, though in a different way: has the state been weakened or restructured? It will also be crucial to look at the role of the European Union (EU) to see whether it empowers non-state actors (Länder and regions, for instance), and whether these actors eventually serve their state.

Setting an example: the German case?

First of all, as stressed above, non-state actors are more or less embedded in particular institutional frameworks which have grown with time, and in a particular institutional culture, which Tanja Börzel defines in chapter 5 as 'the collective understandings about appropriate behavior within a given rule-structure' (p. 111). She puts in evidence the role played by domestic institutional culture: the degree of affectedness – the degree to which non-state actors (Länder and regions, in this case) are affected by European integration – and the availability of resources that these non-state actors may or not possess to face this challenge, explain when non-state actors mobilize at the European level. But within the EU framework, the domestic institutional culture determines solely whether regions, like the Spanish ones, will circumvent the national state, or whether they will cooperate with it, as the German Länder do. Thomas Risse (1995) had earlier stressed the necessity to look at domestic structures as an independent variable. This should argue in favour of case studies; only appropriate case studies will allow us to understand how non-state actors and state actors interrelate with each other.

Of course, the case we examine here, Germany and its non-state actors, is particular, as each case is. It may however be all the more particular as the German institutional make-up is quite diverse and fragmented, as a number of authors, notably Peter Katzenstein (1987), have stressed in the past: bureaucratic fragmentation, ministerial autonomy, coalition governments, and federal structures account for this dispersion of the political system. From the beginning of its inception, the state has been penetrated by various societal actors, in such a manner as to be dubbed a 'semi-sovereign state,' while it has pooled its external sovereignty with that of other countries in the European Community/ Union. Thomas Risse (1995) identified two key variables in the understanding of the impact of transnational networks in shaping international relations: institutional fragmentation of the state and a high degree of international institutionalization. This precisely is the case of Germany: as a corollary of institutional fragmentation and international institutionalization, non-state actors have played a prominent part in Germany for quite a long time. One needs only to recall that most German political foundations were created before or after the Second World War and it is no wonder that a German political scientist, Karl Kaiser, was among the first to address the topic of transnational relations. To that extent, Germany may be a particular case, but at the same time looking at it may help to distinguish certain trends in Europe and in the western world.

Germany is also characterized by a high degree of ideological cohesion, which may be seen as the product of economic, social, and ethnic cohesion – though the social fabric is being progressively altered as a result of integrating both the former German Democratic Republic (GDR) and a large population of immigrants. It is also the product of political, social, and economic institutions which suppose and support consensual approaches. This is crucial in understanding the functioning of interactions between most non-state actors and the state. As Tanja Börzel puts in evidence in chapter 5, the institutional culture in Germany lays stress on cooperation instead of confrontation, as in other cultures. As a result, she underlines that though the Länder put pressure on the central government, they do so within a given legal and political framework which they have shaped, notably thanks to European transnational resources, they do not circumvent the state, as Michèle Knodt contends (Knodt and Kohler-Koch, 2000). Certainly, not all non-state actors support their state: ethnic minorities in particular may be defiant, as Gilles Lepesant shows in chapter 4, depending on the pattern of centre–periphery relations. And, as Sabine Saurugger shows in chapter 7, the same ideology may not be shared any longer; changes in policy paradigms may occur and lead to a complete breakdown in the relation between the state and some non-state actor – in this case, the German nuclear industry after the election of a red–green coalition in 1998. As a consequence, the nuclear industry turned to another opportunity structure, offered by the transnational European networks. Yet, owing to the institutional make-up of Germany and to its prevailing culture which fosters and relies upon a consensual understanding, a number of non-state actors work with their state, and this finding is relevant for the study of other countries which may share the same premises or which have an institutional culture nurturing competition – in which case, counter-examples, too, are relevant.

Europe and beyond: European networks, European frameworks, and policy transfer

Transnational relations may thus offer opportunities – resources – to non-state actors, such as the nuclear industry or the Länder which have seen their influence or their competences curtailed, the former after the overhaul of nuclear policy, the latter after the devolution of sovereignty to European institutions. One could also add to this list, as Fabienne Boudier-Bensebaa does in chapter 8, some enterprises which have been driven to invest abroad by increasing wage costs after reunification. Yet transnational relations may also constitute the framework in which some non-state actors act from the onset, because their aim is to influence or to support the foreign policy of their country, or to shape institutions and practices in other countries. To that extent, not only are they embedded in their culture, they also are firmly rooted in another country, or in other countries. This is the case of firms and also of political foundations and of some of those NGOs which act towards reconciliation between two countries and which Lily Gardner Feldman analyzes in chapter 1: in each of the four cases which come under her scrutiny, she underlines that 'essentially every aspect of societal interaction has been institutionalized and actors rarely have been ad hoc' (p. 40). Even if transactions costs may increase, even if a lack of coherence or consistency between state policies and transnational relations may occur, institutionalized relations sustained by NGOs, to borrow Lily Gardner Feldman's words, may perform a very important function: they make up for deficiencies or operate in areas where governments cannot, as she exemplifies in a number of cases concerning reconciliation between Germany on the one hand, and France, Israel, Poland, and the Czech Republic, on the other. They precede or induce governmental policies. The same may be said of private enterprises in Central – more than in Eastern – European countries, where they may be seen as having integrated the economies of these countries well before the enlargement of the EU – as Fabienne Boudier-Bensebaa shows in chapter 8.

Among these networks and frameworks, the EU plays a particular role. European networks and frameworks often act as opportunity resources for non-state actors whose powers are being challenged or curtailed, legally, or politically, as both Saurugger in chapter 8 and Börzel in chapter 5 demonstrate: in short, they empower them. Saurugger puts in evidence that enlargement has been used by non-state actors to extend their action and influence abroad as well as inside Germany. Some of these actors, the enterprises that Bensebaa and Bluhm scrutinize, even anticipated enlargement. The EU, moreover, may not only offer financial resources but also symbolic power that border regions, 'Euroregions,' resort to in order to overcome tensions and prejudices. However, while the EU is a resource, it is at the same time a paradoxical one, according to Lepesant in chapter 4, as it tightens up external borders and divides peoples and communities. On the whole the EU is, to various degrees, an opportunity – or a cost-structure for those non-state actors which are embedded in their states as well as for those which are transnational from the onset. Beyond the EU, non-state actors do perform very important tasks, too: political foundations are engaged in institution-building, as Soledad Loaeza explains in chapter 2 in the light of one example, the democratization of Mexico's political life and the construction of the Partido Accion Nacional (PAN) as a serious, democratic contestant to the Partido Revolucionario Institucional (PRI) – so serious that it became the first party to oust the PRI in a general election. This underlines a tremendous change in international and transnational relations as compared with the Cold War years. During the so-called 'Cold War,' intervention in what was then considered the 'domaine réservé of national actors,' borrowing Soledad Loaeza's words, was politically incorrect. Now, as Loeaza underlines, intervention is required – as it also had been required in earlier times, if one remembers Lord Byron taking the side of Greek insurgents against the Ottoman Empire. Foreign interventions are seen as a means to foster the democratization process of certain countries and to boost their international credibility or again, as far as Central European countries are concerned, consolidating democracy and paving the way for their integration in the EU. To put it another way, policy transfers are asked for, they are not imposed. In times of uncertainty, domestic and international, certain actors, state or non-state actors, look abroad and turn to Germany for emulation and imitation by policy transfer (Radaelli,1997).

Institutional export . . .

This raises the question of '*cui bono*': in other words, for what or whose purpose should this transfer and export take place? Whereas unwanted intervention served the intervening country during the Cold War years, the tables are now turned. It seems more or less obvious that countries where non-state actors intervene benefit from this intervention – and ask for it – but one may wonder why an intervening country, Germany in this case, and its non-state actors, engage in institution-building and democratization processes. As far as CEEC are concerned, there is one offhand explanation: the complementarity between governmental policies and non-state actions. Geographical proximity and strategic location (in both economic and military terms, i.e. 'soft' and 'hard' security) makes integration, formal – in the EU – or informal – within transnational economic and political networks – a necessity. As far as Latin America or Asia are concerned, the reasons are less compelling, were it not for a clue: up to the 1990s, no German government ever bothered to formulate policy guidelines *vis-à-vis* this continent, which stresses the extent of political foundations' foreign policy role. But why should it be so: why should political foundations play the function that state actors in other countries fulfill? And, generally speaking, what long-term political function(s) do non-state actors fulfill, intentionally or not, besides the obvious short- or long-term aims they pursue, such as institution-building as far as the political foundations are concerned;

improvement of transnational or transgovernmental relations, in the case of political foundations or the NGOs considered by Lily Gardner Feldman in chapter 1; the defense of self-interests in the case of minorities, Länder and enterprises; the integration of CEEC, as far as political foundations, Länder, or enterprises are concerned . . .?

The contributors to this volume were asked to inquire about the possible propagation of a German model. For some, the question was irrelevant, considering the aims assigned to reconciliation, for instance. For most, however, it was relevant but attracted varied and mostly nuanced answers. One should not speak of the export of *a* model, but rather of policy transfers, as David Dolowitz and David Marsh (2001) defined it: i.e. as a transfer of specific policies as a result of strategic decisions taken by actors inside and outside government, including the transfer of policy goals, structures, and contents, the transfer of policy instruments or administrative techniques, of institutions, ideology, ideas, attitudes, and concepts, and the transfer of negative lessons – in other words, the transfer of certain norms, rules, institutions, etc. Interestingly enough, the twin strategy of the Länder, which have profited from transnational channels of access to European policy-making while at the same time applying pressure on the German central government to exact increased legal and political competences to shape the federal policy in Brussels, is looked upon by Tanja Börzel in chapter 5 as having 'externalized' 'the formal and informal institutions of cooperative federalism . . . from the domestic to the European realm of policy-making.' And she goes on to conclude that what she calls a 'flexible adjustment' has 'reinforced rather than changed the existing German territorial structures (p. 129).' By cooperating with their state, and sometimes pressuring it, the German Länder have reinforced the institutional make-up of the Federal Republic.

For Charlie Jeffery in chapter 6, German institutions are being exported, be it 'hard-edged norms,' such as legal requirements, or 'soft-edged' ones, i.e. a collective understanding of what is an appropriate way of doing things – referring, for instance, to policing norms and practices. And they are also being imported, replicated by CEEC in the process of transition and integration to the EU. In other words, Germany, wittingly or unwittingly, performs the role of a model for these countries and it serves the country well as it empowers it: shaping institutions grants Germany a particular privilege. This very concept of 'institutional empowerment' may, however, be put into question as the example of European Monetary Union (EMU) shows. Here Germany played a crucial role in shaping the rules of EMU, yet German decision-makers – bankers or politicians – cannot shape policy outcomes as they formerly did: the question of how connections and contacts, the propagation of norms and rules, and institution transfer and adaptation translate into political power – if they do – still begs explanation (Thielemann, 1999; Le Gloannec, 2001). Katharina Bluhm in chapter 9 comes to a nuanced conclusion. While at a macro-level, a German model is not exported because it cannot be transplanted in an environment which is historically, institutionally, and sociologically different – as Dorota Dakowska and Elsa

Tulmets also underline in chapter 3 – bits and pieces of it are transferred, or rather adopted *and* adapted. 'Institutional export' takes place in three different ways: either elements or practices are transferred, rather unwittingly on the part of German actors, or the core concept of a given practice is transferred and yet reinterpreted in another institutional setting, or normative guidelines are adopted. As a result, a kind of 'hybridization' takes place, borrowing from Dolowitz and Marsh (2001).

Gilles Lepesant, Dorota Dakowska, and Elsa Tulmets (chapter 4 and 3, respectively) meanwhile offer a somewhat different view. The former underlines that Polish elites aim to emulate the German example – that is, to emulate the role Germany has been playing in integrating Poland into the West European community of states and societies: they want to play a similar role *vis-à-vis* the states and societies East of the Bug, from the Baltic to the Black Sea, which would allow their country to decisively shape the geopolitical recomposition of this area. This is indeed something writ large in Polish discourses. And practically, some of the instruments that the German actors resorted to in the management of the border have been transferred to Poland's eastern border. Yet for Lepesant and for Dakowska and Tulmets, German intervention is Europeanized: either because it requires to be Europeanized in order to be accepted, as Gilles Lepesant contends: 'The German concepts for fostering transborder cooperation are accepted when they have a European legitimacy – i.e. when they are perceived as a part of the European system that Polish actors are keen to adopt' (p. 109) – or because, as Dakowska and Tulmets eloquently put it, 'There are no German solutions anymore, there are European solutions.' One might add: or world solutions, as Rolf Knieper does when he analyses the role played by German jurists – including himself – in the codification of law in the area covering CEEC, the Caucasus, and Central Asia: 'There is hardly any room for national genius and pecularities' (Knieper, 2000, p. 167). Put differently, Europe is a resource, either because it offers instruments to the German exporters of institutional practices or because it confers on them legitimacy.

. . . or political credit ?

This means that 'the German model' has come a long way. The notion of 'the German model' was coined in the 1970s by German and other European politicians and political scientists, referring to the successful pattern of economic development that the Federal Republic of Germany (FRG) had followed in the two previous decades. The concept of 'model,' however, did not imply that it could be imitated: one reason for this skepticism was the belief that if other countries successfully copied the German model, the formula could no longer be applied to the FRG, and Germany would lose its position as a major exporter. By the 1980s, however, the original skepticism about the applicability of the German model had dissipated and other countries had come to consider some of its elements worth adopting: the model was being broken down into elements and components which might then be adopted and adapted, such as the close cooperation between banks and industry, the German system of vocational training, or the practice of conflict resolution by gathering employers and trade unions around the same table. However, these very elements have come under heavy criticism. Germany's reunification questions the relevance of a system of wage settlement at the national level, considering the huge disparities between East and West. Globalization, in particular in investment and hence in management practices, leads German enterprises to adopt a more 'Anglo-Saxon' profile. Hence the notion of a 'German model' dissolves in world-wide practices. And political scientists follow suit, acknowledging the post-ontological state of what is being transferred.

If so, the question of 'to whose or which benefit?' is mooted again. Does the action of non-state actors pay back, as Charlie Jeffery asks in chapter 6, and if it does, in which currency? One possible answer is that *political credit* accrues to Germany. Borrowing from Robert Putnam's insistence on trust, we may define 'political credit' as the trust that a particular political actor prompts among its partners, in this case that German governmental and non-governmental actors, 'Germany,' in other words, prompt among their foreign partners. Obviously trust is supported by the belief that Germany is able to deliver, and this belief in turn is nurtured by Germany's performance, based on sustained networks of relations, on permanent contacts, on help and aid, etc. It is based on a political capital which is continuously and patiently fostered by those NGOs, political foundations, etc. analyzed in this volume. It is not an immediate return on investment, it is based on investing in the long term, in developing and sustaining networks in which German non-state actors play a crucial rule.

In these networks, it is not so much the content of what is being transferred which matters. As we wrote above, there is not much of a 'German model' to be transferred: rather, European, or again global, norms, rules and practices are being adopted and adapted. It is rather the actors of the transfer who matter, and the fact that in the case of Germany they are so diverse and that they entertain various types of relations with the state endows the country with a wide repertoire. Soledad Loaeza, Dorota Dakowska, and Elsa Tulmets (chapter 2 and 3, respectively) all emphasize this dimension of trust and the role of political foundations in building it, be it in Latin America, or in the CEEC. Considering the wide variety of non-state and state actors and yet their ideological and practical cohesion, it can be said that a number of non-state actors reinforces the action of the state and contributes to building trust in Germany. If one recalls the four categories of power that Simon Bulmer (1997), following Stefano Guzzini (1993), established, two of them are deliberate power, two categories are not intentional. One is called (too vaguely, in my view) 'unintentional,' which may be equated with 'structural power,' as defined by Susan Strange, while the other is called 'empowerment,' referring to the fact that 'the disposition of a German agent power' may be 'facilitated,' in this case, by the activities of non-state actors which work as conduits of policy transfer towards other countries. They complement the foreign policy of the central state and in some cases they supplement it in times of failure.

This might be the most efficient tool of German diplomacy, the reason for its magnetism, as Loaeza in chapter 2, quoting Timothy Garton Ash, recalls.

Bibliography

Breslin, Shaun (2004) 'Beyond diplomacy? UK relations with China since 1997,' *British Journal of Politics and International Relations*, 6 (3), p. 409.

Bühl, Walter L. (1994) 'Gesellschaftliche Grundlagen der Deutschen Aussenpolitik,' in Karl Kaiser and Hanns Maull (eds), *Deutschlands neue Aussenpolitik, Band I: Grundlagen*, Munich: Oldenbourg Verlag, pp. 175–201.

Bulmer, Simon (1996) *The Domestic Structure of European Community Policy-Making in West Germany*, New York: Garland.

Bulmer, Simon (1997) 'Shaping the rules? The constitutive politics of the European Union and German power,' in Peter Katzenstein (ed.), *Tamed Power: Germany in Europe*, Ithaca, NY: Cornell University Press, pp. 49–79.

Bulmer, Simon, Charlie Jeffery, and William Paterson (1998) 'Deutschlands europäische Diplomatie – die Entwicklung des regionalen Milieus,' in Werner Weidenfeld (ed.), *Deutsche Europapolitik – Optionen wirksamer Interessenvertretung*, Bonn: Europa Union Verlag, pp. 11–102.

Buthe, Tim (2004) 'Governance through private authority: non-state actors in world politics,' *Journal of International Affairs*, 58 (1), pp. 281–290.

Clark, Ann Marie (2001) *Diplomacy of Conscience: Amnesty International and Changing Human Rights Norms*, Princeton: Princeton University Press.

Dolowitz, David and David Marsh (1996) 'Who learns what from whom: a review of the policy transfer literature,' *Political Studies*, 44, pp. 343–357.

Finnemore, Martha (1996) *National Interests in International Society*, Ithaca, NY: Cornell University Press.

Forndran, Erhard (1989) 'Gesellschaft und internationale Politik: Zum Verhältnis von Innen- und Aussenpolitik,' in Hartmut Elsenhans *et al.* (eds), *Frankreich – Europa – Weltpolitik: Festschrift für Gilbert Ziebura*, Opladen: Westdeutscher Verlag, pp. 161–173.

Glaser, Berney G. and Anselm L. Strauss (1967) *The Discovery of Grounded Theory: Strategies for Qualitative Research*, Chicago: Aldine.

Goetz, Klaus (1995) 'National governance and European integration: intergovernmental relations in Germany,' *Journal of Common Market Studies*, 33, pp. 91–116.

Goldberger, Bruce N. (1993) 'Why Europe should not fear the Germans,' *German Politics*, 2 (2), pp. 288–310.

Guzzini, Stefano (1993) 'Structural power: the limits of neo-realist analysis,' *International Organization*, 47, pp. 443–478.

Halliday, Fred (1994) *Rethinking International Relations*, London: Macmillan.

Halliday, Fred (2001) 'The romance of non-state actors,' in Daphné Josselin and William Wallace, *Non-State Actors in World Politics*, Houndmills: Palgrave, pp. 21–37.

Heintzen, Markus (1989) *Private Aussenpolitik: Eine Typologie der grenzüberschreitenden Aktivitäten gesellschaftlicher Kräfte und ihres Verhältnisses zur staatlichen Aussenpolitik*, Baden-Baden: Nomos Verlag.

Higgott, Richard A., Geoffrey, R. D. Underhill, and Andreas Bieler (2000) *Non-State Actors and Authority in the Global System*, London and New York: Routledge.

Josselin, Daphné and William Wallace (2001) *Non-State Actors in World Politics*, Houndmills: Palgrave.

Kaiser, Karl and Markus Mildenberger (1998) 'Gesellschaftliche Mittlerorganisationen,' in Wolf-Dieter Eberwein and Karl Kaiser (eds), *Deutschlands neue Aussenpolitik, Band 4: Institutionen und Ressourcen*, Munich: Oldenbourg, pp. 199–214.

Katzenstein, Peter (1987) *Policy and Politics in West Germany: The Growth of a Semisovereign State*, Philadelphia: Temple University Press.

Katzenstein, Peter J. (ed.) (1997a) *Mitteleuropa: Between Europe and Germany*, Providence, RI and Oxford: Berghahn Books.

Katzenstein, Peter J. (ed.) (1997b) *Tamed Power: Germany in Europe*, Ithaca, NY: Cornell University Press.

Keck, Margaret E. and Kathryn Sikkink (1998) *Activists Beyond Borders: Advocacy Networks in International Politics*, Ithaca, NY: Cornell University Press.

Keohane, Robert O. and Helen V. Milner (eds) (1996) *Internationalization and Domestic Politics*, Cambridge: Cambridge University Press.

Klotz, Audie (1995) *Norms in International Relations: The Struggle against Apartheid*, Ithaca, NY: Cornell University Press.

Khagram, Sanjeev, James V. Riker, and Kathryn Sikkink (eds) (2002), *Restructuring World Politics: Transnational Social Movements, Networks and Norms*, Minneapolis: University of Minneapolis Press.

Knieper, Rolf (2000) 'Begleitung in Umbrüchen und Rechtsreformen,' in Michèle Knodt and Beate Kohler-Koch (eds), *Deutschland zwischen Europäisierung und Selbstbehauptung*, Frankfurt am Main and New York: Campus Verlag.

Knodt, Michèle and Beate Kohler-Koch (eds) (2000) *Deutschland zwischen Europäisierung und Selbstbehauptung*, Frankfurt am Main and New York: Campus Verlag.

Kohler-Koch, Beate and Rainer Eising (eds) (1999) *The Transformation of Governance in the European Union*, London and New York: Routledge.

Koutalakis, Charalampos (2004) 'Environmental compliance in Italy and Greece: the role of non-state actors,' *Environmental Policy*, 13 (4), pp. 754–774.

Kratochwil, Friedrich (1989) *Rules, Norms and Decisions: On the Conditions of Practical and Legal Reasoning in International Relations and Domestic Affairs*, Cambridge: Cambridge University Press.

Le Gloannec, Anne-Marie (2001) 'Germany's power and the weakening of states in a globalised world: deconstructing a paradox,' *German Politics*, 10 (1), Special Issue: New Europe, New Germany, Old Foreign Policy? German Foreign Policy Since Unification, Douglas Webber (ed.), pp 117–134.

Lipschutz, Ronnie (1992) 'Reconstructing world politics: the emergence of global civil society,' *Millennium*, 21 (3), pp. 389–420.

Marks, Gary and Doug McAdam (1996) 'Social movements and the changing structure of political opportunity in the European Union,' in Gary Marks *et al.* (eds), *Governance in the European Union*, London, Thousand Oaks, and New Delhi: Sage.

Müller, Harald and Thomas Risse-Kappen (1993) 'From the outside in and from the inside out: international relations, domestic politics, and foreign policy,' in Thomas Skidmore and Valerie Hudson (eds), *The Limits of State Autonomy*, Boulder, CO: Westview Press.

Palan, Ronen and Barry Gills (eds) (1994) *Transcending the State–Global Divide: A Neo-Structuralist Agenda in International Relations*, Boulder, CO: Lynne Rienner.

Philips, Ann. L. (2000) *Power and Influence after the Cold War: Germany in East-Central Europe*, Lanham, MD: Rowman & Littlefield.

Radaelli, Claudio M. (1997) 'Policy transfer in the European Union: institutional isomorphism as a source of legitimacy,' Jean Monnet Working Papers in Comparative and International Politics, http://aei.pitt.edu/archive/0000391/01/JMWP10.htm.

Radaelli, Claudio M. (2000) 'Whither Europeanization? Concept stretching and substantial chance,' European Integration online Papers, http://eiop.or.at/texte/2000-008htm.

Rhodes, R.A.W. (1997) *Understanding Governance: Policy Networks, Governance, Reflexivity and Accountability*, Buckingham and Philadelphia: Open University Press.

Risse, Thomas (2001) 'Transnational actors, networks and global governance,' in W. Carlnaes, T. Risse, and B. Simmons (eds), *Handbook of International Relations*, London: Sage.

Risse-Kappen, Thomas (1994) 'Ideas do not float freely: transnational coalitions, domestic structures, and the end of the Cold War,' *International Organization*, 48, pp. 185–214.

Rosenau, James N. (1969) 'Pre-theories and theories of foreign policy,' in Barry R. Farrell, *Approaches to Comparative and International Politics*, 2nd edn, Evanston: Northwestern University Press, pp. 27–92.

Sabatier, P. and H. Jenkins-Smith (eds) (1993) *Policy Change and Learning: An Advocacy Coalition Approach*, Boulder, CO: Westview Press.

Smith, Jackie, Charles Chatfield, and Ron Pagnuco (1997) *Transnational Social Movements and Global Politics: Solidarity Beyond the State*, Syracuse, NY: Syracuse University Press.

Strange, Susan (1996) *The Retreat of the State: The Diffusion of Power in the World Economy*, Cambridge: Cambridge University Press.

Thielemann, Eiko R. (1999) 'Institutional limits of a 'Europe of the regions': EC state-aid control German federalism,' *Journal of European Public Policy*, 6 (3), pp. 399–418.

LILY GARDNER FELDMAN

1

The role of non-state actors in Germany's foreign policy of reconciliation: catalysts, complements, conduits, or competitors?

Introduction

The role of non-state actors in reform and revolution in the former Soviet bloc and at the end of the Cold War has stimulated analysis of transnational actors in other settings, both global and regional. This chapter first addresses the relevance for the German case of the more general literature on transnationalism.[1] It then suggests a framework for evaluating the role of non-state actors in Germany's foreign policy of reconciliation. Reconciliation has been a hallmark of German foreign policy, as well as an important feature of intra-state behavior (for example, in South Africa) and inter-state initiatives (for example, in the US and Vietnam).

By 'reconciliation' I mean the process of building long-term peace between former enemies through bilateral institutions across governments and societies. Reconciliation involves the development of trust, empathy, and magnanimity and the capacity to address conflict through cooperative means. It involves both religious and emotional dimensions (Versöhnung) and practical and material aspects (Aussöhnung) (Gardner Feldman, 1999). Historical consciousness is a decisive force in the ability to move forward after conflict. Finally, examples are offered from four concrete cases: Germany's relations with France, Israel, the Czech Republic, and Poland. These four dyads demonstrate that the role of non-state actors is functionally varied, temporally deep, and consequentially broad.

Transnational relations and advocacy networks revised

Bringing Transnational Relations Back In: Non-State Actors, Domestic Structures and International Institutions, edited by Thomas Risse-Kappen (1995), effectively reveals the deficiencies of the original work on transnationalism by Robert Keohane and Joseph Nye, Jr. (1971), but is limited in its applicability to Germany's foreign policy of reconciliation in five respects. First, Risse-Kappen's emphasis on domestic factors and multilateralism as explanations for activity by a transnational actor (TNA) is highly relevant in relations of reconciliation. Yet, in reconciliation the multilateralism applies to the context for intergovernmental relations and, until recently, less so for transnational connections. Second, Risse-Kappen's focus on domestic structures does not seem to include the institutionalized physical presence of a domestic TNA of one country in a second country – for example, political foundations. Moreover, third, his stress on links between a TNA and either the home or host government ignores an equally important third, independent layer of connections essential to reconciliation: between TNAs in two societies – for example, trades unions – as an end in themselves, not as a means to the end of influencing governments (Gardner Feldman, 1999). Fourth, the work's advantage of a variety of functional and geographic cases becomes a disadvantage in understanding single-country cases where a dense network of ties bind two societies and governments in complex and special ways. Finally, the importance of leaders simultaneously holding government and transnational positions – for example, the leader of the political party in power – is largely overlooked.

Activists beyond Borders: Advocacy Networks in International Politics by Margaret Keck and Kathryn Sikkink (1998) shares the benefit of Risse-Kappen's notion of TNAs being both domestic and international at the same time, and of being highly structured and structuring.[2] They also provide a typology for TNA activity and efficacy: '(1) issue creation and agenda-setting; (2) influence on discursive positions of states and international organizations; (3) influence on institutional procedures; (4) influence on policy change in 'target actors'; (5) influence on state behavior' (1998, p. 25).

The authors refer to four types of tactics: information politics, symbolic politics, leverage politics, and accountability politics (1998, p. 16). Keck and Sikkink highlight the explanatory power of issue areas and actor characteristics, including the resources of information and leadership, that Risse-Kappen downplays. In addition, the Keck–Sikkink focus on principled foreign policy and the centrality of norms and values captures much of the essence of relations of reconciliation, as does their appreciation of the role of voluntarism. Yet, reconciliation can also involve motives of pragmatism, and covers the third type of organization Keck and Sikkink identify but then exclude, namely that motivated by 'shared causal ideas, such as scientific groups and epistemic communities' (1998, p. 30).[3] By concentrating on global issues, Keck and Sikkink also fail to take into account that certain countries, like Germany and perhaps Japan, are predisposed to a norm-driven foreign policy due to history, and that networks and ties, thus, can be purely bilateral.

Both works underscore the role of contestation in transnational relations and, therefore, of challenges to governments, echoing some of the initial views of the consequences of non-state behavior (Kaiser, 1971), but competition is but one of four modes to describe the relations between governments and TNAs.[4] The roles of catalyst, complement, and conduit are equally important.

Building on these two works on transnationalism, I rely on the following categories to describe and explain the nature of TNAs in Germany's foreign policy of reconciliation: motives (moral, pragmatic, or both); functional area (economic, political, friendship associations, cultural, religious, academic); domestic context (in home and host setting, including physical presence in the other country); activity (nature, tactics, and resources); and consequences for relations to governments (catalyst, complement, conduit, competitor). The analysis proceeds around the categories of 'consequences.'

As catalyst, conduit, or competitor, it is the TNA that dictates the terms of reference, with the German government performing in a more reactive mode. When TNAs are complements, the government sets the overall tone. The role of catalyst or competitor involves relations of tension with the government, whereas activity as complement or conduit by TNAs suggests harmonious relations. Catalysts are found most often in religious or morally-driven organizations, whereas conduits and competitors occur more often in the political arena. TNAs as complements are the most broadly based, covering most aspects of societal relations. The role of government is hidden when TNAs perform as a conduit, whereas it is open in complementary activity. When TNAs act as complements or competitors, the role of government can be open or hidden.

Transnational actors as catalysts

In all four cases of the German government's policy of reconciliation – with Israel, France, Poland, and the Czech Republic – TNAs were crucial in stimulating official activity, such that we can identify them as catalysts. In all cases, the TNA activity constituted a public demonstration of the desire for change in relations with the other country and a challenge to its own government to act. In the latter three cases, religious groups were particularly important, and in all four, a moral imperative was central.

France

In Franco-German relations, before the initial reconciliation event of the May 1950 Schuman Plan, French and German religious leaders began to interact, both on the Catholic side through the Christian Democracy of Schuman and Adenauer, and on the less well-known Protestant side through the French Protestant church's actions such as its November 1946 involvement in the Speyer Synod, its theological institute in Montpelier for German prisoners of war, and the engagement of Michel Sturm, the French military chaplain in Germany (Hartweg, 1989; Heimerl, 1989). The opportunity for interaction between French and German spiritual and political leaders at the Moral Rearmament's center in Caux helped break the ice between the two sides, as documented by Irène Laure, a French resistance fighter (Piguet, 1985).

Joseph Rovan has pointed to the importance of societal actors in Franco-German reconciliation well in advance of the 1963 Elysée Treaty, citing his own French organization, the International Liaison and Documentation Office (Le Bureau international de liaison et de documentation), created in Paris in August 1945 and later expanded to an office in Bonn, but also the Franco-German Institute (Deutsch-Französisches Institut – DFI), opened in Ludwigsburg in 1948 (1998, p. 15).

The DFI was founded by eleven public figures who were also important politicians – for example, Theodor Heuss and Carlo Schmid, who served as president of the organization from its creation until his death in 1979. Their extensive political contacts garnered support for the institution (Schmid interview, 1975). The DFI's mission also resonated in Germany because of the bilateral connections it had with the French Committee for Exchanges with the New Germany (Comité français d'échanges avec l'Allemagne nouvelle), founded in 1948 by a cross-section of French society: journalists, intellectuals, and politicians (Ackermann, 1994; Bock, 1998; Rovan, 1998). Funding for the DFI was both public (local and regional) and private. In its first stage, from 1948 until 1963, in which it focused on meetings and exchanges between Germans and French, the DFI benefited from cooperative relations with other German societal organizations, whether political, cultural, or media-related, whose interest was France. The DFI's experiences of that period provided a model for the section of the 1963 intergovernmental Friendship Treaty dealing with education and youth (Barzel, 1988, pp. 150–152; Bock, 1998, p. 200).

Poland

Societal actors took the first steps in German-Polish relations almost a decade before the 1970 German–Polish Treaty which began the process of formal 'normalization' and 'reconciliation' between the two governments, culminating in the 1990 'Two Plus Four' agreement and the 1991 German–Polish Treaty on Good Neighborship and Friendly Cooperation. In February 1962, the German Evangelical church published an internal memorandum on domestic and foreign policy, designed to influence parliamentarians, in which eight laymen and theologians called on the government to give up its claim to sovereignty over the Oder–Neisse border and the eastern territories. This initiative was followed by other statements on reconciliation and territories–border issues: the two missives of the Evangelical church in 1963 and 1965; the December 1965 letter of the German Catholic conference of bishops in response to the letter of its Polish counterpart; and the 1968 memorandum of a group of Catholic theologians and lay members (Bensberger Kreis) (Jacobsen, 1992, pp. 35–36, 125–135, 142–145).

Even though the church efforts were criticized by expellee groups (Bund der Vertriebenen – Federation of Expellees), some politicians, and certain segments of the media, according to Jacobsen, said that 'the spiritual dialog could not be stopped' (p. 36). Together with the engagement of public figures like Carlo Schmid (his apology for the crimes of Nazism and call for diplomatic relations at Warsaw University in 1958), Marion Dönhoff, Golo Mann, and Karl Jaspers, the church initiatives contributed to the development of the Grand Coalition's new Ostpolitik in 1966 (Jacobsen, 1992, p. 37).

The Czech Republic

In the Czech case, the churches in the two countries did not play a role similar to the German and Polish churches until after the major breakthrough in relations in 1989; for the post-1968, ideologically doctrinaire Czechoslovakia was far less porous than Poland, and the role of the church far less central. The German Catholic bishops' conference did issue a rapid response on moral obligation and forgiveness in 1990 to the overture of Czechoslovakia's Cardinal Tomasek (as in the 1965 Polish case, Germany did not take the initiative) concerning the expulsion of the Sudeten Germans after the war (Sekretariat, 1990). The Catholic Ackermann Community (Ackermann-Gemeinde) of Sudeten Germans was open to reconciliation before 1989 but ties developed only after 1989 together with the Czech Bernhard Bolzano Society. The Protestant churches also exchanged letters in 1995–96, at a time when official relations were in difficulty over the development of a joint German–Czech declaration on the past and on future ties (Evangelische Kirche, 1996).

Church leaders – the Archbishop of Prague, Cardinal Miroslav Vlk, and the director of the Benedictine School in Ettal, Father Angelus Waldstein – were also included in the 1995 public forum 'Conversations with our Neighbor' organized by the Charles University and Bertelsmann and held in Prague. The forum cut across politics and society in its lectures (Hildegard Hamm-Brücher–Vaclav Havel; Jiri Dienstbier–Kurt Biedenkopf; Jiri Grusa–Antje Vollmer; Günter Verheugen–Josef Zieleniec; Vaclav Havel–Richard von Weizsäcker), kept open public lines of communication, and defined the moral and political obstacles preventing reconciliation and movement at the official level (Bertelsmann, 1997; Verheugen interview, 1997).

Israel

Religious leadership was not a catalyst for the beginning of German–Israeli relations, in part because there were no religious counterparts, but spiritual connections did develop through the Societies for Christian–Jewish Cooperation (Gesellschaften für Christlich-Jüdische Zusammenarbeit), created in 1947 in Hamburg, Wiesbaden, and Munich. The societies were involved in inter-faith discussions within Germany.

Moral inspiration was not absent in the German–Israeli case, but did not take an entirely religious route. In *Many Stones Lay Along the Path* (*Viel Steine Lagen am Weg*), the journalist Erich Lüth describes the absence of political calculation in his founding, together with fellow journalist Rudolf Küstermeier (who had been incarcerated by the Nazis), of the Peace with Israel Movement (Aktion Friede mit Israel) (1966, pp. 270–283). In the summer of 1951, forty-seven states said that they would terminate the state of war with Germany, and only the Israeli government opposed the idea. Lüth regretted the fact that no German official had yet denounced Nazi Germany nor made an overture to the Jews. Peace with Israel then published two articles in *Die Neue Zeitung*, the *Telegraf*, and *Die Welt*, recognizing Germany's responsibility for the crimes, promising to fight any resurgence of anti-semitism, and asking Israel for peace.

Lüth and Küstermeier were intentionally trying to provoke the German government to end its silence regarding the Nazi past, an omission denounced by the Israeli government. Both men have spoken of the overwhelming response of thousands of Germans in letters, newspaper articles, rallies, and lectures (Küstermeier interview, 1975; Lüth interview, 1975). Nahum Goldmann, who was to become the chief representative for world Jewry in the subsequent reparations negotiations, saw the Peace with Israel initiative as a major breakthrough, as he wrote to Lüth on September 14, 1951 (Lüth, 1966, p. 274; Gardner Feldman, 1984, pp. 37–40; Goldmann interview, 1975).

A few weeks after the Lüth–Küstemeier articles, on September 27, 1951, Konrad Adenauer delivered his major statement to the Bundestag, expressing German regret and responsibility, and offering reparations negotiations to Israel. There were domestic and international political pressures on Germany, but the activities of concerned citizens played a role in Adenauer's overture, as noted by *Die Neue Zeitung* (January 18, 1952) and predicted by *Die Welt* (September 7, 1951) (Gardner Feldman, 1984, pp. 56–60). In the final analysis, accountability politics was significant. The Social Democrat Carlo Schmid (active in both Franco-German and German–Polish reconciliation) and the Christian Democrat Heinrich von Brentano also had occasion to interact with Israeli politicians at the the fortieth conference of the Inter-Parliamentary Union in August–September 1951, and these unofficial political contacts also influenced Adenauer (Gardner Feldman, 1984, pp. 57–58).

Summary

In all four cases, German societal actors were propelled by a sense of moral obligation to shape new relations. Where religious or spiritual actors were also politicians, such as in Germany's relations with France and with Israel, there were additional pragmatic motives of the need for German rehabilitation and return to the 'family of nations.' The religious actors were already embedded in their own societies in all cases but Israel, where new organizations had to be created. The difference between the Polish and Czech cases is attributable to the minimal role of the church in communist Czechoslovakia. In the French and Israeli cases, new institutions that cut across society were significant. The activity was both public (exchange of letters, newspaper articles, lectures) and behind-the-scenes (the Caux venue and the Inter-Parliamentary Union). In all four cases, societal actors set agendas, and in all cases except the Czech Republic clearly influenced both rhetoric and reality. In all of the examples, public figures took on leadership roles, and found allies in the other country.

Transnational actors as complements

Societal actors and organizations that complement or run parallel to official activities can be linked to the government in three ways: through public funding; through the presence of an official framework, be it treaty or agreement; and through their reflections on past governmental behavior in fora such as school book commissions. Even where there is no direct governmental linkage, TNAs can influence the official relationship with the other country. Whether direct or indirect relationships exist, for the behavior of a TNA to constitute a complement its effect on official relations must be benign or positive. Their commonality is the fact that the governments themselves do not undertake the activities. Kaiser and Mildenberger characterize these entities, particularly the friendship associations, as 'intermediary organizations' (Mittlerorganisationen) and cite three features: significance of the bilateral relationship for Germany's democracy and its foreign policy; burdened history, both politically and societally, which organizations seek to confront; and importance of the partner country to the FRG economically or politically (1998, pp. 198–199).

France
The DFI has been one of the most durable and comprehensive societal initiatives dealing with Franco-German relations in the last five decades. After the first stage when its activities were more extensive than official policy (Bock, 1998, p. 200), the Institute's work has complemented governmental ties in three stages: consolidation and education of the successor generation, 1963–72; foundation for comparative systems analysis, 1972–89; and national societies in Europe, 1989 until the present (Picht and Uterwedde, 1998, pp. 185–186). The European integration focus and the related topic of globalization define the DFI's current and future agenda (Uterwedde, 2000, pp. 106–112). Today, the chief partner for DFI is the Center for Information and Research on Contemporary Germany (Centre d'Information et de Recherche sur l'Allemagne Contemporaine) in Paris. Exchanges and discussions between elites and between youth in France and Germany, and providing information to a broader public, continue to be the DFI's main activities.

After the initial work of the Catholic and Protestant churches, other religiously based initiatives developed – for example, the Action Reconciliation/ Service for Peace (Aktion Sühnezeichen Friedensdienste), which the German Evangelical church had created in 1958 to promote voluntarism by young people in countries victimized by Nazism. In Franco-German relations, it provided a new spiritual foundation (Aktion Sühnezeichen, 1994).

The Elysée Treaty of 1963, and its supplement of 1988, has provided a framework for the extensive network of contacts in every walk of society. The variety and intensity of societal contacts prompted the appointment of Coordinators for Franco-German Relations, based in the foreign ministries of the two countries, renamed in 2003 'Representative for Franco-German Inter-Societal Cooperation.' The fortieth anniversary of the Elysée Treaty in 2003 occasioned a new wave of societal action across all areas of Franco-German relations, including a common website (Auswärtiges Amt, 2003).

One of the most important endeavors, in terms of funding, numbers of participants and programs, has been the Franco-German Youth Office (Deutsch-Französisches Jugendwerk), created in 1963 within the framework of the Elysée Treaty. Its bilateral Administrative Council is appointed by the two governments, convenes alternately in France and Germany under the chair of the two ministries of youth affairs, and implements its directives through a General Secretary (alternating nationals). Both nationalities serve in all parts of the organization regardless of location, and have responsibility for programs in both countries. As part of the fortieth anniversary celebrations, France and Germany instituted changes in the Franco-German youth exchange framework, including improved participation of civil society actors in decision-making (Bundesministerium für Familie, Senioren, Frauen und Jugend, 2004).

The non-governmental partners who carry out the exchanges include youth associations, sports clubs, language centers, training centers, trade unions, schools and universities, and town twinning organizations. Funding from the two governments stood at 20.5 million Euro in 2004, when some 200,000 young people participated in some 7,000 meetings (Bundesministerium für Familie, Senioren, Frauen und Jugend, 2004a). The initial goal of harmony has been replaced over time by the objective of understanding differences. The organization also promotes trilateral meetings – involving, for example, young people from other Western European countries and from CEE, and to a lesser extent from other geographic regions.

Private activities range across every area of society. Over 2,200 towns are twinned, starting with Ludwigsburg and Montbéliard in 1950. There are French and German bilateral associations of parliamentarians, as well as of former parliamentary interns. Political party connections abound and trade union contacts are extensive (Auswärtiges Amt, 1996). Since 1999, there has been a Franco-German university in Saarbrücken with its own finances, administration, and president and with French and German universities forming its core. Collaboration in science is impressive, including contacts via agreements between the National Center for Scientific Research (Centre National de la Recherche Scientifique) and the German Research Foundation (Deutscher Forschungsgemeinschaft), as well as the Max Planck Society (Max Planck Gesellschaft). There are over 800 agreements in the sciences between French and German universities; and a Franco-German association for science and technology has existed since 1981 (Ficat, 1998). Other disciplines are equally well represented both in university connections and exchanges and in the specialized work of research organizations such as the German Society for Foreign Policy (Deutsche Gesellschaft für Auswärtige Politik), funded through the Robert Bosch Foundation and by the Auswärtiges Amt, and the government-funded German Historical Institute in Paris (Deutches Historisches Institut) (Kaiser and Mildenberger, 1998, p. 202).

Efforts to provide accuracy in historical analysis can be found in the activities of the Franco-German School Book Commission, started in the early 1950s, although both sides feel more comfortable addressing pre-1933 issues, including examination of 'hereditary enmity,' than the Nazi period. Cultural clubs and friendship societies are sufficiently numerous that there is an umbrella Organization of Franco-German Societies (Vereinigung Deutsch-Französischer Gesellschaften in Deutschland e.V.) in Germany, and like the Franco-German Cultural Institutes (Deutsch-französische Kulturinstitute) they parallel the work of the publicly-supported Goethe Institut in France.

Bilateral activity has extended to the economic sphere via trade unions, the Franco-German Chamber of Commerce (Deutsch-Französische Industrie- und Handelskammer), and the German Tourism Office (Deutsche Zentrale für Tourismus e. V.), and here the motives switch from shared values and friendship to instrumental business and economic calculations.

Israel

From the conclusion of the 1952 Luxembourg Reparations Treaty until the establishment of diplomatic relations in 1965, German–Israeli governmental relations were largely out of public view and involved the implementation of the reparations agreement (entailing German goods in kind that built the infrastructure of the Israeli economy), an agreement on German development aid to Israel, and German military assistance.

In the absence of a German ambassador, key individuals, like Rudolf Küstermeier who traveled frequently to Israel, were dubbed 'unofficial ambassadors' by the Israeli side. Private ties, then, assumed a special public importance, and included regular connections between the Social Democratic Party (SPD) and Mapai, starting in 1957–58. Ties between the Free Democratic Party (FDP) and the Independent Liberal Party and between the Christian Democratic Party (CDU) and Likud started much later, improving after the 1977 entry of Likud into national politics in Israel. All three German parties voiced their support of Israel in the German–Israeli Parliamentary Association, founded in 1972 and historically one of Germany's largest parliamentary groups.

Active links had started between the Deutscher Gewerkschaftsbund and the Israeli Histadrut in 1950, extending later to German and Israeli union-owned construction companies investing jointly in projects in Israel. After its founding in 1958, Action Reconciliation was particularly active in Israel, first on kibbutzim, then in social work. The Societies for Christian–Jewish Cooperation were also an important link, with activities ranging from study trips to Israel to public statements supportive of Israel, and a journal. In 2005, there were over eighty societies in Germany. In all of these cases, across a range of ties, the moral obligation to confront Germany's Nazi past and to try to make amends was a powerful incentive. There was also a future orientation with Germans eager to learn about a new and inspiring country.

German students and youth were central actors in the learning and information process concerning Israel. In the mid-1950s, students created German–Israeli study groups at eleven universities, and according to one of the Israeli participants, were a crucial factor in maintaining links between the two countries (Gardner Feldman, 1984, p. 225). On the youth side, private contacts without German government funding began at the end of the 1950s, and often involved the youth sections of the trade unions and political parties. Then, commencing in 1960, the German federal government committed funds for exchanges with Israel. While not paralleling the institutionalization of the Franco-German Youth Office, by 1969 there was a German–Israeli Mixed Commission of Experts involving the German Ministry for Youth, Family, and Health and the Israeli Municipalities Association. Preferring to allow private and local actors to take the lead in this highly sensitive area of young Israelis going to Germany or receiving young Germans, it was only in 1973 that the Israeli Ministry for Education and Culture became partner of the German federal side. Including Germans who choose to do their alternative military service in Israel, some 10,000 young people participate in youth exchange every year. The German–Israeli School Book Commission strove for accuracy of historical interpretation in materials intended for German and Israeli youth (Georg Eckert Institut, 2005a). Although the Commission is no longer active, Germans and Israelis have jointly evaluated Israeli and Palestinian schoolbooks concerning the Arab–Israeli–Palestinian conflict (Firer, Adwan, and Pingel, 2004).

Other public entities were involved in nurturing, but not controlling, societal ties to Israel before diplomatic relations were established, for example in the field of science. Private connections occurred first – for example, Hans Jensen's 1957 visit to the Weizmann Institute and the Fall 1959 lectures by Weizmann Institute scientists in Frankfurt and Düsseldorf, and discussions between German and Israeli scientists about institutional links, but a December 1959 visit by a delegation from the Max Planck Gesellschaft to the Weizmann Institute marked the formal beginning of German–Israeli relations in science. The relationship grew in terms of participants and funding (an annual German contribution of 32 million DM by the mid-1990s) and culminated in the creation of two joint institutions: the German–Israeli Foundation and the German–Israeli Commission on Research and Development (Gardner Feldman, 2003). While the legacy of a common scientific tradition between Germans and Jews facilitated the evolution of German–Israeli partnership, the very nature of science, as an epistemic community, was a major stimulus. Moreover, there were highly practical reasons for German scientists' connection to Israel with its special geographic and climactic conditions unavailable to German scientists at home, and its excellence in science and technology.

After the establishment of diplomatic relations in 1965, the private networks between Germans and Israelis expanded and flourished. Extensive links developed between German and Israeli institutions of higher learning, through Jewish studies programs at German universities (including uniquely one at Humboldt University in the late 1980s devoted exclusively to Israel) and major centers for German Studies at Tel Aviv University, the Hebrew University, and Ben Gurion University in Beer Sheva, funded in large part by private German foundations. Twinning of cities also took off, as did the activities of the German Society for Economic Relations with Israel, founded in 1967. By 1975, the two governments had agreed to the creation of a Mixed Economic Commission involving industry representatives and officials working to promote trade and investment, for reasons of both German history and the German economy.

Since the establishment of diplomatic relations in 1965, the role of umbrella and facilitator for much of the German societal contact with Israel has been played, as with DFI in the French case, by the German–Israeli Society (Deutsch-Israelische Gesellschaft – DIG) created in 1966, with its counterpart Israeli society emerging in 1971. As with the DFI, the political prominence of its leadership, with figures like former chancellor Adenauer, Bundestag president Eugen Gerstenmaier, and the Social Democrat Carlo Schmid, guaranteed a high profile. By 2005, it could boast some forty-eight regional groups and a membership of 5,000 whose dues support the organization. Its goals relate to reconciliation, understanding, and advocacy on Israel's behalf (although on occasion Israel has viewed its positions on the Middle East conflict as too critical) (Gardner Feldman, 1984, pp. 226–228; Kaiser and Mildenberger, 1998, pp. 206–208; Deutsch-Israelische Gesellschaft, 2005).

The fortieth anniversary of diplomatic relations in May 2005 emphasized the importance of societal ties and highlighted their range and depth (Auswärtiges Amt, 2005; Deutschland, 2005). In his speech to the Knesset to kick off the anniversary, President Köhler referred to 'the friendship between many people in our two countries' (Köhler, 2005). The deep commitment registered by German societal institutions was not replicated, however, in public opinion polls, which have been increasingly critical of Israel (Heitmeyer, 2004)

Poland

Before the conclusion of the German–Polish Basic Treaty in 1970, church interactions had provided an important foundation to relations, similar to the activities of various societal actors in German–Israeli relations before official ties. With the signing of the Treaty, and the establishment of diplomatic relations in 1972, ties expanded to include scientific and university exchanges, more media attention, and town twinnings, even as tensions remained significant between the two governments over the issue of German reparations and German minorities in Poland. Contacts between the SPD and the Polish Workers' Party and between the FDP and the Democratic Party continued, consistent with the general pattern of German political party activity in the international realm (Bartsch, 1998, pp. 179–180).

The 1975 governmental agreement permitting ethnic Germans to migrate in exchange for German credits and social security payments stimulated more interactions, including church and union initiatives, youth meetings, the German–Polish Forum (founded in 1977), and regional German–Polish societies. The subsequent intergovernmental cultural agreement stimulated exchanges in yet another arena, although the actors on the Polish side were state-controlled (Jacobsen, 1992, p. 40). Since this expansion starting in the 1970s, trade ties became a fixture of German–Polish relations, involving a variety of German private organizations, with no societal counterpart on the other side, and a framework of German government guarantees and incentives. Since 1994, there has been an active German–Polish Chamber of Commerce (Deutsch-Polnische Industrie- und Handelskammer) in Warsaw.

As with France and Israel, the German–Polish Mixed School Book Commission, involving eminent scholars, has provided a dispassionate approach to the study of history and geography since the 1970s (Georg Eckert Institut, 2005a). Its proposals were criticized in both countries (Riemenschneider, 1998). Similar to the other cases, the purpose of the Commission is not a joint or sanitized view of history, but rather a confrontation with the past and recognition of areas of consensus and disagreement. Its recommendations also offered goals for youth exchange programs (Jacobsen, 1992, pp. 45–46).

The focus on mutual understanding and the appreciation of difference was reiterated in the 1991 German–Polish Treaty on Good Neighborship and Friendly Cooperation, which reaffirmed the importance of the school book enterprise and institutionalized youth encounters in the German–Polish Youth Office, for which the Franco-German experience serves as a model in terms of goals, organization, and administration. In 2003 some 140,000 young Germans and Poles participated (Bundesministerium für Familie, Senioren, Frauen und Jugend, 2004c).

Again building on private practice, the Treaty led to the expansion and formalization of societal ties in a range of areas: the Fund for German–Polish Cooperation, Help for Self-Help (for the German minority in Poland), the German–Polish Economic Promotion Agency, the Committee for Cross-Border Collaboration and the Committee for Interregional Collaboration, parliamentary groups, German political foundations, research institutes, academic exchange (the Deutscher Akademischer Austauschdienst (DAAD) established its Warsaw office in 1998), university partnerships, school projects and language programs, the German–Polish Institute (Deutsches Polen-Institut) the German–Polish Society (Deutsch-Polnische Gesellschaft) (with more than fifty regional groups, and somewhat similar in it purpose and political prominence to the DFI and the DIG), and the German–Polish Forum (Kaiser and

Mildenberger, 1998, pp. 209–210; Cichocki, 1999–2000; Draganovic, 1999–2000; Guz-Vetter, 1999–2000; Deutsch-Polnische Gesellschaft, 2005).

The German–Polish Forum has been guided since 1977 by the Deutsche Gesellschaft für Auswärtige Politik (DGAP), and is charged by the 1991 Treaty with presenting ideas and programs for the enhancement of German–Polish relations, and acting as an early-warning group (DGAP, 2000). Its partner was initially the Warsaw Institute of International Relations and since 1995 the West Institute in Posen. The DGAP also hosts study groups and discussion groups on Poland and German–Polish relations. As with the German–Czech case, since 1999 and with funding from various German private foundations, the DGAP has gone beyond the bilateral focus to organizing these research and dialog efforts into a CEE framework.

2005 was designated by both foreign ministries as the German–Polish Year, with a host of societal events and exchanges. There is now a common website. The degree of activity between the two societies has become so large that German and Polish Coordinators for Inter-Societal and Cross-Border Cooperation were named (following the pattern with France, and with the US) (Auswärtiges Amt, 2004).

The Czech Republic

The private channels that emerged in German–Polish relations prior to formal relations or were enhanced after governmental agreements – for example, churches and German minorities – did not enjoy the same prominence in the Czech case. There were some connections with Charta 77 members, and some Czech dissidents lived in exile in Germany before 1989, but the orthodox nature of Czech communism after the Prague Spring and Czechoslovakia's subordinate position to Poland in the German hierarchy of victimhood precluded the societal foundation present in German–Polish relations as a springboard for accelerated ties after 1989. Thus, the German–Czech Treaty on Good Neighborship and Friendly Cooperation in 1992 could not rival the positive impact in the Polish case.

Due to sporadic interest on the part of Chancellor Kohl and Prime Minister Vaclav Klaus, and opposition from within Germany and the Czech Republic, the subsequent effort to address the shortcomings of the 1992 Treaty took five years to conclude in the 1997 German–Czech Declaration on Mutual Relations and their Further Development. Contacts between the leadership of the Social Democratic parties in Germany and the Czech Republic (Günter Verheugen and Milos Zeman) and of the liberal parties (Klaus Kinkel and Jiri Dienstbier) lubricated the process considerably. Germany took full responsibility for the annexation and occupation of Czechoslovakia, and the Czechs regretted the excesses of the 1945 expulsion of Sudeten Germans and the hardship of expulsion and of property confiscation for those who were innocent. Yet, neither side had its other intentions satisfied: the actual recission of the Benes decrees for Germans; the annulment of German property claims against the Czech Republic for Czechs.

There were major provisions in the Declaration for societal linkages via the jointly financed German–Czech Future Fund: youth exchange, care for the elderly, renovation and upkeep of memorials and cemeteries, minority affairs, scientific research, ecological projects, language programs, and cross-border collaboration (Auswärtiges Amt, 1997). A number of these goals have been implemented, although there was initial difficulty realizing the German–Czech Forum for Dialog (Gardner Feldman, 1999, p. 353; Deutsch-Tschechisches Gesprächsforum, 2005). The DGAP created an additional discussion group in 1999 as an unofficial vehicle for exchanges on bilateral and regional issues (DGAP, 2000). Youth exchange has featured in these new efforts since 1997, and, like the other three country cases, benefits from a coordinating mechanism (Bundesministerium für Familie, Senioren, Frauen und Jugend, 2004b).

A major success story in German–Czech partnership initiatives has been the German–Czech Historians' Commission, established in 1990 by the two foreign ministers. This independent entity has aimed for objective historical interpretation which does not insist on convergence, but does not avoid it either – for example, the joint downgrading of the official number of German victims from the 1945 expulsion (Deutsch-Tchechische und Deutsch-Slowakische Historikerkommission, 2005). The school book effort has been less successful (Gardner Feldman, 1999, pp. 351–352; Georg EckertInstitut, 2005b).

Summary
Parallel to their role as catalysts, private actors as complements to intergovernmental relations have been galvanized by motives of moral obligation and a desire to confront the past, but they also have been driven by pragmatism, whether in the field of commerce, of scientific exchange, or of minority rights. In all four cases, organized ties have occurred in multiple spheres, creating dense networks of societal connections, although the Czech case lags behind the others because it started much later, and was not accorded the same priority as the other three by Germany. In all four examples, connections in specific fields have been accompanied or embraced by more general friendship organizations. Religious ties continue to be central, as do party connections, trade union links, and economic relations. German non-governmental actors were respected institutions before their involvement in bilateral relations (for example, the DGAP); when new, they were led by prominent and esteemed political figures.

Some organizations are physically present in the other country in an ongoing, institutionalized way (for example, Action Reconciliation), whereas others are involved in periodic exchanges with counterpart organizations, sometimes state-controlled (for example, trade unions), and yet others function as bilateral institutions (scientific relations with Israel and with France), sometimes regardless of nationality (for example, youth exchange with France and Poland).

Collecting and disseminating information continue to be primary activities, as does agenda-setting. There is also influence on policy-making via political leaders. In the case of bilateral friendship associations, with France and Israel the stimulus originated with private individuals and was then incorporated into a later intergovernmental agreement, whereas governments have proffered the framework with Poland and the Czech Republic.

Transnational actors as conduits

The German government openly promotes or frames activity when TNAs behave as complements, whereas the government plays a hidden role when TNAs act as conduits. President Roman Herzog has deemed political foundations one of the most reliable channels of German foreign policy (quoted in Phillips, 2000, p. 133). Sebastian Bartsch (1998) refers to German political foundations as 'border crossers' (Grenzgänger) between society and the state, for they operate internationally with public funding, and are subject to some government control, yet they have close relations with political parties which, according to Ann Phillips, protects them from government meddling (2000, p. 130).

The role of conduit, or channel of communication, suggests that party foundations perform public and private functions governments cannot undertake – constant cultivation of relations with opposition parties and parties in power, provision of expert advice, open dialogs with regional or local governments or with societal actors, and frequent utilization of back-channels. The foundations' political affiliations render them authoritative in the eyes of other countries, which is further aided by the foundations' physical presence abroad and their ability to inform German politicians and government officials. This section considers the general contours of political foundation activity in the four countries to show patterns of conduit behavior, and then offers some examples of other actors playing the conduit role (Friedrich Ebert Stiftung, 2005; Konrad Adenauer Stiftung, 2005; Friedrich Naumann Stiftung, 2005; Heinrich Böll Stiftung, 2005; Hanns Seidel Stiftung, 2005).[5]

France
The Friedrich Ebert Stiftung (FES) and the Konrad Adenauer Stiftung (KAS) are the most active foundations in France. The Friedrich Naumann Stiftung (FNS) and the Hanns Seidel Stiftung (HSS) have regional offices in Brussels which cover France, but the Heinrich Böll Stiftung (HBS) is not present in Paris.

For the KAS, cooperation with France enjoys the highest priority because the two countries are neighbors and the motor of European integration. While the political elite in power and in opposition is the main focus – especially during the cohabitation period of the Socialist Prime Minister Lionel Jospin from 1997 until 2002 – the KAS has also developed close ties to business, the media, trade unions, churches, and research institutions. In addition to issues of importance for the bilateral relationship and for European integration, the KAS trilateralizes its discussions to include transatlantic dialogs and third areas such as Russia or the Mediterranean.

The FES also concentrates on European integration and aims at the same range of interlocuteurs. The party connections can be seen in the Franco-German study groups on foreign and security policy and on economic and financial policy set up in 1996 by the then head of the French Socialist Party, Lionel Jospin, and the then chair of the SPD, Oskar Lafontaine. Connections to the French Socialist Party have been even more important since 2002 when the party went into opposition. Like the programs of the KAS, FES activity centers on comparative social, economic, and institutional issues, foreign and security policy, and EU integration.

Israel

All five political foundations have offices in Israel with the FES (1978) and the KAS (1980) being the oldest and the HBS being the most recent (1998). The KAS and the HSS are situated in Jerusalem and the FNS was there also, but the FES and HBS offices are located in Tel Aviv, implying that a united Jerusalem is not the capital of Israel.

The FES deals with issues of the Jewish experience in Europe and the Middle East, but concentrates on the peace process, particularly the need to build support at the grass roots level. The office works closely, therefore, with the FES offices in the Palestinian Authority, Jordan, Egypt, and Lebanon, as well as with the Brussels office, highlighting the role of the EU as a regional peace community. The FES is concerned with the role of the Arab minority in Israel, the religious right, comparative employment issues, and the role of women and youth. In the past, some Israeli elites have feared that the FES was too critical of Israel. German–Israeli relations are also covered, for both reasons of moral obligation and for the national interest of German foreign policy; the focus is on dialog between new generations.

The KAS also emphasizes the weight of the past in its activities in Israel. In addition, it sees its role as building bridges: among Germany, Israel, and Europe, to various groups in Israeli society, and between Israel and its neighbors in the region. It has sponsored Israeli and Palestinian students to attend common seminars. Inter-faith dialog is a new emphasis in its regional programming. Comparative German and Israeli topics have also emerged – for example, a conference on the protection of minority rights in Israel and the FRG under the auspices of President Rau and President Weizmann. The KAS interacts programatically with much of Israeli society – the Supreme Court, universities, women's groups, various ministries, Jewish–Arab organizations, Palestinian groups, and the Knesset. Institutionally, the KAS has solidified its presence through the building of a Konrad Adenauer Conference Center in Jerusalem with funding from various German sponsors. Like the FES, it organizes programs on German–Israeli relations.

The HBS is building networks in Israeli society and Israeli politics, with groups dealing with the environment, gender, culture, and human rights. It sees its office as a venue for critical and innovative debates and dialogs among Israel, its neighbors, and Germany.

Like the FNS, the HSS has a regional orientation in the Middle East, but it does have an office in Jerusalem where it supports rapprochement between Jewish and Arab societal groups, the education of young people in tolerance, democracy, and coexistence, and exchanges over tourism, the environment, communications technology, and the peace process. Its main partners are Beit Berl College and the Palestinian Ministry of Labor.

The FNS has a representative in Israel–Palestine, but its main regional office is in Egypt. The foundation addresses the Arab–Israeli–Palestinian conflict, and also aims to inform German society about societal developments in the region (particularly concerning Islam). It is also helping new Palestinian communities to create democratic structures. Like the FES and the KAS, the FNS has an EU orientation.

The Czech Republic

The KAS, which set up an office in Prague in 1991, sees its mission as threefold: to convey to a German audience the complexities and subtleties of Czech politics and society; to initiate discussions with Czech partners on a range of issues affecting the two countries (from the role of values to the nature of civil society, from privatization to subsidiarity); and to counter nationalism by emphasizing European identity and the EU framework for the political and economic future of the region.

Activities include meetings, student and youth exchanges, and information trips for Czech elites to Germany and for German elites to the Czech Republic. Partners have included political parties from the center to the right, the media, the church, the Czech Institute for Contemporary History, the Czech Christian Academy, and the Center for European Studies at the School of Economics in Prague and the International Institute for Political Science at Masaryk University (Reuter interview, 1997; Starostova interview, 1999). The KAS was close to the Klaus government (Phillips, 2000, p. 153), and did try to keep alive the discussions over the joint declaration when government support in Germany and the Czech Republic wavered (Reuter interview, 1997; Starostova interview, 1999). According to the chief Czech negotiator of the 1997 German–Czech declaration, the KAS played a crucial role as a channel of communication between center-right politicians in the Czech Republic and CDU/CSU politicians. The foundation had the money and the status to bring together people of different perspectives who needed to hear one another (Vondra interview, 2001).

The FES office, established in 1990, has two purposes in the Czech Republic: to promote the German–Czech dialog, particularly in the regional setting of the European Union, and on issues of comparative public policy; and to encourage political and societal discussions of pluralism, rule of law, and economic development. Partners include trade unions (both the umbrella organization and individual unions), the Czech Social Democratic Party, ministries, parliament, local and regional governments, universities, journalists, and foundations. Research and publications, discussion groups, conferences, short-term expert advice, study opportunities, and visiting delegations constitute the main activities (Schmidt interview, 1999). The fact that the Czech Republic has the longest border with Germany of any neighbor explains its importance in CEE for the FES.

The HBS office also opened in 1990 in Prague. Its main focus is energy development, environmental questions, and agriculture, with special projects on local and practical issues such as the quality of drinking water. It sees its goals as providing information and furthering German–Czech understanding (HBS, 2005). Like the KAS, it performed a major function during the negotiation of the German–Czech Declaration as a venue for differing sentiments to be articulated.

The HSS covers many of the same fields as other foundations and has links with political and economic elites and a variety of societal actors, but also deals directly with the Sudeten German issue (HSS 2005; Phillips, 2000, p. 156).

The FNS has a project office in Prague, where activity involves the promotion of the rule of law and of market economy practices through political dialog at all levels, political advice, political education, meetings, and publications.

Poland

The FNS opened its office in Poland in 1991 with a focus on political education, democratization, and marketization, through public events, training workshops, and publications.

The KAS was the first political foundation to open an office in Warsaw in November 1989, much in the spirit of Konrad Adenauer 'for whom reconciliation with France, Poland and Israel was one of the primary goals of German foreign policy' (KAS, 2000). The KAS' work emphasizes political and societal trends in Poland, particularly institutional developments and the growth of civil society. It promotes the German–Polish dialog and christian-democratic positions. Specific projects have dealt with Polish integration into the North Atlantic Treaty Organization (NATO) and the EU, economic transformation, and decentralization and local government.

The main KAS instruments are meetings, publications, exchanges, fellowships, and delegations. Partners have included the Research Institute for Market Economy in Danzig/Gdansk, the Foundation for the Development of the Catholic University in Lublin, the Konrad Adenauer Center for European Law at the University of Breslau/Wroclaw, the Center for International Relations in Warsaw, and the Polish Robert Schuman Foundation in Warsaw.

As with the Czech Republic, Poland's geographic distinctiveness, as Germany's biggest eastern neighbor, accounts for the high priority assigned by the FES to its office in Warsaw. Even before 1989, the FES gave fellowships to future leaders, such as Hanna Suchocka and Lech Balcerowicz. The FES' work has centered on three areas, attuned to the changing nature of governments:

social market economy, democracy, and pluralism; expert advice in the economic and political spheres; and integration of Poland into NATO and the EU. The foundation has paid particular attention to various projects in Silesia, engaging both governmental and non-governmental actors. Other partners are ministries, regional and local administrations, political parties, parliamentary committees, research institutes, regional economic promotion agencies, youth groups, Solidarnosc as well as individual trade unions. Confronting history, as in its programs to take former slave laborers to the places where they worked, and confronting critical policy issues (as in a conference on Kaliningrad) have been central to the FES' goals in Poland (Bünz interview, 2002).

The HBS office in Warsaw is more recent, with the official opening taking place in April 2002. Projects on women, ecology, and EU enlargement dominate the agenda and the foundation works with counterpart organizations in Poland, as well as with its sister offices in Prague and in Brussels. Unlike the other foundations, the HBS office gives full institutional support to all of its undertakings (Rochon interview, 2002).

Other examples

Both German–Israeli and German–Czech official relations have experienced periods of high tension or great difficulty; in both cases, non-governmental connections helped to defuse the situation. With Israel, SPD–Mapai contacts were used to iron out difficulties and misunderstandings over Ostpolitik in 1971, over the release of the Munich terrorists in 1972, and in 1973 when the intervention of SPD friends of Israel, including the Minister of Defense, made the movement of American arms through Bremerhaven possible, even though official policy was to deny German involvement.

In the Czech case, when there was a stalemate in the negotiations over a joint declaration in the mid-1990s and the Kanzleramt was moving very slowly, Foreign Minister Kinkel looked to two actors to keep up some momentum: Milan Horaczek, a Czech dissident who had become a Green Bundestag member in Germany, and later returned to Prague, first as an advisor to Havel, then as the director of the HBS; and Günter Verheugen who had developed excellent ties to the Czech Social Democrats (Reuter interview, 1997; Verheugen interview, 1997; Vondra interview, 2001).

Summary

Most of the political foundations are present in all four countries, usually with a full-scale office and sometimes with a smaller project outlet. The foundations are sensitive in general to the historical background of Germany's relations with France, Israel, Poland, and the Czech Republic, as reflected in their programs, but they are also future-oriented, setting the bilateral relationship in a larger regional context, whether the EU or the Middle East. Bilateralism is not lost but is expressed in new ways, such as comparative public policy, often a sign of maturity in dyadic ties (Gardner Feldman, 2001a).

Physical presence confers advantages in acting as a conduit: regularized contact across the political spectrum, deep networks, expertise, and exchanges that maintain the loop back to Germany. The close relationship between the home offices, which are ensconced in the German political landscape, and the foundations' foreign offices enhances the capacity for influence. In providing expert advice, the foundations are proffering indirect western models for political and economic development.

Much of the foundations' activity entails information gathering and dissemination. Hosting delegations in both directions allows them to play an agenda-setting role both at home and in the host country, and opens the opportunity of exerting policy influence in both places. They provide a crucial link between parties and government both at home and abroad.

Political parties can also act as conduits, as demonstrated in the Israeli and Czech examples in periods of crisis, but it appears that it is the foundations which perform the day-to-day work that renders them significant instruments of German foreign policy.

Transnational actors as competitors

When a TNA acts as competitor, it complicates official policy and/or the bilateral relationship by openly disagreeing with the home government, or by initiating its own activities abroad that conflict with government policy. TNA activity can be critical of either a positive or negative policy toward the partner country. The disagreement can be resolved through change in the government's position, continuing discordance, through prohibition of the TNA's activity by home or host government action, or by a change in the TNA approach. Differences between TNAs and the German government have occurred on various occasions throughout the life of these four cases, but they seemed particularly vibrant during the spring of 2002. We should remember that contention is a regular feature of relations of reconciliation, both between two countries and between the home government and TNAs. It is the capacity for debate and dialog over conflict that distinguishes these ties of reconciliation from relations of enmity. The reappearance of history in the spring of 2002 should be viewed as a necessary productive irritant that tests and authenticates relations of reconciliation.

Israel

There are three main examples of competition in the Israeli case: German scientists working in Egypt in the 1960s; the Action Reconciliation activities in the 1970s; and the German media and public criticism of Israel during the second *intifada* which spiraled out of control in spring 2002:

1   In a period of highly positive German–Israeli relations after the Suez crisis, President Nasser recruited German scientists to help develop rockets for use

against Israel, prompting a successful Israeli request to the German government for their dismissal from a government-funded Stuttgart research center. The scientists' TNA character derived from their identity as an epistemic community, both intellectually (their pursuits as scientists) and in terms of affiliation (from the same institute). When Israel lodged a second complaint on discovering that German scientists had moved to Egypt and were working on atomic, biological, and chemical weapons, the German government was less sympathetic, arguing that they could not stop the activities of private citizens. Despite outcry on the part of the CDU, SPD, and FDP in parliament, and of German public opinion, and Adenauer's replacement by Erhard, the German government did not act and the issue was finally resolved by actions of the Israeli secret service, Mossad.

The issue of the scientists caused a bitter debate in Israel over German–Israeli relations, with Ben Gurion resigning and his successor (Levi Eshkol) issuing the severest attack on Germany since the early 1950s. However, the incident and Germany's inability to stop the German scientists seem to have contributed to Erhard's decision to offer diplomatic relations to Israel in 1965.

2   In the mid-1970s, after some fifteen years of working in Israel to make amends for Nazi crimes, a number of Action Reconciliation volunteers began to involve themselves in questions of Palestinian rights and to be openly critical of Israel (Gardner Feldman, 1984, p. 8). The criticism of Israel was counter-balanced by the work of other members of the movement, but it caused concern within political elites in Germany and Israel (Krupp interview, 1975).

3   A survey of the main German newspapers' reporting on the Middle East by the Duisburger Institut für Sprach- und Sozialforschung during the period September 2000–August 2001 revealed an anti-Israel bias at a time when the German government's position was even-handed regarding the Israeli–Palestinian conflict. The issue became a complicating factor in the spring of 2002 when media criticism seemed to increase and was accompanied by public anti-Israel demonstrations and by harsh attacks on Israel (deemed by some to be anti-Semitic) from the FDP's Jürgen Möllemann and the CDU's Norbert Blüm. In the face of this public activity, Foreign Minister Fischer maintained his understanding of Israel's security needs and his historically based moral commitment to Israel (and the necessity for Palestinian self-determination), and criticized the one-sided view of Israel's detractors in Germany and Europe (Frankfurter Rundschau, April 20, 2002). Moreover, some non-governmental actors came to Israel's defense (Frankfurter Rundschau, April 15, 2002).

Poland

Three cases of competition are noteworthy in German–Polish relations: expellee attitudes regarding the Oder–Neisse line in the 1960s and 1970s; the activity of non-governmental actors during the emergence of Solidarnosc; and the expellee calls from 2000 on for a center to study expulsion featuring Germans as victims:

1   Up until the Grand Coalition of 1966, the Expellee Federation had vigorously influenced and supported official policy which did not accept Polish sovereignty over the Oder–Neisse line or the territories to its East. As a new Ostpolitik of reconciliation and rapprochement emerged, the Expellee Federation launched fierce attacks against the government, reinforced by its tight relationship with the CSU and, initially, with the CDU. The CDU, however, was increasingly splitting into fundamentalist and reformist camps (older figures like Richard von Weizsäcker, Rainer Barzel, and Alois Mertes, as well as young Christian Democrats) (Clemens, 1989, chapter 1). The expellee condemnation of Ostpolitik grew with the new SPD/FDP government in 1969, which pursued a more conciliatory and status quo-oriented policy. The signing and ratification of the Eastern treaties, including that with Poland, aroused deep political divisions between government and opposition and within government. In the ratification, 230 deputies, mainly from the CDU/CSU opposition, abstained, leaving the government with 248 affirmative votes and seventeen votes in the negative.

2   Whereas some 60% of public opinion had supported the SPD/FDP government's policy of reconciliation and rapprochement with Poland in the early 1970s, ten years later there was a major divergence between German societal actors and the government over martial law in Poland and the emergence of Solidarnosc, for German officialdom was far less critical of General Jaruzelski than other western governments. In the 1970s, the Bensberger Kreis (following its earlier role as catalyst) and a group led by Bernhard Vogel (as President of the Central Organization of German Catholics) built extensive relations with Polish dissidents, such as Adam Michnik and Wladyslaw Bartoszewski, and church as well as lay groups. Over 2 million care packages were sent to Poland by German private citizens, an act long remembered positively by Poles. It was this extensive networking by TNAs, intensified in the early 1980s in contradistinction to the policy of the SPD/FDP government, that permitted Germany and Poland to declare a 'community of interest' (Interessengemeinschaft) in the 1990s (Jacobsen, 1992, pp. 32, 46–47; Tomala, 1992, pp. 17–18; Kerski, 1999).

3   Reconciliation has proceeded vigorously at both the societal and governmental levels since the early 1990s, but TNAs still can cause tensions in relations and demonstrate that history lies only skin-deep. In June 2000, Erika Steinbach, the president of the Expellee Federation and CDU parliamentarian, proposed a Center for the Remembrance of Expulsion (Zentrum gegen Vertreibung) in Berlin that would permanently showcase the victimhood and plight of German expellees and periodically address other expulsions. The expellees emphasized that they were moved by the 'spirit of reconciliation' (Associated Press, June 6, 2000). The government's

initial response to the request for funding was lukewarm, preferring a special exhibition in the House of History (Haus der Geschichte) located in Bonn (*FAZ*, September 21, 2000).

Frau Steinbach persisted and was joined in her efforts by political luminaries like the SPD's Peter Glotz (himself an expellee from Czechoslovakia), and by the spring of 2002 the Minister of State for Culture broadened the government's earlier response by proposing an information center on expulsion, albeit with a European, rather than a German, focus. The Polish response to Steinbach's proposal was negative or uninterested until the SPD parliamentarian Markus Meckel (also the German head of the German–Polish parliamentarians' group) countered with a proposal for a center in Breslau that would expand and denationalize the perspective by including the Polish expellees' history (*Süddeutsche Zeitung*, March 26, 2002). The Polish historian Wlodzimierz Borodziej seconded Meckel's proposal, the Polish President Alexander Kwasniewski responded positively, and the two Polish journalists Adam Michnik and Adam Krzeminski in an open letter to Chancellor Schröder and Prime Minister Miller elaborated on the need for a European and future-oriented framework, although public opinion remained reluctant (*FAZ*, June 18, 2002).

Frau Steinbach's activities and pressure and Edmund Stoiber's candidacy for chancellor in the September 2002 elections together elevated the issue into a major parliamentary debate in Germany, with motions by all parties. Stoiber expanded the topic of history and victimhood even further, and provoked the Poles even more, in his address to the East Prussian expellee association in June 2002 when he called for a rescission of the Polish Bierut decreees of 1945–46, which dealt with expropriation and expulsion of German minorities for their wartime activities (*FAZ*, June 26, 28, 2002). The ferocity of the negative Polish reaction was dissipated by the subsequent survey of the Sejm (parliament) archives which indicated the decrees had in fact already been lifted by communist governments in 1949, 1951, and 1985.

The idea of a Center has continued to animate German–Polish relations. For example, Erika Steinbach mounted an exhibition on expulsion in Berlin in August 2006. The German government has continued to respond to these stimuli, for example in its own plan for an exhibition in 2006, and in the February 2005 creation (together with Poland, Hungary, and Slovakia) of a European Network on Remembrance and Solidarity (Europäisches Netzwerk Erinnerung und Solidarität),which includes among other activities addressing the issue of expulsion in a pan-European sense (Bundesregierung, 2005; *Die Welt*, February 3, 2005).

German–Polish relations had been further complicated in the fall of 2004 when the Prussian Claims Society, representing Germans expelled from Poland, announced its plans to sue Poland for lost property (*Deutsche Welle*, 2004). In a unanimous vote, the Polish Sejm in response demanded reparations from Germany for Second World War damage (*International Herald Tribune*,

September 11, 2004). The two governments dealt with this development in a coordinated manner by jointly commissioning a legal evaluation, which concluded that there was no basis for claims on either side.

The Czech Republic

Two of the German–Czech cases of competition relate to Sudeten German influence from 1999 on, and the third relates to the Greens:

1   The Sudeten German Expellee Association (Sudetendeutsche Landsmannschaft) was sufficiently influential to prevent inclusion in the 1992 Treaty of a clause annulling their property claims (Kopstein, 1998, p. 58). Their opposition to the 1997 Joint Declaration was just as vigorous, but with a new twist. In both the European Parliament (EP) and in Bavaria, through the vehicle of the CSU, the Sudeten Germans linked Czech EU membership to the resolution of outstanding claims (Kettle, 1996, p. 24). The Sudeten Germans could not stop the 1997 Declaration, but their opposition slowed down the negotiations considerably.

2   The linkage strategy resurfaced in September 2001, when at an expellee meeting Edmund Stoiber also made the connection between rescission of the Benes Decrees and EU membership (*AP*, September 21, 2001). The issue of the Benes Decrees became fully politicized in February 2002 when Czech Prime Minister Zeman referred to Sudeten Germans as a pro-Nazi fifth column during the German occupation of Czechoslovakia, and much of the German political scene denounced his view. While Foreign Minister Fischer tried to downplay the issue, he could not prevent the fallout: the cancellation of Chancellor Schröder's plan to visit Prague in March, and the direct involvement of EU Commission officials and the EP to look into whether the Benes Decrees violated EU norms. The Czech parliament was as upset as the Bundestag, but in the opposite direction, with a clear majority voting for legal retention of the Benes Decrees.

    German government officals continued to maintain that there would be no barriers to Czech membership of the EU, but the explosive potential of the Benes Decree issue was seen in Stoiber's May 2002 speech to the Sudeten German reunion and Interior Minister Schily's subsequent attack on Stoiber for ignoring the letter and spirit of the 1997 Declaration where Czechs did regret the harm to innocents during the expulsion. In Schily's speech to the Sudeten Germans, he called for a rescission of the Benes Decrees as a symbolic gesture, and for an attendant commitment by the Sudeten Germans not to set in train property claims against the Czechs. He also reminded his audience that the Czechs themselves were the first expellees with the German annexation of 1938. Stoiber continued to insist on recission of the Benes Decrees even after Czech membership of the EU (May 2004), for example in his May 2005 address to the Sudeten German Society meeting in Augsburg.

3   Zeman repeated his rejection of Sudeten German demands in a visit to
     Theresienstadt in May 2002, arguing that satisfaction of their claims would
     dishonor the memory of Theresienstadt's victims. He also proposed com-
     pensation to anti-fascist Sudeten Germans, demonstrating that gestures
     of reconciliation can emerge from profound tension. Until the 1997
     Declaration, the Czech Republic was the only country whose victims of
     Nazism had never received any payment from Germany (Sitler, 1998,
     pp. 32–33). Additionally, Jewish victims received some compensation as
     a result of a January 1998 agreement between the German government
     and the American-based Claims Conference on Material Claims Against
     Germany. A large part of turning around a German government that was
     reluctant to address the issue of compensation can be attributed to the ini-
     tiatives of the Greens working with other political forces in Germany, but
     particularly with the American Jewish Committee, which at the same time
     was collaborating with the Czech Jewish community to advance its views in
     meetings in the Czech Republic, Germany, and the US (Gardner Feldman,
     2001b; Kraus interview, 1999).

France

There was no crisis of history in Franco-German relations in the first years of
the new millennium as there was in the other three relationships. Yet, there were
deep tensions between the two governments since the open disagreements at the
December 2000 Nice European Council meeting and France's refusal to entertain the idea of more German votes in the Council of Ministers. Areas of tension
included agricultural subsidies and the EMU's Stability Pact. Observers viewed
'two partners who have drifted apart' (*Financial Times*, February 2, 2001). Both
sides recognized these differences, which derive from different social and economic philosophies and not from the behavior of TNAs, and after Nice a new
framework for more regular meetings at more levels was put in place at the
Blaesheim talks.

Despite the differences between the two governments, public opinion in
each country has been very positive concerning the partner. In a survey published in the *Süddeutsche Zeitung* and in *Libération* at the end of January 2001,
86% of the Germans and 81% of the French interviewed thought the Franco-
German tandem was essential for the future development of the EU (Agence
France Presse, January 31, 2001). 'Competition' in the sense of the other three
cases is thus not relevant in the Franco-German case, although one could talk of
'contradistinction' between periodic governmental attitudes and the sentiments
of non-governmental actors.

Summary

In the three country cases, German TNAs were motivated by what they saw as a
moral imperative, except regarding German scientists in Egypt, where the

involvement was much more instrumental. All of the cases were played out in the political realm. Concerning Israel, German private actors undertook initiatives at home and abroad that were harmful to German–Israeli relations. In the first Polish and Czech cases, German TNAs were critical of emerging conciliatory policy toward the other country, and tried to prevent it. In the second and third Polish examples and the second and third Czech examples, German TNAs saw dereliction in official German positions and sought to counter it through changing policy in the Czech cases and the third Polish case in the years 1990–2002, and through its own initiatives to counteract official policy in the second Polish case in the 1970s and 1980s.

In the first Israeli case, the German government initially countered the TNA, but then refused to act. Regarding the second, there was nothing for the German government to do, except feel embarrassed. In the third case, the German government has continued to pursue its even-handed policy. With Poland in the first case, the German government felt its room for maneuver lessened, but it still prevailed. With respect to the second Polish case, discordance remained. In the third Polish case, the government slightly altered its position. In the first Czech case, after giving in to the TNA, the German government finally resisted in the next stage, and has largely maintained its position during the second case. The German government changed its position totally for the third Czech case.

The third Czech case was entirely successful for two reasons: the strong domestic anchoring of the Greens, and the triangular transnational alliance, in which the American Jewish Committee was instrumental through its traditional political lobbying in advertising the plight of Czech Jewish victims of Nazism.

Conclusion

The analysis of Germany's relations of reconciliation have displayed both moral and pragmatic motivations, and they are sometimes combined in the same actor. Functionally, in each of the four cases, essentially every aspect of societal interaction has been institutionalized and actors rarely have been ad hoc; religious actors, political foundations, and friendship associations have been particularly active.

TNAs for the most part have been rooted in German domestic politics, as opposed to global TNAs with a German affiliate, and have found counterparts or partners in the other country. The political foundations have been particularly effective due to their physical presence abroad. The range of issues on which TNAs interact with the other country has been broad and bilateral, although increasingly the bilateral relationship has been couched in a multilateral setting. Collection and dissemination of information has been the most frequent task and will grow in the light of technology. Agenda-setting is a second regular feature of TNAs, while policy influence is clear, but harder to establish. Tactics to affect the government include highly public campaigns for catalysts and competitors and very private lobbying for conduits. Consistent financial resources, from the government in the case of political foundations, permit the gradual accretion of networks in society and the corridors of power that are the essence of the foundations' work in the host country.

TNAs as catalysts have been active before the establishment of official relations, and as complements sometimes were a product of intergovernmental agreements. Much of the reconciliation activity of TNAs is complementary to official ties. The categories of conduit and competitor are less frequent, but still significant in their consequences for official policy. Conduit behavior can be ongoing, as in the case of the political foundations, or can arise over specific events. Competitive behavior bears some elements of crisis. In terms of consequences, TNAs have influenced their own government and the government of the other country. They have provoked their own governments to act, shaped their behavior, and acted as surrogates.

Rather than proffering snapshots, these four cases demonstrate the evolution of ties and TNA activity over long periods of time (more than five decades in relations with France and Israel, three decades with Poland, and some fifteen years with the Czech Republic). Their role has been significant, multifarious and central to the German government's foreign policy of reconciliation.

Notes

1   There is a recent literature on transnationalism in German foreign policy, but it tends to be general and downplays the role of reconciliation (Bühl, 1994; Bartsch, 1998; Kaiser and Mildenberger, 1998). German discussions of transnationalism as an international phenomenon also do not incorporate analysis of reconciliation. See, for example, the work of the two sections of the Wissenschaftszentrum Berlin – 'Transnationale Konflikte und Internationale Institutionen' and 'Zivilgesellschaft und transnationale Netzwerke.' Other German literature on transnational networks has focused on their role in European integration and in global governance. See, for example, Kohler Koch and Eising (1999); Wolf (2000); and Jachtenfuchs and Knodt (2002).

2   Similar to the early efforts by Keohane and Nye, neither work accords priority to German cases, even though many would share Walter Bühl's view that Germany surpasses most other nations in its degree of transnational (and multinational) connections (1994, p. 176).

3   Keck and Sikkink (1998) exclude MNCs because of their instrumental goals. They are largely omitted from my analysis not because of their pragmatism (in fact, in the German–Israeli case, German industry has cited moral as well as instrumental reasons for activity in Israel), but because their activities are too broad to capture here.

4   Unlike Kaiser, neither Risse-Kappen nor Keck and Sikkink see competition as negative.

5   For a more detailed analysis of specific party foundations, see chapter 3 in this volume by Dorota Dakowska and Elsa Tulmets.

Bibliography

Books and articles

Ackermann, Alice (1994) 'Reconciliation as a peace-building process in postwar Europe: the Franco-German case,' *Peace and Change*, 19 (3).

Aktion Sühnezeichen Friedensdienste e.V. (1994) '6 Juin 1944. 50 Jahre danach. Über 30 Jahre Aktion Sühnezeichen Friedensdienste in Frankreich,' *Zeichen*, 2.

Auswärtiges Amt (1996) *Wege zur Freundschaft: Adressbuch der deutsch-französischen Zusammenarbeit*, Bonn.

Auswärtiges Amt (1997) 'Deutsch-tschechische Erklärung über die gegenseitigen Beziehungen und deren künftige Entwicklung,' Prague, January 21.

Auswärtiges Amt (2003) 'Kompendium der deutsch-französischen Zusammenarbeit', at www.auswaertiges-amt.de/www/de/laenderinfos/elysee/kompendium (accessed June 9, 2005).

Auswärtiges Amt (2004) 'Bundesminister Fischer würdigt neue Koordinatorin für die deutsch-polnische Zusammenarbeit Gesine Schwan,' November 10, at www.auswaertiges-amt.de/www/de/ausgabe_archiv?archiv_id=6391 (accessed November 10, 2004).

Auswärtiges Amt (2005) '40 Jahre diplomatischer Beziehungen zwischen Deutschland und Israel,' at www.auswaertigesamt.de/www/de/laenderinfos/40jahre_bezisr/index.html (accessed June 9, 2005).

Bartsch, Sebastian (1998) 'Aussenpolitischer Einfluss und Aussenbeziehungen der Parteien,' in Wolf-Dieter Eberwein and Karl Kaiser (eds), *Deutschlands neue Aussenpolitik*, Band 4: Institutionen und Ressourcen, Munich: Oldenbourg.

Barzel, Rainer (1988) '25 Jahre, 1963–1988: Deutsch-Französische Zusammenarbeit,' Bonn: Presse- und Informationsamt der Bundesregierung.

Bertelsmann (1997) *Gespräche mit dem Nachbarn*, Prague: Bertelsmann/Charles University.

Bock, Hans-Manfred (1998) '"Stillwirkende Kraft der politischen Bemühungen": Zur Gründung des Deutsch-Französischen Instituts vor 50 Jahren,' in *Dokumente: Zeitschrift für den deutsch-französischen Dialogs*, 3.

Bühl, Walter L. (1994) 'Gesellschaftliche Grundlagen der deutschen Aussenpolitik,' in Karl Kaiser and Hanns W. Maull (eds), *Deutschlands neue Aussenpolitik*, Band 1: Grundlagen, Munich: Oldenbourg.

Bundesministerium für Familie, Senioren, Frauen und Jugend (2004a) 'Reform des Deutsch-Französischen Jugendwerks beschlossen,' October 26, at http://bmfsfj.de/Kategorien/Presse/pressemitteilungen, did=21138.html (accessed October 27, 2004).

Bundesministerium für Familie, Senioren, Frauen und Jugend (2004b) 'Deutsch-Tschechischer Jugendaustausch,' September 7, at http://bmfsfj.de/Kategorien/Presse/pressemitteilungen, did=20210.html (accessed June 14, 2005).

Bundesministerium für Familie, Senioren, Frauen und Jugend (2004c) 'Deutsch-Polnisches Jugendwerk,' September 7, at www.bmfsfj.de/Politikbereiche/kinder-und-jugend,did=20226.html (accessed June 14, 2005).

Bundesregierung (2005) 'Statement von Kulturstaatsministerin Weiss zum künftigen "Europäischen Netzwerk Erinnerung und Solidarität,"' February 2, at www.bundesregierung.de/rede-,413.782741/Statement-von-Kulturstaatsmini.htm (accessed June 10, 2005).

Cichoki, Marek A. (1999–2000) 'Der Nachbar, den es nicht gibt,' *Dialog: Deutsch-polnisches Magazin*, Winter.

Clemens, Clay (1989) *Reluctant Realists: The Christian Democrats and West German Ostpolitik*, Durham, NC: Duke University Press.

Delors, Jacques (1988) *France-Allemagne: le bond en avant*, Paris: Odile Jacob.

Deutsch-Französisches Jugendwerk (2005), at www.dfjw.org.

Deutsch-Israelische Gesellschaft (2005), at www.dig-frankfurt.de/orga/dig.htm.

Deutsch-Polnische Gesellschaft Bundesverband e. V. (2005) at www.deutsch-polnische-gesellschaft.de/info.html.

Deutsch-Polnisches Jugendwerk (2005), at www.dpjw.org.

Deutsch-Tschechisches Gesprächsforum (2005), at www.diskusniforum.org.

Deutsch-tschechische und deutsch-slowakische Historikerkommission (2005), at www.dt-ds-historikerkommission.de.

Deutsche Gesellschaft für Auswärtige Politik (DGAP) (2000), at www.dgap.org/fopr5.htm.

Deutsche Welle (2004) 'Warsaw–Berlin tensions rise over expellee claims,' September 6, at www.dw-world.de/dw/article/0,1564,1319213,00.html (accessed March 1, 2005).

Deutschland (2005) '40 Jahre diplomatischer Beziehungen Deutschland und Israel,' Sonderheft Israel, January, at www.magazine-deutschland.de.

Draganovic, Julia (1999–2000) 'Junge Universitäten im Aufwind,' *Dialog: Deutsch-polnisches Magazin*, Winter.

Duisburger Institut für Sprach- und Sozialforschung (2002) 'Die Nahost-Berichterstattung zur Zweiten Intifada in deutschen Printmedien, unter besonderer Berücksichtigung des Israel-Bildes: Analyse diskursiver Ereignisse im Zeitraum von September 2000 bis August 2001,' Duisburg.

Eberwein, Wolf-Dieter and Karl Kaiser (eds) (1998), *Deutschlands neue Aussenpolitik*, Band 4: Institutionen und Ressourcen, Munich: Oldenbourg.

Evangelische Kirche (1996) 'Kundgebung der 8. Synode der evangelischen Kirche in Deutschland auf ihrer 7. Tagung zur Versöhnung zwischen Tschechen und Deutschen,' November 7.

Ficat, Charles (1998) 'Die deutsch-französische Zusammenarbeit in der Wissenschaft,' *Dokumente*, 2.

Firer, Ruth, Sami Adwan, and Falk Pingel (2004) *The Israeli-Palestinian Conflict in History and Civic Textbooks of Both Nations*, Hannover: Verlag Hahnsche Buchhandlung.

Friedrich Ebert Stiftung (2005), at www.fes.org.il; www.fes.war.org.pl; www.fesprag.cz.

Friedrich Naumann Stiftung (2005), at www.fnst.de.

Gardner Feldman, Lily (1984) *The Special Relationship between West Germany and Israel*, London: Allen & Unwin.

Gardner Feldman, Lily (1999) 'The principle and practice of 'reconciliation' in German foreign policy: relations with France, Israel, Poland and the Czech Republic,' *International Affairs*, 75 (2).

Gardner Feldman, Lily (2001a) 'Gesellschaftliche Beziehungen in drei Dimensionen 1968–90,' in Detlef Junker *et al.*, *Die USA und Deutschland im Zeitalter des Kalten Krieges 1945–1990: Ein Handbuch. Band II: 1968–1990*, Stuttgart: Deutsche Verlagsanstalt.

Gardner Feldman, Lily (2001b) 'Die Rolle von Juden und jüdischen Organisationen in den deutsch-amerikanischen Beziehungen,' in Frank Trommler, *Deutsch-amerikanische Begegnungen. Konflikt und Kooperation im 19. und 20. Jahrhundert*, Stuttgart: Deutsche Verlags-Anstalt.

Gardner Feldman, Lily (2003) 'Annäherung, Widerstreben und Ablehnung. Das Dreiecksverhältnis zwischen Deutschland, Israel und dem amerikanischen Judentum,' in Frank Stern and Maria Gierlinger (eds), *Die deutsch-jüdische Erfahrung. Beiträge zum kulturellen Dialog*, Berlin: Aufbau-Verlag.

Georg Eckert Institut für internationale Schulbuchforschung (2005a), at www.gei.de.

Georg Eckert Institut für internationale Schulbuchforschung (2005b) 'Projekte: Deutsch-tschechische Schulbuchgespräche. Historischer Rückblick,' at www.gei.de/deutsch/projekte/d_t_projekt.shtml (accessed June 14, 2005).

Guz-Vetter, Marzenna (1999–2000) 'Wir werden uns auf die bereiche Wissenschaft und Kultur konzentrieren,' Gespräch mit Eugeniusz Gorczyca, *Dialog: Deutsch-polnisches Magazin*, Winter.

Hanns Seidel Stiftung (2005), at www.hss.de.

Hartweg, Frédéric (1989) 'Introduction: quelques réflexions sur les protestantismes allemand et français et leurs relations,' *Revue d'Allemagne*, 21 (4).

Heimerl, Daniel (1989) 'Les églises évangeliques et le rapprochement franco-allemand dans l'après-guerre: le conseil fraternel franco-allemand,' *Revue d'Allemagne*, 21 (4).

Heinrich Böll Stiftung (2005), at www.boell.de.

Heitmeyer, Wilhelm (2004) 'Texte zu Ergebnissen der Umfrage 2004 des Projektes 'Gruppenbezogene Menschenfeindlichkeit' mit Schwerpunkten zum Antisemitismus,' Institut für interdisziplinäre Konflikt- und Gewaltforschung Universität Bielefeld.

Jachtenfuchs, Markus and Michèle Knodt (eds) (2002), *Regieren in internationalen Institutionen*, Opladen: Leske & Budrich.

Jacobsen, Hans-Adolf (1992) 'Bundesrepublik Deutschland – Polen: Aspekte ihrer Beziehungen,' in Hans-Adolf Jacobsen and Mieczyslaw Tomala (eds), *Bonn-Warschau 1945–1991: Die deutsch-polnischen Beziehungen*, Cologne: Verlag Wissenschaft und Politik.

Jacobsen, Hans-Adolf and Mieczyslaw Tomala (eds) (1992) *Bonn-Warschau 1945–1991: Die deutsch-polnischen Beziehungen*, Cologne: Verlag Wissenschaft und Politik.

Kaiser, Karl (1971) 'Transnational relations as a threat to the democratic process,' in Robert O. Keohane and Joseph S. Nye, Jr. (eds) (1994), *Transnational Relations and World Politics*, Special Volume of *International Organization*, 25 (3).

Kaiser, Karl and Hanns W. Maull (eds) (1995), *Deutschlands neue Aussenpolitik*, Band 1: Grundlagen, Munich: Oldenbourg.

Kaiser, Karl, and Markus Mildenberger (1998) 'Gesellschaftliche Mittlerorganisationen,' in Wolf-Dieter Eberwein and Karl Kaiser (eds), *Deutschlands neue Aussenpolitik*, Band 4: Institutionen und Ressourcen, Munich: Oldenbourg.

Keck, Margaret and Kathryn Sikkink (1998) *Activists Beyond Borders: Advocacy Networks in International Politics*, Ithaca, NY: Cornell University Press.

Keohane, Robert O. and Joseph S. Nye, Jr. (eds) (1971), *Transnational Relations and World Politics*, Special Volume of *International Organization*, 25 (3).

Kerski, Basil (1999) 'Die Rolle nichtstaatlicher Akteure in den deutsch-polnischen Beziehungen vor 1990,' Discussion Papers, Arbeitsgruppe Internationale Politik, Wissenschaftszentrum Berlin für Sozialforschung, Berlin, January.

Kettle, Steve (1996) 'Czechs and Germans still at odds,' *Transition*, 2 (3), February 9.

Köhler, Horst (2005) 'Ansprache von Bundespräsident Horst Köhler vor der Knesset, Jerusalem,' February 2, at www.bundespraesident.de.Reden-und-Interviews,11057.66215/Ansprache-von-Bundespraesident.htm (accessed February 5, 2005).

Kohler Koch, Beate and Rainer Eising (eds) (1999), *The Transformation of Governance in the European Union*, London: Routledge.

Konrad Adenauer Stiftung (2000), at http://otto.kas.de.

Konrad Adenauer Stiftung (2005), at www.kas.de/proj/home/home/24/1/; www.kas.de/proj/home/home/48/1/; www.kas.de/proj/home/home/11/1/.

Kopstein, Jeffrey (1998) 'Die Politik der nationalen Aussöhnung. Erinnerung und Institutionen in den deutsch-tschechischen Beziehungen seit 1989,' *WeltTrends*, 19.

Lüth, Erich (1966) *Viele Steine Lagen am Weg*, Hamburg: Marion von Schröder Verlag.

Mildenberger, Markus (1999–2000) 'Versöhnung als Fünfte Kolonne,' *Dialog: Deutsch-polnisches Magazin*, Winter.

Phillips, Ann L. (2000) *Power and Influence after the Cold War: Germany in East Central Europe*, Lanham, MD and Oxford: Rowman & Littlefield.

Picht, Robert and Henrik Uterwedde (1998) 'Europäische Zukunft gestalten: Neue Aufgaben für das Deutsch-Französische Institut,' *Dokumente*, 3.

Piguet, Jacqueline (1985) *For the Love of Tomorrow: The Story of Irène Laure*, London: Grosvenor.

Riemenschneider, Rainer (1998) 'Transnationale Konfliktbearbeitung: Die deutsch-französischen und die deutsch-polnischen Schulbuchgespräche im Vergleich,' *Internationale Schulbuchforschung*, 20.

Risse-Kappen, Thomas (ed.) (1995) *Bringing Transnational Relations Back In: Non-State Actors, Domestic Structures and international Institutions*, New York: Cambridge University Press.

Rovan, Joseph (1998) 'France-Allemagne, 1948–1998,' in Jacques Delors, *France-Allemagne: le bond en avant*, Paris: Odile Jacob.

Sekretariat der deutschen Bischofskonferenz (1990) 'Worte der Versöhnung: Erklärungen der Bischöfe Deutschlands und der CSFR,' Bonn, September 5.

Sitler, Jiri (1998) 'The forgotten victims,' *Transition*, 5 (11).

Tomala, Mieczyslaw (1992) 'Die Beziehungen zwischen Polen und der Bundesrepublik Deutschland,' in Hans-Adolf Jacobsen and Mieczyslaw Tomala (eds), *Bonn-Warschau 1945–1991: Die deutsch-polnischen Beziehungen*, Cologne: Verlag Wissenschaft und Politik.

Uterwedde, Henrik (2000) 'Gemeinsam an der Gesellschaft von morgen bauen,' *Dokumente*, 2.

Wolf, Klaus Dieter (2000) *Staatsräson – Die neue zwischenstaatliche Kooperation als Demokratieproblem in der Weltgesellschaft*, Baden-Baden: Nomos.

Interviews

Bünz, Hermann, FES, Warsaw, June 5, 2002.

Goldmann, Nahum, Paris, June 9, 1975.

Kraus, Tomas, Jewish Community, Prague, February 1, 1999.

Krupp, Michael, Aktion Sühnezeichen, Jerusalem, April 15, 1975.

Küstermeier, Rudolf, Berlin, May 1, 1975.

Lüth, Erich, Hamburg, June 28, 1975.

Reuter, Franz-Josef, KAS, Sankt Augustin, March 5, 1997.

Rochon, Agnieska, Warsaw, June 5, 2002.

Schmid, Carlo, Bonn, June 16, 1975.

Schmidt, Heidulf, FES, Prague, February 3, 1999.

Starostova, Barbara, KAS, Prague, February 2, 1999.

Verheugen, Günter, Bonn, March 11, 1997.

Vondra, Alexandr, Czech Ambassador to the United States, Washington, DC, July 18, 2001.

Soledad Loaeza

2

The political dimension of Germany's unintentional power: the KAS and Mexican democratization

KAS and democratization

The participation of international and transnational actors (TNAs) in the democratization processes of the last quarter of the twentieth century in Latin America was a distinctive feature of the vast wave of political change that swept the region in those years. Events that in the past had been considered the *domaine réservé* of national actors became a legitimate concern for foreign governments, as well as for non-governmental and non-state organizations and groups. Initiatives and actions that according to the traditional notion of national sovereignty would have been considered illegitimate interference became a public fact broadly accepted and, in many cases, a resource for domestic actors. This change was based on a profound transformation of attitudes regarding the relationship between citizens and the state by which human rights took precedence over the national interest. However, the change also suggests that in Latin American countries democratizing domestic actors were too weak on their own to sustain the process and that deteriorating authoritarian actors were unable to stop it. National, international, and transnational actors thus converged in the promotion of regime change. So much so that 'it may be artificial to dichotomize the analysis [of democratization processes] into domestic and international elements.'[1] The activities and the weight of non-state and non-governmental actors in these processes were so important that they deserve close examination

Mexico's democratization illustrates the combined influences of foreign and domestic actors. It stretched throughout the 1980s and 1990s and led to the gradual dismantling of a hegemonic party system in place since the early 1930s. Old and new political parties and government authorities were the main protagonists in the building of a multi-party system and of institutions that were a warrant of competitive and clean electoral processes. Nevertheless, these political changes were introduced at the same time as profound economic reforms were encouraged by foreign governments and intergovernmental agencies. Domestic and foreign NGOs, non-state actors, the media, opinion-makers, and influential academics also played an important role in the articulation of social protests and demands. They contributed to set the agenda of change and shaped political debate. In this protracted process of democratization[2] national political actors benefited from the support of external actors that provided ideological references and material and moral resources of different kind.

This chapter discusses the contribution of the Konrad Adenauer Stiftung (KAS) to Mexico's democratization. It focuses on the relationship between the German foundation and the Partido Accion Nacional (PAN), the long-standing opposition party that in the 2000 presidential election defeated the legendary Partido Revolucionario Institucional (PRI), in power since 1946. Nevertheless, the hegemonic 'official party' tightly linked to the state, that held a virtual monopoly of elective offices had two predecessors, the Partido Nacional Revolucionario (PNR, 1929–38) and the Partido de la Revolución Mexicana (PRM, 1938–46). The PAN was founded in 1939 but until the early 1980s it painstakingly survived as a marginal minority in the hostile environment of an authoritarian system that barely tolerated any form of opposition. In the unfavorable circumstances of systematic and persistent electoral fraud and governmental control of political participation, and of very scarce material and political resources, the PAN could aspire to be only an 'interest group' sporadically representing limited political discontent. This situation hindered the party's organizational and ideological development, keeping it in a state of weakness that in several instances threatened its continuity.

It is argued here that the KAS played a significant part, albeit indirectly, in the consolidation of the PAN by supporting its institutionalization, providing the party with the means to define a more precise ideological identity. Acting as a reference, too, the German foundation fostered the modernization of the party's platform and policy programs. Given its traditional identification with Catholic thought, the PAN was a natural counterpart to the KAS and an organization particularly receptive to its programmatic influence, a receptivity that was further enhanced by the party's relatively low level of institutionalization. But the KAS also contributed to the training of a new PANista elite. These transformations turned the PAN into a credible alternative for the Mexican electorate. Moreover, the relationship between the PAN and the KAS led to the introduction of Christian Democracy in the newly pluralized Mexican political spectrum, a significant innovation in a country where, given the historical conflict between church and state, religious references in politics had been considered unacceptable and illegitimate. This experience represented an important shift for German foreign policy that in Mexico until then had concentrated almost exclusively on the promotion of its economic interests. In the 1990s the KAS' activities translated into a discrete but effective diplomacy of political influence. The recently unified Germany successfully fulfilled the role of the democratizing power that

Chancellor Kohl had designed for his country in the post-Cold War international order.

This positive assessment of the performance of the KAS in Mexico contradicts more pessimistic evaluations that were made at the end of the 1980s when, according to Michael Pinto-Duschinsky, the 'Adenauer Foundation [had] not been very successful in Latin America.'[3] This author argues that by 1989 the KAS had been forced to recognize that it had not achieved the spread of Christian Democracy throughout the region it had worked for in the previous two decades. As evidence of this failure, Pinto-Duschinsky mentions the need Christian Democrats had to enter in coalition with other political forces in Argentina, Brazil, and Colombia, among others, and the marginality and fragmentation of Christian trade unions in the region. The success of the KAS in Mexico in the following decade, the position it achieved during the democratization process in this country, and the role it played in the consolidation of the PAN, could not have been predicted on the basis of this negative balance.

As it will be seen below, in the late 1950s German Christian Democracy sought to establish a close relationship with the PAN, a project that was strongly rejected by the party leadership at the time. This previous experience indicates that the effectiveness of the KAS' influence three decades later was made possible first by changes in the international and in the domestic environments: on the one hand, the end of bipolarity and the emergence of multiple international actors and, on the other, the weakening of authoritarianism. The first part of this chapter therefore looks at the changes in the international context: the impact of the US policy of democracy assistance and at the activities of proliferating non-state and non-governmental actors; the following section examines the shift in German foreign policy in Latin America after the end of the Cold War and describes the characteristics, strategies, and instruments of German political foundations in the promotion of democracy in Latin America. The second part of the chapter discusses the role of the PAN in the democratization process. Here the party's doctrine and ideology are emphasized, because during authoritarianism the PAN claimed these as its most distinguishing features, even if vague and relatively inarticulate; and, secondly, because the social doctrine of the Catholic Church and Christian values and beliefs seemed to provide a natural connection between the KAS and the party. In the 1990s the PAN leadership found in the KAS an inspiration and a reliable source of material, but most of all ideological support. This, in turn, fostered the institutionalization of the PAN.

Democracy assistance and new international actors in domestic processes

At the beginning of the 1980s President Ronald Reagan initiated a new wave of democracy assistance in US foreign policy.[4] Although this was related to a new anti-communist crusade, it was different from past experiences in which the potential threat of communism had mostly received a military response. This evolution in policy led to the creation of programs to assist elections, strengthen civil institutions, and the administration of justice, and for the dissemination of democratic ideas. In June 1982, before the British parliament, President Reagan announced that his administration would develop a 'global program of democracy assistance' that would foster 'the infrastructure of democracy' that allows a 'people to choose their own way to develop their own culture, to reconcile their own differences through peaceful means': a free press, political parties, unions, and universities.[5]

This announcement was received with mixed feelings in Latin America where US interventionism went back to the nineteenth century. President Reagan's words produced anxiety in a number of countries in the region because they were understood as a response to the Frente Sandinista de Liberacion Nacional (FSLN) that, since proclaiming the victory of the revolution in 1979 over the Somoza dictatorship, had undertaken the construction of a socialist regime with the support of the Cuban government. However, at more or less the same time, democratic aspirations were mobilizing anti-authoritarian protest and demands in countries under military rule, such as Argentina, Brazil, and Chile. Authoritarian regimes were also shaken by a severe financial and economic crisis that seemed to dominate the whole region. Several Latin American countries were subject to International Monetary Fund (IMF) stabilization programs (SAPs) and to the World Bank requirements for economic reform.

In these difficult circumstances, almost inevitably, domestic politics were deeply penetrated by international actors. It could be argued that there was little new in this form of foreign interference in domestic processes in the region. However, the international context of the 1980s and its evolution into the twenty-first century gave the traditional forms of influence – that came close to imposition – and the undertakings of non-state and non-governmental actors an entirely different meaning. Their involvement in democratization processes was deemed legitimate and desirable due to the precedence human rights took over the national interest. Also these actors are invested with a moral authority that derives from their commitment to the defense of human rights and from their non-participation in party politics. Their major endeavor is the promotion of 'civil society empowerment' and their strategy the strengthening of local groups *vis-à-vis* their government. Churches, political foundations, human rights organizations, aid agencies from Amnesty International to Global Exchange or Caritas, gave a new meaning to transnational relations by pursuing principled goals and by promoting 'civil society empowerment.' This orientation set them apart from the economic organizations that used to dominate the non-state area of world relations and concentrated on instrumental gains. Their influence on domestic processes did not replace that of governments of western democracies and intergovernmental organizations such as the World Bank, the IMF, or the EU, that continued to impact political and economic change by explicitly conditioning their relations to national governments demanding the creation or modification of rules, most of which had important implications for domestic institutions and processes. Although these demands referred mainly to stabilization policies, privatizations, and economic deregulation, many of them entailed political reforms. In some cases these were explicit – for instance, adhesion treaties or more limited trade liberalization agreements with the EU, include a 'democratic clause' to which signatory countries must conform; but the political conditionality of economic cooperation was not always so specific, and regime change was perceived as an inevitable consequence of economic liberalization.[6]

The legitimacy of international pressures on domestic actors to democratize political regimes was further encouraged by increased economic integration and internationalization that tended to erode the traditional notion of sovereignty. Moreover, many Latin American political leaders and political forces assumed that openness to external political influences and demands was a measure of modernity. This context propitiated the activities of non-state and non-governmental actors also committed to the democratic cause. Since the 1980s, the support from abroad for domestic anti-authoritarian opposition gained an unprecedented and widespread support, even in countries like Mexico that had been a ferocious defender of non-intervention.

Germany's foreign policy and the promotion of democracy

Following in the steps of US foreign policy, in 1984 at the conclusion of the London Summit, the EU issued the 'Declaration on Democratic Values' that introduced the promotion of democracy as a priority of European diplomacy. In the subsequent decade, most European democracies steered their own aid programs in the same direction and placed democratization among their priorities. (It should be noted that transnational non-state actors – political foundations and party internationals – had already been present in the successful Spanish democratization of the late 1970s.) After the collapse of the bipolar international order and in the face of decaying socialist regimes, liberal democracy became the only valid formula of political organization and 'special arrangements' that in the past masked authoritarian regimes were no longer tolerated.

In 1993, the rule of law and respect of human rights and fundamental freedoms were stated as the goals of the Common Foreign and Security Policy (CFSP). These initiatives were a precedent for the foreign policy of a reunified Germany that found in the promotion of democracy a vehicle of international influence and a platform for its own diplomatic projection. The promotion of democratic values and institutions became an important chapter of international cooperation and development aid on the basis of two assumptions: first, that to be effective and long-lasting, political reform has to be supported from outside – a belief strongly felt in Germany on the basis of its own historical experience; and, secondly, that political change is a necessary condition for economic reform. The implication of these two assumptions was a profound reversal of previous paradigms in international relations – namely, those that derived from the strict separation of the international and the domestic realm of politics.

German unification had long-range consequences for an international system that had already been transformed from Cold War bipolarity by the emergence of an increased number of actors. Beyond the momentous impact of this event on regional and world balances, the fall of the Berlin Wall was a symbol of the triumph of civil society over the totalitarian state that had for decades denied its citizens their basic rights. The events of November 9, 1989, almost immediately took on a historical dimension of universal proportions. They represented the materialization of ideals of freedom and democracy. This historic experience also invested political change with a sense of moral restoration that enhanced the international image of Germany as a country that had defeated the ghosts of the past and could rightfully claim a position of legitimate political influence.

Germany gained a new international assertiveness with the fall of the Berlin Wall. It sought to reinforce its image as a country firmly committed to the defense of democratic values and institutions, the promotion of which was a natural extension of its own identity. The pursuit of this goal would also invest its foreign policy with a moral authority that could be translated into a basis of influence more effective than economic power. After 1990 Chancellor Helmut Kohl inaugurated a foreign policy characterized by what he defined as a 'culture of restraint': 'the conscious avoidance of assuming a high profile and a strong leadership role.'[7] In 1999, on the occasion of the German parliament's change of seat from Bonn to Berlin, Chancellor Kohl made an appeal to prudence and to resist self-complacency and the temptation of arrogance to avoid compromising Germany's new position of international influence,[8] from which it could participate in the shaping of a new international system. Within this program, the promotion of democracy was a strategy to participate in what Chancellor Kohl called the 'universalization of human rights' that was part of a wider conception of the desired changes in the international system.

German foreign policy in Latin America since the end of the Cold War

The international structure emerging after the end of the Cold War signified new options for German foreign policy. The minister of Foreign Affairs, Hans-Dietrich Genscher, extended its reach to non-European regions, strengthening its bilateral connections and its individual foreign policy, while maintaining its commitment to European integration.[9] In Latin America, the goals of German diplomacy shifted from emphasizing economic interests[10] to stress ideas, values, and arguments, as the main content of a 'soft diplomacy.' These guidelines did not change after the Kohl government was replaced by the Socialist–Green alliance led by Gerhard Schröder. In 2002, the Bundesministerium fur wirtschaftliche Zusammenarbeit und Entwicklung (BMZ) issued a *Strategy Paper for Latin America* that stated the 'promotion of democratic political systems' as a central motive for German development cooperation.[11]

The document still underlines the economic dimension of cooperation with Latin America, identifying the region first as an important area of potential growth for German business and industry: 'In the newly industrializing countries in particular both German development cooperation and German manufacturers and traders have provided a vital impetus to economic development.'[12] Nevertheless, the discussion of the political dimension of the cooperation strategy confirms Germany's commitment to the consolidation of the 'incipient reform process' and describes the following areas of involvement for German agencies: state reform and the roles of the private sector and civil society, good governance, equal rights, free trade unions, the promotion of human rights, the set up and development of self-help-oriented structures, state regulatory policy and democratic controls, judicial reform, decentralization, the promotion of community development, and land rights.[13] The width and breadth of German political development cooperation seems boundless. The favored instruments of this ambitious cooperation program were development services and programs of political foundations, churches, and other NGOs that received support from the BMZ budget.

Until the late 1980s the overwhelming economic presence of the US in the region was ever- present in any European consideration of its options in Latin America. According to Wolf Grabendorff the primacy of the economic dimension in their relations was explained by this implicit acknowledgment, whereas any political or strategic consideration ties were considered 'intolerable.'[14] Accordingly Germany wanted to be perceived as an economic power that did not threaten or challenge US hegemony in the region.

However, after 1990 Germany abandoned this policy and sought to establish itself as an alternative political interlocutor for Latin American countries always distrustful of US pressures and interventionism. Latin American perceptions of Europe also changed. In the past, Western European countries were mainly considered as an alternative for trade and investments, whereas ideologically they were perceived as subordinate to US interests, so much so that Latin America did not expect much from European countries concerning the transformation of the international order.[15]

The change in the Latin American perceptions of Europe's international role was a reaction to the success of the democratization processes in Portugal, Spain, and Greece, and it was further sustained by the presence of socialist parties in power in various European countries. In the 1990s anti-imperialism disappeared as a cause of mobilization in many Latin American countries and the 'European world view' was more readily acceptable and seen more favorably than US policies dedicated to the 'export of democracy.' In this period, the 'apolitical' approach of Europeans towards Latin America started playing to their advantage as they could promote democracy with 'clean hands' and adopt a 'moral stance' that could not be claimed by the US.[16] The difference between the proposals of change advanced by the US and those of the Europeans explains the openness in Latin America to the latter's policy of promotion of democracy. Since the beginning of the 1980s European support had been directed to the strengthening of civilian elites. The purpose of European strategy in the region was to familiarize Latin American elites with the pluralist conception of democracy.[17]

In Latin America, the end of the Cold War also meant new opportunities for democratic reform. The goals of regional elites and German 'soft diplomacy' thus met on democratization. Globalisation also provided an equally powerful incentive for Europeans to approach the region in a new light and this new international context brought responsiveness to German political strategies and initiatives in most Latin American countries. Transnational relations were nothing new in the region; Manfred Mols recalls that the transnational set of networks was for decades more important than intergovernmental relations even in sensitive political areas. Political foundations, for instance, began their activities in this region in the early 1960s, advising political groups and governments.

In 1990, Josef Thesing, Director of the International Institute of the KAS recognized the opportunities for an 'objective cooperation' in the region once the Soviet Union had disappeared. According to him this event had put an end to the political game many developing countries had played for decades, oscillating between East and West.[18] However, these countries were also expected to engage in profound reforms and 'put their house in order.'

The new perception of Latin America demanded a closer coordination between different German actors present in the region. According to Manfred Mols and Christoph Wagner, this reassessment of Latin America by the German government brought for the first time the development of an 'independent concept of the region.'[19] In June 1994 the 'Work Group for Latin America' (Gesprächskreis Lateinamerika) was created, intended to formulate a broad approach to Germany's relations with the region.[20] The result of this was a document, *Lateinamerika-Konzept der Bundesregierung*, that stressed the German intention to broaden and intensify political relations on the basis of shared values associated with representative democracy and market economy. In this approach, political reform is the basis of a sound economic development.

German diplomacy in Latin America was intended to increase official political exchanges between heads of state and relations between parliamentary groups, and to promote the inclusion of social groups in any initiative of cooperation and dialog, emphasizing the role of political parties and foundations, churches, unions, sport associations, and other cultural organizations. Through them German diplomacy – official and informal or 'parallel diplomacy' – creates a wide network that is the basis of an ambitious program in which a number of NGOs receive public funding. In 1999 religious organizations such as Misereor, together with assistance programs to combat hunger and health problems, totaled some 100 and received 8% of the total BMZ budget. This official support is based on the assumption that private initiatives are more effective than official actions.[21]

In the *Lateinmerika-Konzept der Bundesregierung*, redemocratization was understood as having brought a qualitative progress to the region, creating new opportunities for the consolidation of democratic institutions. Nevertheless, as has already been mentioned, the political and cultural objectives of German foreign policy are not entirely altruistic and devoid of economic interest. Latin America is an important market for the expansion of German interests that find new opportunities in the region thanks to economic reforms such as liberalization and privatization undertaken in the last two decades. The consistency between diplomatic instruments and economic interests is expressed in the official document that recognizes political influence and cultural presence as instruments that deepen the commitment of German business in the region and help develop friendly attitudes towards Germany among 'future Latin American business executives.'[22]

Political foundations: an instrument of Germany's unintentional power

In 1962 Chancellor Konrad Adenauer decided to channel public funds destined for foreign aid to political foundations. The goal was the promotion of democratic values and the diffusion of German political culture. This decision was a first step towards building an instrument of 'soft power' to sustain a 'parallel diplomacy' that would be the equivalent to the French *diplomatie de prestige*: a *politique de grandeur* without the grandiloquence. The importance of political foundations in the Latin American policy of the German government has been so great that Mols and Wagner contend that, thanks to political foundations, there was a specific German policy towards Latin America.[23] Wolf Grabendorff goes even further, and asserts that West German foundations are not only linked to political parties, 'but they can also be considered as the 'executive organs' of their political mother organizations, allowing the party to participate to a certain extent in the domestic politics of another country at a non-governmental level without violating the rule of non-interference in intergovernmental relations.'[24]

Germany has five political foundations each affiliated, albeit tenuously, with the main German political parties: the KAS (Christian Democracy, CDU), the Friedrich Ebert Stiftung (FES, Social Democracy, SPD), the Friedrich Naumann Stiftung (FNS, Liberal, FDP), the Hanns Seidel Stiftung (HSS, Christian Social, CSU), and the Heinrich Böll Stiftung (HBS, Green, GP). Among TNAs these foundations hold a somewhat ambiguous position. They operate with public funding and are subject to some government control; their programs and budgetary spending are under parliamentary supervision. Nevertheless, they present themselves as NGOs; in the functions they perform they come close to think-tanks, also because they are non-profit organizations, and their strategies show some similarities with those of human rights organizations. Their activities are private, but their goals are distinctly political: the promotion of peace and freedom, the strengthening of the democratic order, the introduction of safeguards to human rights, development aid, and the pursuit of international understanding and cooperation. Most of these could not be undertaken by official agencies; if they were, they could be a source of diplomatic tension: for instance, in establishing and sustaining relations with opposition parties and getting involved in various political activities they run the risk of infringing the law.

To accomplish their goals, political foundations engage in a wide range of activities working with the parties that share their political beliefs. However, and as has already been mentioned, in Latin America, depending on the domestic context and balance of power, political foundations have agreed to work with parties that hold different, and even opposed, ideological identities. Thus, the FES established an office in Mexico in 1970 and it worked very closely with the then hegemonic PRI; traces of the foundation's influence are still evident in Mexico's labor legislation. This relationship was based on the PRI's somewhat vague claims to a social democratic identity. Before the 1990s the KAS also maintained cooperation with the PRI, however limited. Nevertheless, the resources and efforts of the KAS turned to the PAN during the 1980s, when the party made important inroads in the PRI's electoral hegemony.

Political foundations organize publications, seminars, meetings, and dialogs between different political forces. They supply information and expertise, encourage consultation and national and international exchanges between official and private actors, and provide fellowships and 'neutral ground' for closed discussions between political actors. Political foundations interact and develop close and stable ties with business, the media, trade unions, churches, and research institutions. They organize programs for the education and training of elites and support assistance programs for the underprivileged; they also promote social organizations and self-help groups.

In these ways political foundations contribute to the broadening and the setting of the agenda for political debate, and they also help the identification of policy options. However, the leadership programs of political foundations may be their most powerful instrument of influence, because they define the ideological and programmatic identity of political parties.[25] The importance of their activities seems to be greater in a context of collapse or gradual deterioration of authoritarianism – as will be shown below – for political foundations provide a framework of reference for the discussion between government and opposition, between different political forces, and between academics, politicians, and businessmen.

The fundamental distinction between political foundations and other transnational NGOs lies in the fact that their goal is institution-building whereas, for instance, the goal of think-tanks may be purely scholarly research and academic debate and policy-making; while human rights institutions are more interested in non-institutional ends, organizing civil society groups or mobilizations. [26] There is also an important difference between think-tanks and human rights groups and political foundations, in that their networking with local actors targets economic, academic, and political elites; think-tanks have more restricted targets – mainly the academic community or business and governments; while human rights organizations work with wider social groups.

In Latin America, political foundations are perceived as independent organizations because they are committed to universal values, and are thus seen as public interest bodies that produce information and analysis as a public good. They are considered expert organizations free from vested interests or power ambitions. Their purported aims are to contribute to the enhancement of a tolerant, plural, and democratic citizenry, and this perception has also been supported by their non-profit organization character. Thus, in spite of their political affiliation and of the open involvement of the World Christian Democratic Union and the Socialist Union in democratization processes in the region, in both of which German political foundations play a central role, they are accepted as policy research institutes, 'facilitators' that are not seeking immediate economic or political gains.[27] They have built trust by cultivating an image of altruistic organizations while maintaining a low profile.

Latin American receptivity to political foundations is an almost spontaneous search for balance in a region overwhelmed by US hegemony; the German political foundations' presence in Latin America is seen as a countervailing influence. The political foundations' ties to specific political parties in Germany tend to disappear in the eyes of their Latin American hosts because they are not associated with US foreign policy and interests, which are always bound to raise suspicions. Their particular European identity, the restrictions they have – they do not fund political campaigns or parties – and their links to the German state lend them authority and legitimacy in the region.

The success of political foundations in Latin America lies also in the fact that, as Laurence Whitehead wrote in the mid-1980s, European definitions of democracy stress social and economic participation, whereas the US notion of democracy emphasizes almost exclusively electoral aspects. Whitehead also noted that the European political spectrum 'is reasonably congruent with that likely to emerge in Southern Europe and Latin American nations as they redemocratize.'[28] This assessment was confirmed by the fact that European political parties' organization and programmatic basis facilitated identification with similar currents in Latin America more than with US political parties.

The KAS in Latin America in the 1990s

The KAS first started its international cooperation programs in Latin America in the early 1960s. The region became a priority for Western democracies that feared the potential impact of the Cuban revolution on neighboring countries that had also suffered poverty, social inequalities, and anti-democratic political regimes. The political foundations' main objective was to sustain democratic alternatives to revolution. However, the 1970s and the beginning of the 1980s witnessed the ascent of the FES and the Socialist International (SI) over local political actors sharing social democratic beliefs and aspirations, although Christian democratic organizations played a crucial moderating role in the El Salvador civil war.[29] The association of the SI with a critical view of Ronald Reagan's policy in Central America and Margaret Thatcher's liberalizing reforms favored social democratic influence in Latin America. However, its pillar was Willy Brandt's charisma.[30] Brandt's disappearance and the discredit of socialism (even the defeat of the PRI) weakened the SI's and the FES' influence among Mexican political actors.

In the 1990s, the KAS gained a position of influence in many countries in the region – for instance, Mexico – where in the past its activities had been limited. (In 2005, it had representation offices in seventeen Latin American countries.) This new position was as much a reflection of Helmut Kohl's prestige as the leader of German reunification as an indirect consequence of the breakdown of socialist regimes in Eastern Europe, and of the sequels of military dictatorships on the Latin American left, among which the rise of a strong anti-statist feeling was decisive. The Christian Democratic message of economic reform and social responsibility was also consistent with the criticisms of a growing number of political and opinion groups against the technocratic policies adopted by Latin American governments under pressure from international agencies. Moreover, in a region still predominantly Catholic, the distinctly Christian values held by the KAS appealed to long-standing local traditions. The KAS also provided a basis for policy proposals that responded to some of the main concerns of conservative currents of opinion: the primacy of a personalized approach to politics, human welfare in a capitalist regime, and tolerance and pluralism.

The 1996 KAS international cooperation report stated that it had more access to social and political elites in Latin America than in any other region of the world. The KAS officials therefore believed that they had a wider array of possibilities 'to contribute to the shaping of political systems.'[31] Since then, and in accordance with this general goal, the KAS' main interlocutors in the region have been political parties, parliaments, small- and mid-sized business, local and regional authorities, unions, and the media. The KAS' priorities are the strengthening of these interlocutors and their consolidation as effective political actors, the promotion of the rule of law, democratic constitutions, and sound and coherent social policies. The KAS advisory and study programs are intended to help Latin American countries find solutions to close the gap between constitutional forms and reality: decentralization, the consolidation of parliaments, the reorganization of law enforcement agencies, the stabilization of party systems, the integration of the military in the democratic state and in democratic processes, the fight against corruption and human rights violations, and the protection of the environment. The 1996 report credits the KAS with electoral reforms in El Salvador; the support of the Chilean Christian Democratic party during the dictatorship years; advising Brazilian governmental authorities, parliamentarians, and political parties on the design of judiciary reforms; municipal government modifications; and economic and environmental policies.

Mexico's PAN and democratization

The international context and internal conditions prevailing in Mexico in the 1990s facilitated the actions of the KAS. Its success in a country that traditionally condemned and rejected any form of external influence can be seen as a measure of the change of attitudes that accompanied Mexican democratization. In the past, a staunch nationalism inspired a profound distrust of any political or economic foreign influence; however, during the 1980s a profound economic crisis led Mexican elites, and also underprivileged Mexicans, to look for solutions outside their own country and history. Thus, while politicians and government officials opted for policies of economic liberalization and internationalization, the unemployed migrated to the US in search of opportunities. Thanks to this evolution the outside world was no longer a threat: it became an opportunity in the eyes of millions of Mexicans.[32] Deteriorating economic conditions upset the political system, precipitated internal discontent, and stimulated debate. It also fostered unprecedented diversity and the emergence of new political actors including transnational non-governmental actors, many of which were prominent in the dynamics of change. Among them, the KAS holds a distinguished position as a discreet and effective organization and the PAN was among the main beneficiaries of its activities.

The PAN was founded in 1939 to represent social groups and political interests that had been excluded from the revolutionary coalition rallied around the official party. A characteristic feature of Mexican authoritarianism was the existence of an unbalanced party system in which an overpowering official party coexisted with a limited number – never more than four – of small opposition parties that represented minor currents of opinion. For most of the second half of the twentieth century these organizations were irrelevant and almost marginal; nevertheless, their participation in the electoral processes that since 1920 took place regularly every three and six years for the renewal of authorities at the municipal, state, and federal level, contributed to sustain the democratic *facade* that separated the Mexican system from the dictatorships.

The PAN stood out among these parties. It was generally perceived as the most authentic and independent opposition, however small or weak.[33] In spite of electoral fraud, rigged elections and repeated disappointments, the PAN survived over four decades in a hostile authoritarian environment that rejected political pluralism and claimed a hypothetical 'revolutionary unanimity' as the basis for the official party's hegemony. Traditional public perceptions associated the PAN with the wealthy, the Catholic Church, and with groups and organizations identified with the most conservative interests in society. Nevertheless, the distinctive political identity that set the party apart from other opposition organizations were not its alleged political allies but its loyalty to the values of liberal democracy and to the social doctrine of the Catholic Church. By contrast with almost all other political forces actives in Mexico in the second half of the twentieth century, the PAN unfailingly upheld the superiority of elections, a multiparty system, and the legal means of political change with respect to the revolutionary alternative or the collective mechanisms of direct democracy dear to the revolutionary tradition. For the PAN, democracy was a long-term educational project.

The development of the PAN was conditioned by the institutional framework provided by the 1917 constitution that established a system of universal and direct suffrage as the basis of popular sovereignty and elections as the legitimate route to political power. However, there existed a fundamental tension between the liberal, representative model that inspired the constitutional order and the revolutionary origins of the state. This translated into unwritten rules and patterns of behavior – associated in particular with the exercise of presidential power – and these imposed themselves on formal institutions and even prevented them from operating. These informal institutions set strict limits on the representation of interests and the workings of opposition. The development of political parties was thus handicapped by the overbearing weight of the state, the nature of presidentialism, and the impulse towards unanimity exercised by the official party. These general characteristics of the political system impaired the development of autonomous political organizations. For example, parties helped facilitate socialization, the aggregation of interests, and, at times, the transmission of demands. But they did little to set limits on the power of the executive branch (given the weakness of the legislature) or to offer an alternative to the party in office.

The Mexican authoritarian system did not forbid opposition parties and it could even be said that it promoted a multi-party system, by supporting their existence – albeit precarious – through electoral legislation and certain fiscal privileges and material support. Nevertheless party organizations remained under-institutionalized as their logic and internal workings could be subject to the arbitrariness of personal leaderships; also, their continuity depended on personalized politics. This situation was aggravated by the fact that opposition parties lacked experience in governmental responsibilities; as their possibilities to influence the decision-making process were slim there were no incentives for the formulation of policy platforms or programmatic proposals. PANista criticisms of authoritarianism centered on electoral fraud, but they remained silent with respect to other areas of government and were ignorant of the complexities of these responsibilities, to which they were indifferent as power seemed completely inaccessible. Rather than acting as political parties, they worked as limited interest groups, without either the ability or the desire to widen their horizons. In the worst cases, they became simply a mechanism by which the state could transmit certain messages to society – such as the importance of holding elections to maintain a 'democratic aspiration.' They helped defuse some political tensions and provided a secondary safety valve in a system that had other methods to resolve conflict, such as repression, cooptation, and extra-institutional negotiation.

The Mexican authoritarian regime did not collapse suddenly in 2000. Since 1982 it had shown severe symptoms of exhaustion. A powerful component of political mobilization was added to the combined effects of the accumulation of some these symptoms and of the impact of liberalizing reforms intended to attack them and to transform the Mexican state. This was the beginning of a gradual dismantling of authoritarianism, the point of departure of which was an ambitious electoral reform (introduced in 1977) followed by a severe financial crisis in 1982 that triggered an electoral mobilization that favored the PAN. Thus was launched a democratization process that followed a pattern of reform through elections. In 1996 an autonomous electoral authority was created to guarantee impartiality and fairness in the competition.

Gradualism gave the PAN the opportunity to achieve its own modernization by defining a clear ideological affiliation and a platform of policy options. Thanks to this definition the party gained autonomy, and reinforced its identity as an anti-authoritarian party, that was also a viable alternative to the PRI. During the 1980s and 1990s the PAN leadership was renewed, the party experienced a recruitment drive that significantly increased the numbers of militants and sympathizers, and its share in the national vote went from 18% in 1988 to 43% in 2000. Thus the PAN contributed to the structuring of the Mexican electorate and constructively channeled the anti-PRI feelings that had been feeding extra-institutional protests.

Several elements converged in the modernization of the party: first, the mobilization of anti-PRI voters that went to the polls initially at local elections and for whom the PAN was an instrument of protest; secondly, changes in the legislation that guaranteed respect of the vote and impartiality of electoral authorities; and, thirdly, the mobilization of a democratizing coalition that backed the opposition demands to the government and its initiatives. The KAS support for the PAN in this period could be counted as part of this third element.

The institutionalization of the PAN meant that the party overcame the powerful obstacles that had hampered its development – namely, the restrictions imposed by the authoritarian nature of the regime during most of the twentieth century, in which the state was the fundamental political actor.

The KAS and Christian Democracy in Mexico: the doctrine and policies of the PAN in power

In the early 1980s the PAN was the only Mexican opposition party that had some credibility as an organisation independent from the state. The years of political marginality had contributed to build the image of a serious political organization sincerely committed to electoral democracy. This last feature, that could have jeopardized the party's chances of becoming the main beneficiary of discontent, was remedied with the support of local Catholic and business organisations. Their infrastructure enabled the party to capture an increasing anti-authoritarian vote. Initially the wave of opposition took form in the northern states of the country, bordering on the US that are also considered emblematic of modern Mexico. In the following years the rise of the PAN extended to other regions of the country, and became the expression of a center–periphery cleavage that undermined centralized Mexican structures.

The sociological characteristics of these new PANista voters defied conventional ideas regarding political identities in Mexico. Surprisingly, the PAN candidates that were voted in at municipal elections in several important cities of the region, and the party that historically had been identified with the forces of conservatism, became the choice of voters that were younger, better educated, and better paid than the average PRI voter. This electorate posed a serious challenge to the PAN itself. In order to stabilize these protest votes and its new position as an influential political actor, the party had to offer its electorate structured and viable policy choices. In this respect, the support of the KAS was crucial.

One of the constants in the history of the PAN has been its insistence on the importance of political doctrine. The variety of norms and values adopted since 1939 to bolster the culture of its militants received sustenance from the social doctrine of the church and Catholic thinking. This affiliation was the origin of the mistaken notion, that lasted decades, that the PAN was a party of the Catholic Church. Moreover, this identity set the party distinctly apart from other political organizations that insisted on connecting with the Mexican revolution; the Catholic identity of the PAN (at its strongest in the 1940s and 1950s) went against the anti-clerical tradition of the Mexican state, and one of the reasons given by the original leaders of the party for their reluctance to affiliate to Christian Democracy was that the electoral legislation forbade the political use of religious names or symbols. Later on the party's Catholic inspiration, that had provided the cornerstone for its development as an institution and for its survival during the tough times of authoritarianism, would be the touchstone of its modernization.

PANista doctrine fulfilled various different functions. First, it provided the basis for a more precise political identity than was the case for other currents of opinion, whose general (but rather vague) point of reference was the ideas generated by the Mexican Revolution. Second, thanks to its doctrinal identity, the party was able to maintain an internal consistency when it stood alone in an authoritarian context. Finally, the links with Catholic thinking provided a connection between the party and developments in the field of ideas beyond Mexico.

A diffuse doctrinal identity was crucial for the internal cohesion of the party during the years when it represented a marginal political minority. The PANista doctrine also had a stabilizing influence in the long period of transition from authoritarianism to a multi-party system, and when the severe crisis of the 1980s hit the general framework of reference of the old state-centered political system, PAN doctrine was also a reference – even if a negative one – for other parties that did not share its beliefs and creed. Knowledge of this doctrine became the standard for legitimacy within the party. Such was the case that during the years of the party's rapid growth in the 1970s and 1980s acceptance of the doctrine became a condition for belonging, for authority and for legitimacy in the party. By implication, the 'doctrinaires' were those in the party with a strong sense of service, while the 'pragmatists' were driven by ambition for power. Ignorance of the doctrine became a matter of reproach.

In the 1980s, there was a fresh attempt at defining the doctrine undertaken by the then president of the PAN (1990–93), Carlos Castillo Peraza. The main difference between this readjustment of doctrine and others in the past was that the PAN was already a party in government. It had a fifth of all the seats in the House of Representatives, in which the PRI held only a half. It also governed numerous important municipalities and the state of Baja California. In such circumstances, doctrinal redefinition had gained considerable practical importance because it needed to be translated into effective programs and policies. For this reason, the PAN – for the first time in its history – took its commitment to Catholic thought to its logical conclusion by adopting the Christian Democrats' proposals for government and in 1998 it became a member of the Organización Demócrata Cristiana de América (ODCA).

German political foundations had been active in Mexico since the 1960s, performing their normal advisory activities concerning labor and electoral legislation,[34] unionization, training programs for industrial and agricultural workers, and assistance and programs of various kinds. The FES, KAS, and FNS maintained close relations with Mexican political parties, although before the 1980s they all concentrated on the official PRI.[35] In the mid-1970s the KAS established a small representation office in Mexico. In the following twenty years it developed strong ties with political and academic elites; it thereby successfully became part of a wider network – or coalition[36] – of democratizing actors that included opinion-makers, political parties, academic institutions, and informal groups, and gained access to the political system. As the pluralization of Mexican political life proceeded, the foundation adjusted to the new conditions thus created. Hence, the electoral progress of the PAN meant that the KAS could concentrate its efforts and resources on a party that shared its beliefs and political creed. Moreover, in the 1990s and in the light of the Mexican government's modernizing efforts – namely the signing of the North American Free Trade Agreement (NAFTA) between Canada, the US, and Mexico (1994) – the latter became a priority in the German foreign policy agenda.[37]

In Mexico the receptivity of the PAN to the KAS' influence since the 1980s stood on the same ground as in other Latin American countries: the familiarity with the Christian message, and the discredit of the technocratic policies and political organizations and parties associated with a strong state tradition. Nevertheless in the area of formal relations there were important differences that set Mexico apart from most Latin American countries. Until the beginning of the 1990s Mexican–German relations followed the same pattern that had developed in other Latin American countries and emphasized trade and investment over political relations. However, the signature of NAFTA opened up new opportunities for European interests in a promising North American market. The new ties linking the Mexican economy to its northern neighbors also guaranteed the stability of Mexican economic policies.

The stamp of the KAS' influence on the PAN had been present since 1985 in party platforms that up until then had been repetitious or poor. In the 1988 presidential campaign the PANista candidate, Manuel J. Clouthier, made frequent references to different German experiences – for instance, Ludwig Erhard's stabilization policies. Ever since then the social economy market had become the centerpiece of every party program and proposal. These programmatic changes gave the PAN an air of modernity and pragmatism that responded to the everyday concerns of ordinary people. The party stopped being looked on as an organisation of out-of-touch idealists guided exclusively by philosophical considerations and ethical motives.

In the modernized PAN, the social economy market is at the heart of a vast program of reforms that include issues and proposals directly taken from the international cooperation programs of the KAS: fiscal decentralization, a strengthened federalism, the fight against corruption, agrarian reform, development of small and mid-size business, and the moderating influence of state mediation. The influence of German Christian Democracy over the PAN was very clear in the 1990s, especially with regard to its critique of the overextended state and economic policy-making. The party adopted the principles of the social market economy, respect for property rights, private initiative, and individual rights, basing its approach on the belief that different sectors of society were partners in the creation of wealth, and not rivals or enemies.[38]

In the 1980s and 1990s the KAS worked closely with PAN sections which relied on its standard instruments and activities: publications, exchange programs, training programs, seminars, and conferences. The KAS was also a facilitator of the dialog between the PAN and other parties, and participated intensely in the democratizing network that emerged in Mexico in the 1990s, including a diverse constellation of NGOs and TNAs. However, the foundation concentrated on political, economic, and academic elites. The KAS was the inspiration of the PAN foundation, Fundación Rafael Preciado Hernández, it takes part in an ambitious program of rural development, Fundación Mexicana de Desarrollo Rural, and it has established solid institutional ties with elite research institutions, such as El Colegio de México.

This impressive development of the KAS' influence bears a striking contrast with a previous attempt to affiliate the party to Christian Democracy Then, in the eyes of the US and its western allies, poor social and economic conditions in

Latin America heightened the potential of the communist threat in the region, as the recent experience of the Cuban Revolution had shown. Thus even before the KAS was created, German Christian Democrats were active in Latin America, in Chile, in El Salvador and in Venezuela, where they endorsed the organization of Christian Democratic parties. In Mexico in 1957 they contacted young PANista leaders and invited them to adhere to the party international. German Christian Democrats proposed to sponsor different activities to support the PAN's programs and development. However, the young PANistas' enthusiastic response was not shared by the leadership of the party, particularly by its main political figure, Manuel Gómez Morin, who firmly opposed any connection with the CDU/CSU. In 1961, the young leaders who had accepted German support were expelled from the party.

In the early 1970s the PAN leaders' response to the intimations to internationalize, at first from western Europe, then from Latin America, was very positive. However, doctrine was at the heart of the relationship between the KAS and the PAN. The appeal of the Christian democratic message in Mexico lies in the connection it establishes with cultural traditions still present at the end of the twentieth century,[39] and in the anti-liberal implications of the Catholic proposal of 'Solidarismus': the principle that man is the foundation of the social order and that the relations between persons are naturally ones of solidarity. The rejection of collectivism also responds to the upper and middle classes' anti-communism and their fears of revolutionary movements. Solidarismus, the doctrine advanced by Pope John Paul II and Catholic political thought, also repudiates the liberal idea that the individual can fully realize herself only if she manages to define her autonomy and liberty in relation to society and rejects the indifference of liberalism towards the spirituality of being human.[40]

In Mexico 'third-way' solutions find fertile soil because of the severe social inequalities and also because the programs of the Mexican revolution were also presented as a third option between liberalism and socialism, as with Christian Democracy. Hence, this message is not entirely new or alien to the Mexican electorate. It promotes moderate and limited state interventionism in certain areas: in cultural matters and education, as well as over the market itself. So far as the first of these is concerned, it argues that the state should guarantee a philosophical vision of education. As regards the second, it rejects the idea of a natural harmony in the market,[41] considering necessary regulation and the exercise of public authority over economic actors. The idea is to create a regulatory state that limits its own involvement in productive activities and dedicates most of its energies to correcting market distortions and ensuring a better distribution of income.

The KAS' democratic endeavors in Mexico seemed to have been rewarded with the victory of the PAN's candidate in the presidential election of 2000, Vicente Fox. The defeat of the PRI was not a small feat for all of the national political actors involved in the process; however, it can also be seen as a success for German parallel diplomacy.

Conclusion

International and domestic conditions explain the success of the KAS in Mexico in the 1990s, because they created opportunities and incentives for Mexico and for German foreign policy. On the one hand, the end of the Cold War produced a framework favorable to the development of new options for European actors as well as for Latin American countries: on the other hand, the crisis of the authoritarian state made Mexican political actors, particularly the PAN, susceptible and responsive to the influence of a TNA that in a not-so-remote past would have been considered 'interventionist' and therefore rejected.

Political foundations as TNAs have a wide margin of autonomy, at least in Latin America. This may be an unavoidable consequence of Germany's geopolitical position that sets its priorities in CEE and absorbs governmental authorities' attention and resources. Moreover, the absence of a EU framework shaping German foreign policy in the Latin American region lends more meaning to informal diplomacy in this region where 'German magnetism' may find an unexpected receptivity. This 'magnetism,' that constitutes what Timothy Garton Ash calls the 'third dimension' of German power – different from economic and military power – that derives from a particular society, culture, and way of life, and stands for an overall attractiveness 'is loosely related to a country's relative prosperity, but by no means simply a function of it.'[42]

The end of the Cold War bipolarity meant new options for German foreign policy in less developed countries (LDCs); specifically in Latin America where, after the collapse of the Soviet bloc, the US became more tolerant of non-hemispheric influences. In this period Latin America also became a place where the foreign policy of a unified Germany could pursue a *diplomatie de prestige* and strengthen the international role it has assumed as a country committed to the promotion of democratic values and institutions. The analysis of political foundations, a unique German diplomatic instrument, shows how a unified Germany deals with its 'unintentional power,'[43] pursuing a consensual foreign policy that is an expression of long-term state strategy. Thus, although political foundations are well identified with specific ideological programs and political parties, they are also a state policy instrument.

The comparison between the two episodes of the relationship between the PAN and CDU/KAS – 1957–62 and 1982 onwards – sheds light on the prevailing meanings of national sovereignty and self-determination at each point in time. In the 1950s the influence of foreign organizations – state and non-state – on national processes was considered as illegitimate interference in domestic affairs. In the last quarter of the twentieth century these notions seemed to wane under the moral superiority of democracy over national sovereignty, so much so that international public opinion – as represented by state and non-state actors (the media, churches and a wide variety of NGOs) – became a legitimizing force as powerful as voters in the national context, and in some cases even more so.

To the surprise of many the signature of NAFTA, the free-trade agreement (FTA) between Canada, Mexico, and the US in 1992, found weak internal opposition; this was an expression of a profound change in Mexican attitudes towards the outside world that began to be perceived as an opportunity and stopped being considered as a threat. In this new context, when a domestic political actor explicitly referred to a 'foreign model,' it was perceived as modern and democratic whereas in the past, these ties would have been a liability. However, the German political foundations' experience in Mexico could also serve the formulation of a general hypothesis: the greater the economic influence of a country on another, the lesser the latter's tolerance to the potential political influence of the former. The lesser the economic influence, the greater the tolerance to its political and cultural presence.

The KAS' experience in Mexico in the 1990s exemplifies the potential reach of TNAs; it also illustrates the profound transformations the international system has undergone resulting from globalization, the erosion of the traditional concept of national sovereignty, and the proliferation of non-state actors.

Notes

1 Whitehead (2001), p. 24.
2 Cf. Loaeza (2000), pp. 93–116.
3 Cf. Pinto-Duschinsky (2001), p. 248.
4 Carothers (1999), pp. 29–37.
5 *Ibid.*, p. 31
6 For a discussion on political conditionality in the third wave of democratization, see Schmitter (2001), pp. 26–54.
7 Kohl (1999), p. 117.
8 *Ibid.*
9 Rummel (1996), pp. 40–67.
10 Cf. Alba Vega (1996).
11 BMZ (2005).
12 *Ibid.*
13 *Ibid.*, p. 8.
14 Grabendorff (1982), pp. 39–57.
15 *Ibid.*
16 Cf. Whitehead (1986), p. 42.
17 Grabendorff (1982), p. 50. For the differences between the American and the European political strategies in Latin America see also Whitehead (1986).
18 Thesing (1990).
19 Mols and Wagner (1999), pp. 116–135.
20 'Lineamientos' (1995), pp. 157–180 (document approved by the German government in May 1995); Auswärtiges Amt (1995). Cf. Mols and Wagner (1999).
21 KAS (1999).
22 *Ibid.*
23 Mols and Wagner (1999), p.127. However, the authors insist that economic interests continue to dominate the German perspective on Latin America.

24 Grabendorff (2001), p. 217.
25 Keck and Sikkink (1999), p. 409.
26 Stone (2000), pp. 211–225.
27 In 1984, nineteen parties or political movements in the western hemisphere were full members of ODCA, founded in 1947 by Eduardo Frei, as an affiliate of the World Christian Democratic Union. By 2000, the number of Latin American parties in that organization had increased to thirty-one in twenty-six countries. Their electoral strength added represented close to 30% of Latin American voters.
28 Whitehead (1986), p. 17.
29 President Reagan recognized the importance of European democratizing endeavors after 1982 in a speech delivered to the UK Houses of Parliament, when he stated that Social Democrats, Christian Democrats, and Liberals had offered open assistance to fraternal, political, and social institutions to bring about a democratic process, and also recognized that the German political foundations had become a major force in this effort. Cf. Whitehead (1986), p. 42. See also Pinto-Dutschinsky (2001).
30 Grabendorff (1982), p. 53. Furthermore, according to Laurence Whitehead, as soon as the German Social Democrats were out of office in 1982, West Germany cut off an aid program that the Schmidt government had been funneling to Nicaragua. Cf. Whitehead (1986), p. 30.
31 KAS (1996), p. 54.
32 Loaeza (1994), pp. 145–180.
33 For a history of PAN, see Loaeza (1999).
34 In 1970 new labor legislation was passed, based on a document prepared by the FES.
35 Alba Vega (1996), pp. 11–12.
36 Risse (1999), p. 384.
37 Cf. Alba Vega (1996).
38 The main precepts of the social market economy include decentralization, the notion that the businessman (especially the small- and medium-scale businessman) is the key economic agent, the primacy of the price mechanism and perfect competition, the autonomy of the central bank, free access to markets, freedom of contract, and continuity in economic policy-making. As regulatory precepts, the following are proposed: state control over monopolies, a redistribution policy with regard to income, the regulation of labour markets and a minimum wage.
39 In comments on an earlier version of this chapter, Hans Jürgen Pule pointed out that the central importance of doctrine in the relationship between PAN and KAS was an exception, as political foundations did not usually influence the political programs or the policy platforms of the organizations they supported. German political foundations tended to be more pragmatic and to concentrate their efforts on the material support of political organizations – i.e. office equipment or campaign material.
40 Solidarismus made its first appearance in the mid-nineteenth century, the work of a German Jesuit, Heinrich Pesch. Pesch was an economist who insisted that welfare was the only objective of economics. He put forward a way of thinking based on scholasticism and Catholic social philosophy. Its main tenets were developed later on by another Jesuit, Oswald von Nell-Breuning, a canon of the Saint Georges University in Frankfurt. Von Nell-Breuning was responsible for the diffusion in 1931 and 1932 of the encyclical *Quadragesimo Anno* of Pius XI, produced to celebrate the anniversary of Rerum Novarum. It likewise decried liberalism and individualism, and its main proposals revolved around social policy and work legislation. Von Nell-Breuning is one of the founding fathers of the market social economy, the main tenet of European Christian Democracy as it developed in Germany after 1947; see Von Nell-Breuning (1946). See also Kösters (1989), pp. 7–16. The Mexican thinkers that

have worked on Solidarismus are all related to PAN; Efraín González Morfín and
Raúl González Schmall are among the most distinguished of them.
41 Dierickx (1994), pp. 15–30; Kleinmann (1993).
42 Garton Ash (1994), p. 383.
43 'Germany exercises power not so much strategically as by its sheer weight,' Katzenstein
    (1997), p. 120.

Bibliography

Alba Vega, Carlos (ed.) (1996) *México y Alemania: Dos países en transición*, Mexico: El
    Colegio de México.
Carothers, Thomas (1999) *Aiding Democracy Abroad: The Learning Curve*, Washington
    DC: Carnegie Endowment for International Peace.
Dierickx, Guido (1994) 'Christian Democracy and its ideological rivals: an empirical
    comparison in the low countries,' in David Hanley (ed.), *Christian Democracy in
    Europe: A Comparative Perspective*, London and New York: Pinter.
Eisenstadt, Todd (2000) 'The neglected democrats: protracted transitions from author-
    itarianism,' *Democratization*, Special Issue, 7 (3).
Garton Ash, Timothy (1994) *In Europe's Name: Germany and the Divided Continent*, New
    York: Vintage Books.
Grabendorff, Wolf (1982) 'Las relaciones entre America Latina y Europa occidental:
    actores nacionales y transnacionales, objetivos y expectativas,' *Foro Internacional*, 23–1.
Grabendorff, Wolf (2001) 'International support for democracy in contemporary Latin
    America: the role of the party internationals,' in Laurence Whitehead, *The
    International Dimensions of Democratization: Europe and the Americas, Expanded
    Edition*, Oxford: Oxford University Press.
Higgott Richard A., Geoffrey R.D. Underhill, and Andreas Bieler (eds) (2000) *Non-State
    Actors and Authority in the Global System*, London and New York: Routledge.
Katzenstein, Peter J. (1997) 'United Germany in an integrating Europe,' *Current History*,
    96 (608).
Keck, Margaret and Kathryn Sikkink (1999) 'Redes transnacionales de cabildeo e
    influencia,' *Foro Internacional*, 39 (158).
Kleinmann, Hans-Otto (1993) *Geschichte der CDU: 1945–1982*, Stuttgart: Deutsche
    Verlags-Anstalt.
Kohl, Helmut (1999) 'Cuarenta años de labor parlamentaria en Bonn (alocución del ex
    Canciller Federal de Alemania con motivo del traslado de la sede del Parlamento
    Federal desde Bonn a Berlín),' *Contribuciones*, 63 (3).
Konrad Adenauer Stiftung (KAS) (1996) 'Por la paz, la democracia y la justicia: la labor
    internacional de la Fundación Konrad Adenauer,' Departamento de Cooperación
    Internacional.
Konrad Adenaeur Stiftung (KAS) (1999) 'Cooperar en un solo mundo: la cooperación
    internacional de la Fundación Konrad Adenauer,' Departamento de Cooperación
    Internacional.
Kösters, Wim (1989) 'Economía social de mercado: antecedentes históricos, desarrollo
    pricipios y elementos funadamentales,' *Contribuciones*, 6 (1).
Loaeza, Soledad (1994) 'The changing faces of Mexican nationalism,' in M. Delal Baer
    and Sidney Weintraub (eds), *The NAFTA Debate: Grappling with Unconventional
    Trade Issues*, London: Lynne Rienner.
Loaeza, Soledad (1999) *El Partido Acción Nacional: La Larga Marcha, 1939–1994.
    Oposición Leal y Partido de Protesta*, Mexico: Fondo de Cultura Económica.

Loaeza, Soledad (2000) 'Uncertainty in Mexico's protracted transition: the National Action Party and its aversion to risk,' *Democratization*, 7 (3).

Mols, Manfred and Christoph Wagner (1999) 'El significado relativo de America Latina en la politica exterior alemana,' *Foro Internacional*, 39 (15).

Pinto-Duschinsky, Michael (2001) 'International political finance: The Konrad Adenauer Foundation and Latin America,' in Laurence Whitehead, *The International Dimensions of Democratization: Europe and the Americas, Expanded Edition*, Oxford: Oxford University Press.

Risse, Thomas (1999) 'Avances en el estudio de las relaciones transnacionales y la politica mundial,' *Foro Internacional*, 39 (158).

Rummel, Reinhardt (1996) 'Germany's role in the CFSP: 'Normalität' or 'Sonderweg'?,' in Christopher Hill (ed.), *The Actors in Europe's Foreign Policy*, London and New York: Routledge.

Stone, Diane (2000) 'Private authority, scholarly legitimacy and political credibility: think tanks and informal diplomacy,' in Richard A. Higgott, Geoffrey R.D. Underhill, and Andreas Bieler (eds), *Non-State Actors and Authority in the Global System*, London and New York: Routledge.

Thesing, Josef (1990) 'El desarrollo de los acontecimientos en los países de Europa del este y su impacto en el Tercer Mund,' *Contribuciones*, 28 (4).

Von Nell-Breuning, Oswald (1946) *La reorganización de la Economia Social Desarrollo y Análisis de la Enciclica Quadragesimo Anno*, Buenos Aires: Editorial Poblet.

Whitehead, Laurence (1986) 'International aspects of democratization,' in Guillermo O'Donnell, Philippe C. Schmitter, and Laurence Whitehead (eds), *Transitions from Authoritarian Rule: Comparative Perspectives*, London: Johns Hopkins University Press.

Whitehead, Laurence (2001) 'Three international dimensions of democratization,' in Laurence Whitehead (ed.), *The International Dimensions of Democratization: Europe and the Americas, Expanded Edition*, Oxford: Oxford University Press.

Dorota Dakowska and Elsa Tulmets

3

Transnational relations and foreign policies: the interactions between non-state and state actors in the German assistance to Central Europe (political foundations in Poland and the program Transform in Estonia)

German engagement with CEE countries

The main purpose of this chapter is to establish the role played by German non-state actors in the assistance to CEECs over the 1990s until their accession to the EU on May 1, 2004. Of numerous countries which engaged in the reform process immediately after the liberalization of 1989, Germany and the US particularly developed a bilateral level parallel to their participation in multilateral action.

Actors from civil society today have a growing influence on political decisions. As everyday contacts develop confidence and loyalty, and lead to the institutionalization of professional relations between ministries, NGOs, companies, foundations, and epistemic communities, one cannot any longer speak of a strict separation between public and private actors (Czempiel and Rosenau, 1989; Strange, 1996). The two worlds described by James Rosenau, the state-centered, and the multi-centered, are irremediably interconnected. Furthermore, following the 'double-edged diplomacy' theory of Robert Putnam (1988), domestic and foreign policies are linked. Through foreign assistance to transformations, there has been a blurring of lines between the external and internal context (Pridham, 1994; Whitehead, 1996).

German foreign policy is strongly transnationalized, through semi-public or private actors. We therefore contest the (neo)-realists' vision of Germany as a '(united) power.'[1] Owing to its federal structure, Germany may be qualified as a semi-sovereign state, embedded in a multilateral (European) context (Katzenstein, 1987, 1997a).

These contributions help us to shape our analytical framework. We ask two major questions:

- How is German semi-sovereignty reflected in the assistance to CEEC – i.e. how do TNAs mobilize in foreign policies?
- How does the EU enlargement prospect affect German engagement in the region? Our hypothesis is that German assistance to CEE has been transnationalized owing (1) to the specificity of the semi-sovereign administration[2] and (2) to the growing importance of the EU dimension.

The specificity of German expertise is to be sought in both structural features of assistance (the relationship between public and private actors), and in its ideal components (the diffusion of elements of German political culture such as the social market economy and the unification experience). What are the expected and the effective results of the German assistance investment? Considering that the financial amounts engaged are not the only relevant measure of influence, an empirical study of actors, their instruments, and beliefs is required.

German cooperation with CEEC is realized through: (1) focusing on the requirements of the adaptation to the *acquis communautaire*; (2) delegating national programs to a supranational level. One of our hypotheses is thus that German non-state actors, supported by state actors, actually anticipated the enlargement process, in as far as they helped to associate their Eastern partners to European transnational networks:

- How far did German initiatives facilitate EU enlargement?
- How far was Europe an opportunity window and multilateralism an instrument for German actors?
- What kind of financial and symbolic resources did the European integration process represent for those actors?

The evolution of German engagement in Estonia and Poland will be analyzed in the light of the explanatory variable of EU enlargement.

In this chapter, we focus on two cases which may be considered as representative for German cooperation with CEEC. The first case analyses the engagement of German political foundations in Poland after 1989. Formally considered as NGOs, the political foundations are associated to German development policies through the Bundesministerium für wirtschaftliche Zusammenarbeit und Entwicklung (Federal Ministry for Economic Cooperation and Development – BMZ) and the Auswärtiges Amt (Foreign Ministry – AA). Unlike most NGOs, they are financed by public funds and the amount each foundation receives depends on the weight of each political party in parliament. Being party-associated (parteinah) is one of the foundations' main resources. This example is relevant for the importance attached in German foreign policy to non-state and semi-formal relations helping to deepen bilateral relations and to bind partners to transnational networks.

The second case focuses on the functioning of the German inter-ministerial bilateral program Transform on the Estonian example. Built on the logic of transnational networking, Transform is the major initiative of Germany's bilateral technical cooperation with CEEC to help them introduce democracy and a social market economy. Created in 1992 in order to coordinate the assistance begun in the 1980s in CEE, Transform mainly comprises education and formation of selected partners from eleven countries which, according to criteria determined by the Organization for Cooperation and Development (OECD), are involved in a transformation process.[3]

Even the definition of 'non-state actors' is problematic. NGOs are formally *non-profit* organizations; however, their budget may be partly public. Even if the political foundations do not respond to the classic definition of NGOs, they consider themselves as such. The German non-state actors which we take into consideration cooperate closely with ministries. They are usually financed by public funds and have close links to parties, industry, or state agencies. German governmental agencies have a special status, as they are totally subsidized by public administrations (like the Kreditanstalt für Wiederaufbau – KfW, the Carl Duisberg Gesellschaft – CDG, and the Gesellschaft für technische Zusammenarbeit – GTZ), but their legal status may be public (KfW . . .) as well as private (GTZ . . .) and take the form of a foundation (Institut für rechtliche Zusammenarbeit – IRZ Stiftung . . .). The framework of their tasks is determined by the ministries to which they are related. They nevertheless have an important leeway and responsibility for their actions and work daily with private actors and professionals from industry, the judiciary, and civil society.

The precise nature of the relationship of state administration/non-governmental actors, in which some see mutual instrumentalization, whereas others describe it as a virtually perfect symbiosis, remains difficult to define. In using the concept of 'transgovernmental coalition' in German assistance policies towards CEE, we follow Thomas Risse's (1995) definition.[4] We focus on networks, which associate non-state actors, but also state agencies. We adopt Tanja Börzel's definition of policy network as 'a set of relatively stable relationships which are of [a]non hierarchical and interdependent nature linking a variety of actors who share common interests with regard to a policy and who exchange resources to pursue these shared interests with regard to a policy acknowledging that cooperation is the best way to achieve common goals' (Börzel, 1998). The mission of the political foundations focuses on the transfer of styles, ways of doing, beliefs, and norms (for the distinction, see Radaelli, 2000), which may be qualified as 'soft' elements. The transfer of 'hard' elements (rules, procedures) will be discussed in the second part of this chapter. Finally, the general concept of 'state' may be deconstructed at different levels and fields of public administration. In relationships between federal ministries, as well as between services, competition relationship and bargaining are not unusual.

Political foundations: autonomous foreign policy instruments and the transnational socialization of Polish elites in the context of EU enlargement

The example of political foundations bears some specificity: they are situated at the intersection of different poles of power – the political parties they cooperate with, the federal ministries they are financed by:

- What values and norms embedded in the mandating institutions influenced the foundations' strategy in CEE ?
- How did the EU enlargement factor shape their engagement ?

Non-state political actors between ministries and political parties

Because of their particular position and the work they do abroad, political foundations are generally considered as being an integral part of German foreign policy. Created mainly in the post-war years,[5] they were traditionally committed to political education, to encourage civic engagement in political life, and to promote pluralism in the post-war FRG.[6]

The international engagement of German political foundations is only a part, though an important part, of the foundations' activity as a whole. Each foundation has a three- or four-decade experience of development aid in Latin America, Africa, and Asia (Vieregge, 1977; Schürmann, 1989). Since the 1970–1980s, political foundations have also set up their offices in industrialized countries, where they lead political dialog and organize conferences on current issues. The activity in CEE combines the characteristics of both approaches. Although Central European states are not 'developing countries' according to OECD criteria, the liberalization of 1989 required a substantial transfer of know-how in the economic, political, and judicial spheres. Political foundations participated indirectly in that process, but at the same time developed political dialogs with the clear objective of helping to stabilize the party landscape in the target countries and to find potential partners for German political parties.

The activities of political foundations reflect the orientations of German foreign policy enhanced by the specific preferences of each party. In relations with EU candidate countries, the official strategy consisted in promoting economic stability and ensuring markets and a political and institutional rapprochement, a reconciliation dimension realized through the deepening of the dialog and the creation of networks and forums aimed at the enlargement of the EU.

STIFTUNGEN: ON BEHALF OF POLITICAL PARTIES

The existing studies on political foundations vary greatly in the importance they accord to the party–foundation relationship. Some consider foundations as classical NGOs, taking their political dimension almost for granted (Biagiotti, 1996), while others describe them as instruments or mailboxes of the parties (Vieregge, 1977). The party affiliation seems to be an essential characteristic of the foundations' international engagement (Grabendorff, 1996, p. 217).[7] Still, the establishment of the effective role played by foundations in German foreign policy and external relations of each political party requires a thorough case study:

1. How does foundation analysis influence the perception of party members interested in foreign affairs?
2. What incentives do German politicians give to foundation employees?

The foundations' representatives usually stress their independence from the political parties, citing the 1986 decision of the German Constitutional Court, which reaffirmed the separation between them. However, although the foundations are independent legally and financially, they are based on ideological and personal links with the party. Important party officials sit on the foundations' administration board.[8] For German parties, foundations are important platforms facilitating the access to virtually the whole political scene of the partner country. In the foundations' international activity, two kinds of resources directly serve the parties: information and confidence capital:

(1) Staying in constant touch with foundation representatives abroad permits a direct information flow to the parliament. The foundation offices provide a great deal of knowledge and expertise on foreign and domestic policy issues, especially those which are too specialized or long-term-minded to be elaborated by usual party political advisors. This communication system may prove efficient provided there is enough interest among German Members of the Bundestag for international affairs. The effectiveness of the information activity also depends on the directors' personality. In some cases, foundation representatives can become a kind of lobbyist for 'their' country, publishing political manifestos, sending information letters to key political decision-makers in Germany, and trying to focus attention on their zone of activity.

(2) The need for transfer of confidence is stressed in official documents concerning foundations

Especially when the past burdens relations with a country, the activity of foundations bears unquestionable advantages: it allows the deepening of the society dimension of bilateral relations, and the multiplication of links, while guaranteeing the necessary attention to the sensitivity of some questions. Foundations act as NGOs, thus diminishing the degree of German state intervention, the predominance of which could hamper bilateral relations.[9]

Unquestionably, the value added of the foundations, as compared with state assistance programs, is the direct access to key decision-makers in host countries. Foundations have the opportunity to inform their parties about the last internal evolutions, in some cases advise their partners in a reform discussion, or even encourage coalition-building, initiatives that would be unacceptable if coming from the German government.[10] The foundations' privileged position within German institutions relies on a well-balanced exchange of resources; it is very advantageous that, while using party resources (contacts, prestige, information), foundations are not bound by their constraints. Thus, field representatives may very well disagree publicly with a party orientation or statement (although it seems improbable that they would propose a discussion subject opposed to party interests).

ESSENTIAL INSTRUMENT OF FOREIGN AND DEVELOPMENT POLICIES

The success story of political foundations is inextricably linked to the history of the BMZ. The foundation of the BMZ in 1961, charged with the coordination of growing German international cooperation, constitutes the starting point for the long-term establishment of NGOs in the public policy spectrum. In fact, the weakness of the newly created institution implied the reliance on the NGO network, which eventually formed a kind of lobby, aimed at strengthening its own position and at the same time the funding ministry (Schürmann, 1989, p. 20). Throughout the decades of cooperation many relationships were institutionalized. The autonomy of an NGO depends on the preservation of a correct equilibrium between the ministerial subventions and its own resources (Glagow and Schimanck, 1983). While the party support emanating from the Bundestag provides the political foundations with the necessary resources for their activity,[11] it guarantees an ideological independence from a possible ministerial influence.

The relationship between the BMZ and the political foundations relies on an overall recognition of the latter's effectiveness. The formulation of administrative directives leaves the foundations an important leeway for action. Foundations submit their projects to the BMZ, which evaluates them for accordance with the general directives and provides them with subsidies. The AA checks all the projects under the criterion of their compatibility with foreign policy principles. Existing ministerial control is thus largely negative (Phillips, 2000, p. 129), and the rejection of a project submitted is rare. Ministerial documents, since the beginning of the cooperation with the foundations, bear witness to the stability of general cooperation concepts.

First, the notion of pluralism is stressed, in as far as the foundations are committed in their overseas activity to reflect the diverse political tendencies coexisting within the FRG at the individual, society, and state level.[12] The idea is that you can teach pluralism only while practising it, through the transmission of different values, which may compete, complete, and overlap with each other. This plural approach enables the discussion-oriented 'export of ideas' (Ideenexport), while avoiding the proliferation of a monolithic 'Germany model' (BMZ, 1999, pp. 2–3). A key to German assistance performance lies in the fact that there is a consensus common to the BMZ officials and to the foundation that the state alone is unable to fulfill the tasks of development policies (BMZ, 1999, p. 17). As compared with the state-run programs, the foundations have the advantages of leading a direct social dialog, and being a guarantee of continuity, a long-term presence, and having an independence from government changes.

Second, the use of the NGO status can fulfill the objectives of state policies, embodied in the principle of limited publicity (eingeschränkte Publizität). Following government suggestions, the foundations present themselves in their work abroad as NGOs (BMZ, 1973, p. 59, 1999, p. 15). This shows the importance accorded to Germany's international image and also explains the difficulties in understanding the effective status of the Stiftungen, that exploit their flexible profile, appearing as more or less state- or party-affiliated, according to circumstances (Bartsch, 1998, p. 193). Illustrating the thesis of 'pluralism without competition' (Phillips, 2000, p. 130), the BMZ encourages the cooperation between the Stiftungen in their work abroad. Furthermore, BMZ officials may prevent the foundations from working too closely with the same institution, the aim being to reach the largest partner spectrum.[13] In any case, a kind of agreement takes place between the foundations concerning their activity abroad, which completes their traditional division of labor linked to the specific profile of each foundation.[14]

Speaking of a 'symbiosis' between the BMZ and the political foundations is justified by their historical interdependence. The BMZ bureaux regularly consult foundation officials over the formulation of new regional or sector concepts. Foundation foreign offices provide reports about their projects and the general situation in host countries. Proof of the waning cleavage between public and private actors is the coalition composed of ministry officers and foundations, aimed at defending the latter's funds and statute. The BMZ director in charge of the Stiftungen defends them from budget cuts required by the Ministry of Finance, or from external attempts for more centralization, which occasionally haunt German institutions.

Preparing for EU enlargement: rapprochement through transnational networking

In the first stage of the transformation process, political foundations had the advantage of being among the first foreign 'NGOs' implemented in the region,[15] and the capacity to mobilize the necessary expertise from Germany relatively quickly. However, democracy assistance is not a unidirectional movement; it may be considered as an *interactive learning process*. The EU enlargement variable will be used to analyse both the multilateralization of political networking and the tightening of bilateral relations. However, the obvious limits of a transfer demand caution in any conclusions about foundations' influence.

FOCUS ON EU ENLARGEMENT: THE BEST USE OF MULTILATERALISM . . .

Since the mid-1990s, the foundations' activity has been increasingly focused on European issues and the Central European partners embedded in a multilateral context. The EU enlargement may be considered as an international socialization to liberal norms and values (Schimmelfennig, 1998). The candidate states must adapt 80,000 pages of the *acquis communautaire* to their legislation. It may be asked in how far this constraint is a resource for the German NGOs as it may facilitate the taking over of some of the institutional solutions that they propose. According to foundations' representatives, their aim is to develop links between CEE partners and both Bonn and Brussels. It may be argued that the EU enlargement prospect gave political foundations an important leeway for the transfer of both political ideas and transnational legitimacy. The strong normative context created by the EU (Katzenstein, 1997a) seems to have increased the demand for foreign advice during the pre-accession period. The European dimension has thus provided huge resources for German factors in terms of receptivity and prestige. As a foundation representative stated: 'there are no German solutions anymore, there are European solutions.'[16]

LEGITIMACY TRANSFERS IN EUROPE: IT'S ALL NETWORKS

The EU eastward opening paved the way for the enlargement of European transnational networks. The parties represented in the EP wished to associate with as many and strong CEE partners, potential full members after enlargement, as possible. Political foundations were more than just intermediaries in this process. Owing to their network of personal contacts in the European institutions, foundation field representatives could influence decisions in an informal way. By diffusing information through party networks they participated in the process of legitimization of CEE parties.[17] The party affiliation meant that a foundation representative spoke not only on behalf of his foundation and party, but also of the Chancellery, in the case of a government party foundation, so that a distinction between them was sometimes difficult to perceive (Grabendorff, 1996, p. 213). On the transnational scale, foundation representatives supported contacts between the members of EP or party Internationals and politicians of the partner countries.[18] Foundations helped the parties to identify their partners, observing (sometimes also supporting) their political evolution, and finally assessing their readiness to being admitted to the party as observer or associate member.

Thus, the KAS gave a substantial support to the anti-Meciar opposition in Slovakia. It presented Mikulas Dzurinda as the viable interlocutor on the international scene, providing him with contacts and advice before and following his electoral victory. The KAS has been active in helping Central European parties to become associate members of the European People's Party (EPP). This was the case of the Magyar Demokrata Forum (Hungarian Democratic Forum – MDF) in Hungary; the (ODA), the Unie Svobody (Union of Freedom – US), and Krestanské a Demokratické/Cs Strany Lidové (Christian Democratic Union/ Czech People's Party – KDU/CSL) in the Czech Republic; the Union of Freedom (UW), Stowarzyszenie Lewicy Demokratycznej (Conservative People's Party –

SKL), RS, AWS, then also the PO and Polskie Stronnictwo Ludowe (Polish Peasant Party – PSL) in Poland; but also Christian Democratic parties in Slovakia, Estonia, Latvia, and Bulgaria. The European scene of transnational party interactions occasionally reminded one of a market where different parties propose their affiliation to the same client.[19]

Any definition of the role of political foundations in the interactions with European parties must take into account the fusion between these *milieux*. One can hardly speak of foundations lowering transaction costs in a network whose members describe themselves as a 'team.' However, it should be possible to consider them as a kind of 'epistemic community' (Haas, 1992) based on experts familiar with EU policy-making and able to diffuse their knowledge and contacts. We can also use the concept of 'advocacy coalition' (Keck and Sikkink, 1998) to describe the networks created by the foundations associating with their partners in order to support the EU enlargement perspective at both the European as well as the national level.

EUROPE ENABLES THE DEEPENING OF BILATERAL RELATIONS . . .
Transnational networking aimed at the international legitimization of a political partner makes up the framework of the foundations' activity. The foundation could engage in friendly dialog with a partner, but political bilateral party cooperation does not occur before the eventual association of a Central European partner to the European Party or International. Only such an association could provide the new member party with sufficient political legitimacy and allow it to be considered as an equal partner by the German political parties. Transnational lobbying may thus be considered as a precondition for the further deepening of the cooperation on a bilateral level.

The case of the SPD/Sojusz Lewicky Demokratucznej (Democratic Left Alliance – SLD) cooperation during the 1990s, when internal developments gave the first impulses to tighten relationship, is representative. The 1993 electoral victory of the post-communist SLD and the PSL in Poland marked an important point for the social democrat FES in the legitimization process of Central European post-communist parties.[20] A close cooperation did not really occur before the admission of the (SdRP, the predecessor of the SLD) to the Socialist International (SI). Since then, the SPD and the SLD have entered a closer relationship, embodied by a bilateral parliamentary group, which has enabled communication, coordination, and convergence of views.

The foundations do not have the right to participate directly or indirectly in electoral campaigns. However, they can increase the professional abilities of the social and political actors in dispensing media training or political rhetoric courses. An important field of foundations' engagement is the 'pre-political' space. Thus, the youth associations close to political parties were generously subventioned by the foundations (some of them up to 80%). This gives the foundations access to the future political elite, potentially more receptive to ideas on European integration

. . .. BUT THERE ARE LIMITS

Looking for institutional transfers, we should not forget that there are structural and cultural incompatibilities as well as continuities. Thus, the SPD wished to cooperate with social democratic parties that arose from the opposition or from emigration *milieux* as was the case with Spanish or Portuguese social democrats in the 1970s (Ortuño Anaya, 2002). However, the majority of Central European social democratic parties emerged from the former communist parties, owing to their financial, informational and professional resources, and these realities had to be taken into account by the SPD, which eventually multiplied contacts to post-communist parties and led its own evaluation of their internal democratization (see also Phillips, 2000, pp.166–168). The KAS for a long time presented federalism and social market economy as objective 'models' to be sought and taken over in transformation countries. However, for different reasons, the concept of a social market economy forged by the German ordoliberals in the 1950s has been more recently called into question.

Notwithstanding the difficulties with quantifying this kind of activity, it is worth asking what the results of this transnational link-building are, and if any loyalties have followed. The latter is not necessarily guaranteed as a return on German political investment. Following Rosamond (1999), to deconstruct political discourse on enlargement in Poland would show that 'European integration' as a concept may serve very different purposes according to social actors (internal legitimization, justifying a political decision . . .). Moreover, while German decision-makers were often the privileged interlocutors for the Polish politicians in the early pre-accession period, things changed in an enlarged EU with a multiplicity of actors and communication levels which have dramatically increased the complexity of interactions.

Still, discussion habits and communication channels may be considered a lasting investment. Polish political parties, having a close relationship with German partners may be bound to carry on with exchange and dialog even in a period of political tension. Notwithstanding the crises observed in the European or bilateral context, politicized think-tanks on both sides have good chances to continue to discuss the European Neighbourhood Policy, the future of the European Security and Defense Policy (ESDP), etc.

Overall, it may be stated that political foundations won an important political credit in Poland. They managed to ensure a certain return on their investment: direct information flow and contact networks. Some of the foundations' field representatives became an authority in EU matters and their voice counted in the local press. Their support for the Polish case in the German debate about EU enlargement was significant. German engagement in Poland cannot be compared with that of any other EU country; a concluding image, recalled in a discussion with a Polish NGO leader is that 'Owing to the foundations, the Germans ceased to be perceived in Poland as Teutonic Knights.'

The German foundations may be considered as 'change agents,' mobilizing in the Polish context, persuading their partners to redefine their identities

(Börzel and Risse, 2000). They can hardly be seen as intermediaries in a study of the Europeanization of Polish political parties. While the Transform program overtook the classical assistance activity of the political foundations, they concentrated on more elite-oriented and political issues. Still, the presence of political foundations in CEE has been ensured, as they remain a traditional, reliable, foreign policy instrument, appreciated by German politicians and envied abroad (Bartsch, 1998, p. 196).

The Transform program: expand markets in CEEC, export the model of 'social market economy,' and change Germany's image abroad

Implemented between 1992 and 2002, the Transform program officially consisted in the presentation of the German 'model' of social market economy, of federalism, as well as of the experience of reunification. It was conceived as a complement to the Poland–Hungary Assistance for Economic Reconstruction (PHARE) program,[21] where 'Germany contributes 28% of the budget,' but 'participates [in its implementation] in an unsatisfactory way' (Federal Cabinet Decision, 1992, 1993). In the framework of Transform, German ministries strengthened their links to societal organizations such as NGOs and companies,[22] and especially relied on networks developed during forty years of development policy abroad: (1) After having identified these networks of actors retracing various sectors of German society, their origins and their evolving tasks, do we observe transfers of German 'models' to CEEC, or rather a growing focus on EU enlargement issues? (2) After a short analysis of the Estonian example, a country more anchored to Finland's and US assistance, may we still speak of a German 'influence' spread over Eastern and Central Europe?

The promotion of German economic experience through transnationalized foreign assistance

Official documents and interviews with officials[23] reveal that the main aims of the program are to expand markets in CEEC, build strong networks of long-lasting contacts, and change Germany's image abroad. But do all of the actors identified participate in this specific program? Do other societal actors act parallel and/or complementary to the German official assistance?

THE PROGRAM: A PRODUCT OF GERMAN EXPERTS FOR ASSISTANCE IN CEEC
The coordination of German bilateral assistance is the result of a conjectural situation – many German ministries developed their own policies towards the transformation countries up to 1988. In 1992, the Federal Cabinet decided to implement the Transform program for CEEC and Newly Independent States (NIS), by coordinating the actions of the federal ministries under a single concept entitled the 'General concept of consulting on democracy building and on market economy in transition countries.' Know-how transfers would, for

instance, concentrate on these items, and be distributed among different actors and sectors related to them – i.e. economics, politics, agriculture, law, environment, social matters . . . The main idea of the program is the same as in assistance for third world countries: 'help the countries to help themselves' (Hilfe zur Selbsthilfe) in their transformation.

The assistance to CEEC, in particular Transform, was developed for different reasons. The German discourse on relations with Eastern Europe entails at least three kind of norms: responsibility, solidarity, and chance (Ecker-Ehrhardt, 2002):

- *Political reasons*: the discourse was above all part of the negotiation for the East–West rapprochement process (the Kohl–Gorbatchov agreement of 1988). The action of German pressure groups suggested it was a duty of the German government to help German minorities in CEEC after the Two Plus Four agreement of 1990 (Sudetendeutsche and Aussiedler associations, like the Bund der Vertriebene were granted some public funds for the development of their actions). In the discourse, however, political leaders preferred to emphasize the role of history, Germany's responsibility in the fate of CEE, and its will to help these countries democratize. Germany's image abroad is another reason often quoted.

- *Economic reasons*: German companies had already invested in those countries for several decades, and wanted to increase their market shares there. These new markets were perceived as a chance for the German economy but the discourse also expressed a fear of mass immigration from Eastern Europe to Germany.

Between 1993 and 1996, more than 800 projects were implemented through Transform (Bafoil, 1997, p. 165), whose consulting activities encompassed the following issues:

- Back-up economic policies in order to create the conditions for a social market economy and to establish medium-size companies and other relevant economic structures;
- restructuring of companies, privatization, and breaking up of monopolies;
- setting up a fiscal system to include taxes, customs and excises, and budgets; establishing the banking, stock market, and insurance systems;
- technical assistance to the agricultural sector;
- job training and specialized training in business (i.e. management training, vocational training), as well as measures leading to qualifications;
- the law, with an emphasis on economic law;
- helping both to create and to improve administrative structures;
- back-up advisory services in labor market policy and social policy, environmental protection, house-building and urban development.

Although all sectors were linked together, the German program mainly focused on economics (46% of the expertise). The other sectors, and especially the social and environmental ones, represented only a marginal part of the assistance (4 % and 2%, respectively, in 1998).[24] Between 1990 and 2000, a total of 2,377 billion DM (about 1,15 billion Euros) was spent on consulting activities as well as other matters, mostly under the label of the Transform program. Since 1995, the annual budget significantly decreased: in 1997 it was comparable to the UK's, and represented a sixth of the US bilateral technical assistance (GTZ, 1999, p.10).[25] In fact, German ministries (and their mandated partners) developed bilateral projects more and more in the EU framework, benefiting from EU financing, which had almost doubled by 2000.

THE ACTORS: MOBILIZING NETWORKS FROM ALL SECTORS OF GERMAN SOCIETY

The concept of a 'policy network' may again be useful to explain how the German program, apparently structured and shaped by public actors, was in fact implemented by non-state actors. As the Transform program used the resources of *Ostpolitik*, as well as of development assistance and of the process of German unification, almost every German ministry and their main (public and private) partners were represented. The networks were made up of experts in federal, regional, and local administrations, in health care systems, in NGOs or companies' foundations, in chambers of commerce, and consulting companies . . . With some exceptions, German assistance in CEE was not really different from that carried out in third world countries since the 1970s.[26]

All of these organizations had their own networks of relations, related to other public levels (cities, Länder), to companies (services, banks . . .), and to societal actors (professional associations, academics . . .). For example, the IRZ Stiftung, a foundation working for the Bundesministerium der Justiz (Ministry of Justice – BMJ), relied on a large web of contacts for the organization of seminars, meetings, and training on current judicial and legislation issues. The members of the IRZ were in fact politicians (national and European Members of Parliament), economists (heads of companies, banks, Deutscher Industrie- und Handelstag, the chamber of commerce (DIHT), academics (management or law professors), and people from the judicial sector (advocates, lawyers, fiscal advisors . . .).

SOCIETAL ACTORS AS INSTRUMENTS OF GERMAN'S FOREIGN ASSISTANCE TO EASTERN EUROPE, OR INFORMAL DIPLOMATS?

The German government adopted an integrated approach for the coordination of the program: all the actors officially worked together under the leadership of the Lenkungsausschuss, a triumvirate composed of the Bundesministerium für Wirtschaft und Technologie (Ministry of Economics and Technology – BMWi), the AA, and the BMZ. Until the election of Gerhard Schröder in 1998, former State minister for Agriculture Walter Kittel was responsible for the general coordination. Eleven local offices were set up in the German embassies in CEEC by the KfW for the management of the various projects. KfW experts acquired a sort of monopoly on transition matters, using links to a large network of economic as well as diplomatic contacts. On many occasions, congresses and seminars were organised in CEEC with other German actors, such as political foundations, chambers of commerce, trade representation of the Länder, etc. . . .

However, the coordination reflected political rivalries and power relations between German actors: for the ministries, the control of the Lenkungsauschuss (coordination committee) and the repartition of the annual budget was at stake, whereas many state agencies and NGOs, which already communicated every day, believed that annual coordination meetings in Bonn were a waste of time. Another contradiction lay in the implementation of the program. While Eastern partners officially spontaneously asked for German assistance, the reality showed that most Eastern partners, on the contrary, had been directly contacted by German companies or state agencies. Most of the time, German companies had already built contacts in CEEC in order to evaluate (or even to create) the need, and help their partners elaborate a project to be submitted to German governmental agencies, and then approved by German ministries. In this sense, one should not speak of the 'instrumentalization' of NGOs by public actors as these are processes of mutual influence. The analysis of societal organizations, agencies, private (companies') foundations, expert organizations – or, as shown above, political foundations – were most of the time followed up or partly taken over by administrative organizations.[27] In a sense, if we consider the thesis of 'privatization' of state's policies (Hibou, 1999; Brühl, 2001),[28] we may call them places of informal diplomacy.

A TRANSNATIONALIZED ASSISTANCE

Many agencies, NGOs, and (mostly consulting) companies involved in Transform developed transnational networks in Europe and contacts with international organizations, which rather contradicted the hierarchical structure of the program. One example is the IRZ Stiftung: it helped with the implementation of PHARE and Technical Assistance for the CIS (TACIS) projects, but also developed ties with other EU judicial associations like the Dutch Centre for International Cooperation in Leyden, or the French Association pour le renouveau et la promotion des échanges juridiques avec l'Europe centrale et orientale (ARPEJE) in Paris. Together, they organized seminars on general and EU-related issues for CEE partners, mostly with the help of EU financing.

Another reason explaining the difficulty of a bilateral hierarchical coordination was the federal structure of assistance, which at the same time encouraged overlapping actions;[29] thus German regions (Länder) as well as cities (Hamburg, Bremen, Munich), universities, and other public administrations built their own networks of relations.[30] Sometimes, individuals were the source of these connections between local, federal, and even supranational levels, as they were working for the German parliament, were part of a local NGO, and/or had contacts at the European Commission. The personal address book of some influential people (political, business . . .) situated at the cross-section of these networks may have proved more efficient than a whole organization.[31]

LINKS TO OTHER SOCIETAL ACTORS, AND AUTONOMIZATION PROCESSES
Many members of civil society (retired professors, churches, charitable organizations) have granted aid parallel to official bilateral assistance. Some of them were partly connected to Transform actors, like the political foundations, especially as far as financial matters were concerned. Their actions were mostly complementary to those taking place in the framework of the German program. Companies' foundations such as the Robert Bosch Stiftung (Bosch) and the Herbert Quandt Stiftung (BMW) considered that their duty was to act where traditional actors of Germany's foreign policy did not want to or could not intervene. For example, the Robert Bosch Stiftung (with a budget of 64 million DM in 1997, i.e. 32 million Euros) developed projects promoting the German language, complementary to those driven by the Goethe institutes. Bilateral (friendship) associations (German–Estonian associations . . .) played an important role in mutual understanding and the implementation of local projects, as did individual people (academics, wealthy persons with personal ties to CEEC), clubs (Rotary club . . .), or religious organizations (Caritas . . .). As a general observation, most of the protagonists seemed to care less about the federal level: they concentrated on wider non-territorial-limited actions, or they worked directly for European institutions and in the framework of transnational European and international networks.

THE PROGRAM TRANSFORM IN ESTONIA: PREPARING FOR ACCESSION TO THE EU
For several reasons, Estonia is an interesting case study among the eleven countries targeted by Transform, as it stresses the growing importance of EU issues in German assistance. It shows, for example, that long-lasting contacts with Eastern partners, be they small or big, may be interesting for German actors, as these contacts may be decisive for coalition-building in the framework of multilateral (EU) decision-making processes (Adam, 1995). While on the economic side German investments in Estonia remained rather insignificant, the influence of German actors in specific sectors like the judiciary and law have been decisive. Since Estonia is one of the countries where the Transform program can be considered as complete (as in the Czech Republic and Hungary in 1998), it was easier to draw early conclusions from this case during our research project.

As German technical assistance is embedded in a multilateral level, and German actors are plural, can we still speak of the transfer of a German 'model' to CEEC? Furthermore, the process of European integration leads to the production of 'hard norms' (Radaelli, 2000): do these norms act as constraints or as resources for the different actors participating in the transformation in CEEC? Finally, how can we qualify the role played by German actors between Western and Eastern Europe?

THE IMPROBABLE TRANSMISSION OF A GERMAN 'MODEL'
One should not speak of the transfer of a German 'model' to CEEC.[32] Even if German institutions and practices have more or less inspired the reforms intro-

duced since 1989, the practice was different. Political decisions, historical paths, and cultures influenced the reshaping of the state, as did the (neo-liberal) ideas diffused by international organizations such as the IMF, the World Bank, and the European Bank for Reconstruction and Development (EBRD).

Some examples of projects implemented by Transform experts in Estonia show that Germany's contribution to reforms in Estonia was rather marginal:

- *Privatization in Estonia*: the US helped to build the whole framework, the GTZ and the Treuhandanstalt Osteuropa Beratungsgesellschaft (TOB) came later. The Estonian privatization agency was shaped by the TOB, but the input of the GTZ experts remained marginal. One Treuhandanstalt/ GTZ expert, Schmidt, played an important role, as he personally advised Prime Minister Vähi.
- The *Estonian Central Bank (Eesti Pank)*: while the Estonian Crone was linked to the DM, the Eesti Pank was mostly built on the British example.[33] German experts gave advice on the German banking system, and especially on the Euro and on the functioning of the European Central Bank (ECB).
- The *Estonian Chamber of Agriculture*: this was built with the help of experts from different countries, especially from Nordic ones (Finland, Denmark).
- The *Estonian constitution*: this was mostly reshaped with Canadian consultants.
- *Education*: a lot of money was invested by the German government in order to open German schools, but they competed with American and British ones.
- *Social and environmental assistance*: this was mainly provided by Nordic countries (Finland, Denmark, Sweden) which were concerned by the consequences of pollution in the Baltic Sea.

The assistance on commercial law may be the only field of a really important transfer, as 80% of German trade laws were taken over.[34] According to Estonians it was decided to re-establish the former Estonian laws elaborated in the nineteenth-century Bismarckian period for a quick transition to western standards. The structures of German companies (GmbH . . .)[35] and the internal organization of German chambers of commerce served as examples for a fast transformation on the economic level. The assistance of the IRZ Stiftung and of the Institut für Ostrecht created in 1958 is notable, as well as the twinning between Kiel and Tallinn, which was crucial in building the Estonian chamber of commerce. While further investigations need to be made, one thing is certain: there has been no transfer of a 'social market economy,' as Transform's financing did not concentrate on the social field, and because this question largely depended on the political orientation of the benefit country, which was ultraliberal in Estonia.

Despite the diverse public encouragements and local trade representations of German Länder (Schleswig-Holstein, Mecklenburg-Vorpommern) in Tallinn, the number of German joint ventures (JVs) remained rather low in Estonia (some fifty in 1999). The main direct investments came from Nordic countries like Finland, Denmark, Sweden, and Norway. As most of the cooperation projects were implemented through different donors (US, UK, Finland . . .), a 'cross-breeding' process seems to have taken place among the manifold CEEC administrations, institutions, and organizations. This idea is reinforced by the fact that German assistance to Estonia and other CEEC increasingly concentrated more and more on the preparation for EU integration.

A Growing Reference to Europe in German Cooperation Policy
We may speak of an ever-increasing focus on the EU dimension in two ways: the content of the assistance was more and more oriented on the transmission of the *acquis communautaire*, and the preparation for the Euro. As far as organization and practice are concerned, most of the Transform experts working for German organizations operated more and more on the supranational level, especially in the implementation of EU programs (PHARE, Twinning, the Instrument for Structural Policies for Pre-Accession (ISPA), and the Special Accession Program for Agricultural and Rural Development (SAPARD)).

On the eastern side, partners who used at the beginning to accept any kind of assistance, progressively began to pin down their real needs, and to select projects more relevant to EU questions. They made their own experience, while noting that the western answers were not always the most suitable for their specific problems. In turn, western strategies also evolved: social and environmental norms were, for example, more frequently used as symbolic resources by German experts for the negotiation of a contract, as their involvement was often presented as 'a condition for a successful integration in the EU.'

However, one should not neglect the importance of the local, mostly informal coordination in CEE, because it fosters a more integrated Europe in many ways. The presence of western permanent experts in eastern administrative and professional structures helped to develop unexpected ties: not only between West European agents (for whom 'it is a way to be better informed about what other EU countries do'), but between East European countries too (Estonians now organize training in Ukraine and in the Balkans). Furthermore, German actors helped to shape the Northern Dimension of CFSP, and took part in the regionalization process around the Baltic Sea: a good example is the fact that the respective directors of the chambers of commerce in Kiel and Tallinn were at the same time presidents of the Council of Northern Countries. There are many other examples of this kind.

The 'Bridging' Role of German Actors
German experts encountered, and still encounter, many difficulties in implementing assistance. Beside the political color of the government, and sometimes a clear rejection of German assistance, the local culture and traditions represent strong barriers to institutional or know-how transfers, as do corruption and organized crime. But as a result of the approach built on partnership, interaction, and the making of 'opinion relays' (politicians, administrators, professors,

heads of companies, journalists. . .) and socialization processes (i.e. relations built on confidence and loyalty, Keck and Sikkink, 1998) everyday contacts were a first step to a more integrated Europe. German actors were glad when they saw that they could participate in modifying perceptions on values such as freedom, private property, or the respect for the law. They seemed particularly satisfied when they managed to keep regular personal contacts with Estonian (and CEEC) partners, and saw that they were informally called on for advice on 'mostly technical and very precise questions, even several months after the end of projects.'[36]

While financial means remained modest and even decreased after 1995,[37] interviews with local actors revealed that the actions of these experts were more important than expected, and that German experience was appreciated and respected in CEEC. This may be interpreted as a growing political credit accruing to German actors. Furthermore, many eastern partners preferred to work in the framework of bilateral assistance, and especially of the German one, because of its flexibility compared to EU programs. As far as financing is concerned a progressive and strong increase in responsibility of Eastern partners was evident after 1998: participants now have to share the costs of training courses, journeys, and meetings.

Thus, one cannot speak of a general German influence over Eastern Europe. We agree with the concept of 'Tamed Power'[38] developed by Peter Katzenstein (1997a) – i.e. German (political, economic, educational . . .) structures and European construction acted as constraints on Germany's sovereignty. But so did EU norms on other West and East European countries. The Estonian case also revealed that many other countries participated in the transformation processes of each CEEC. If one could find links between Western and Eastern European countries, one could point to the fact that while Poland and Hungary were, for example, more connected to German and US assistance, and Romania more to France (partly for historic, economic, and geographic reasons), Estonia was linked to Finland, to other Northern countries, and to Northern America. However, with regard to Germany's long-standing boundaries with CEE and to the unique experience of reunification, many German actors felt that they had accomplished an important 'bridging' role between West and East, more than any other West European actors could ever do. That at least is what many Eastern actors now think about their German partners.

Conclusion

As non-state actors' influence in political decision processes grows, we have demonstrated that the public and private sectors are irremediably interconnected. As internal and external affairs are two sides of the same coin, German assistance to the CEEC was embedded in the European context: a result of many interacting actors from ministries, political parties, epistemic communities, political and companies' foundations, associations, and other NGOs, corporations, professional groups, and even individuals. The political foundations reflected German cooperative federalism, allowing political parties to shape public policies. The activity of German political foundations in the EU candidate countries anticipated and prepared the process of EU enlargement by creating informal communication channels and by assisting the early enlargement of some of the European transnational networks. As much of the information flow inside the EU is at the same time both informal and politicized, this part of German assistance seemed quite well adapted to the requirements of EU policymaking.

Between 1989 and 2004 – the year of accession of the candidate countries from CEE to the EU – we could observe the development of links between bilateral and multilateral assistance and a growing participation of transnational actors in the intensification of interaction between the western part and the eastern part of Europe. These actors acted more and more in a European/multilateral context, and not only over financing. Generally speaking, their actions did not really differ from those led in other (non-European) countries, although in the case of CEEC, re-unification and EU norms were strong resources for German assistance.

The examples chosen here show that there is no strict transfer of a German 'model' to CEEC, but of certain German institutional features, of the experience of democratic state-building, and of knowledge about European decision-making process. As a matter of fact, German experts supported the liberalization of CEE markets in the context of globalization. Social and environmental problems were thus not the main priorities of German coordinated assistance to CEEC, although Germany is known as a pioneer in these fields. These questions were relegated to private actors, who did not have the appropriate means to defend these causes in a world of growing competition. The government and its institutionalized partners still had the responsibility for the orientation of cooperation policies, and especially in the distribution of resources needed for their implementation. As bilateral assistance was vanishing and being replaced by multilateral programs, citizens, especially those involved in transnational networks, were likely to feel more concerned by the importance of environmental or social questions, which were directly related to collective security.

As shown in Peter Katzenstein's Tamed Power, Germany adapted very well to the EU framework of collective decision-making: it managed to push forward solutions which suited its interests, although usually in consultation with other countries. The factors facilitating the adoption of institutional solutions were: (1) The existence of a dense communication network inside the EU; (2) Institutional similarities between Germany and some 'smaller' EU states. This analytical framework applied to the analysis of the (material and immaterial) resource 'Europe' in German policy towards CEE. German policy was also a European one. The EU enlargement required institutional harmonization and the integration of a powerful communication network. Both were highly important for Germany, especially in relations with neighboring countries. In a sense, the focus of assistance on European norms was already a first step to more mutual understanding, as they acted as a reference for the conscience of both the western and the eastern actors.

Notes

We thank Anne-Marie Le Gloannec and Peter Katzenstein for the useful remarks on this chapter.

1 There exists a substantial theoretical literature on the relevance and different meanings of concepts of power, influence, and eventual German hegemony over the 'smaller' European states: see Maull (1990); Schwarz (1994); Davis and Dombrowski (1997); Reich and Markovits (1997); Tewes (1997).

2 According to the sociological–institutionalist view, a broader institutional context, in which actors are embedded, shapes their expectations and may thus influence policy outcomes (Thielemann, 1999).

3 They include Belarus, Bulgaria, the Czech Republic, Estonia, Latvia, Lithuania, Hungary, Poland, Slovakia, Russia, Ukraine, and, since 1998, Slovenia.

4 Transgovernmental coalitions are 'networks of government officials, which include at least one actor pursuing her own agenda independent of national decisions' (Risse-Kappen, 1995, p. 9), a reflection based on Keohane and Nye (1974, pp. 39–62).

5 The exception is the social democratic FES, created in 1925, forbidden in 1933, and revived in 1945. The KAS was founded from two institutes in 1964, the Christian Social HSS was founded in 1967, and the liberal FNS in 1958. The Green HBS was founded 1997 out of the Regenbogen Stiftung created in 1989. In 1999 the Rosa Luxemburg Stiftung (RLS), affiliated to the post-communist (PDS), was awarded its first grants by the Bundestag.

6 For a more thorough analysis, see Dorota Dakowska, 'Les fondations politiques allemandes dans la politique étrangère: de la genèse institutionnelle à leur engagement dans le processus d'élargissement de l'UE,' dissertation prepared at the Institut d'Etudes Politiques de Paris, based on a research in different public and private archives as well as on 100 interviews with foundations representatives and their partners in Germany, Poland, Hungary, and Brussels.

7 Grabendorff (1996) qualifies foundations as 'executive organs of the political mother organization, allowing the party to participate to a certain extent in the domestic politics of another country at a non-governmental level without violating the rule of inter-governmental relations.'

8 Among the members of the Board of the KAS we could name Helmut Kohl, Peter Hinze, Angela Merkel, Volker Rühe, Bernhard Vogel. Johannes Rau was the vice-chairman of the board of the FES until 1998.

9 On the foundations' evolution under the Hallstein doctrine, as an instrument of counteracting the communist influences in the third world, see Pinto-Dushinsky (1996).

10 'Without the resources, organisatory force and influence networks of the foundations, the German parties would be less able to play an important role on the international scene of the expanding transnational party cooperation' (Bartsch, 1998, p. 192).

11 The budget of political foundations is made up mainly of state subsidies, decided in the annual budget vote. The funds come from the Ministry of Interior, the AA, and the BMZ. They are divided between the foundations according to a repartition

mechanism, depending on the results of the political parties during the last two parliamentary elections. In 2001 the percentage was as follows: the KAS and the FES: 32.5 per cent each; the FNS, the HSS, and the HBS: 11.66 per cent each (after the subtraction of 0.5 per cent of the whole sum for the RLS) (BMZ).

12 ' Pluralism is not only the message but also the medium,' *Die Tätigkeit der politischen Stiftungen in Mittel- und Osteuropa*, Bonn, May 1995, p. 6.

13 In Poland, both the FES and the KAS initiate projects with the liberal, pro-European UW. While organising conferences with the same research institute can happen, continued financing of one institution by two different foundations is forbidden.

14 For instance, the FES has a close traditional cooperation with the German trade unions, the KAS insists on local government in accordance with the Christian Democrat subsidiarity concept. The Greens concentrate on ecological issues and women's rights, the liberals stress economic issues and human rights, while the HSS specializes in administration training and security questions. All foundations are committed to the propagation of the rule of law, political pluralism, and social solidarity.

15 The role of the past must be stressed. As early as the 1970s, in the wake of Ostpolitik, the FES proposed journalist exchanges and conferences on the schoolbook commission. Both the FES and the KAS awarded unofficial scholarships to Polish academics like Hanna Suchocka (Prime Minister and Minister of Justice in the 1990s), Leszek Balcerowicz (Minister of Finance and father of the economic 'shock therapy'), or Janusz Reiter, the first Polish Ambassador to Germany after 1989. Foundations set up offices in Warsaw as early as 1989.

16 Interview Berlin, July 2000.

17 Providing political partners with legitimacy is the main function of party internationals (Grabendorff, 1996). For more details about the German political action within transnational party families, see Soledad Loaeza's chapter 2 in this volume.

18 For a more detailed analysis of these aspects, see Dakowska (2005).

19 Thus, the FIDESZ, initially affiliated with the liberals, became an associated party of the EPP at the end of 2000, which was considered as a big success for the KAS Budapest. In a similar way, the UW left the EPP in 2003 to cross over to the Liberal International. Because of the mobilisation of Polish pro-European voters during the European elections on June 13, 2004, the UW managed to send four representatives to the EP, among whom was its historical leader Bronislaw Geremek.

20 Interviews with members of the SLD in Poland, September 2000.

21 PHARE – Pologne-Hongrie, Aide à la Reconstruction Economique.

22 In its *Journalistenhandbuch*, the BMZ explains it had to develop stronger cooperation with civil society – through Public–Private Partnerships (PPP), for example – in order to cope with the modern global context (BMZ, 2000).

23 About fifty interviews were conducted between 2000 and 2004 with German officials in ministries, governmental agencies, foundations, and NGOs working in the framework of Transform and PHARE/twinning. First-hand material was often provided after these interviews (annual reports, internal reports, etc.).

24 For 1998, the repartition of Transform's budget in each sector was as follows: commercial sector (46%), training and qualifications (12%), financial sector (9%), consulting on government and law (8%), agricultural sector (7%), research (7%), consulting on administration (5%), labor, social, health (4%), environment (2%) (BMWi, 1997, p. 23).

25 While the budget of Transform is significantly decreasing, it is put to the test by the re-orientation of German assistance to South Eastern European countries: the German financing of reconstruction and democratization in the Balkans was in 1999 as high as the Transform budget in 1995: 300 million DM, about 150 million Euros.

26 The main organizations involved in Transform have existed since the 1950s and 1970s. The activity of the KfW and the CDG, set up for the implementation of the Marshall Plan in Germany, and the GTZ, related to the BMZ, has been entirely dedicated to assistance to third world countries. Other organizations were created more recently to promote German reunification (Treuhandanstalt) and assistance to CEEC (TOB, IRZ Stiftung).

27 Nevertheless, it is not easy to judge what precisely was exactly adopted or not, as some interviews revealed that some analyses were not even read by administrators because of their length.

28 Béatrice Hibou, for example, thinks that states adapt to domestic and international constraints by cooperating more and more with semi-public and private actors. As a result of the ever- increasing role of transnational actors in political decisions, public actions are more and more focusing on economic matters and integrating economic and financial questions in their discourse.

29 However, the move of the German government to Berlin partly contributed to the reshaping of this federal structure: Bonn, where the BMZ and BMA stayed, and the Ruhr region have turned into an institutionalized pool of expertise and development assistance, whereas Berlin has become the centre of political decisions. A Centre for International Cooperation (CIC) was created on July 1, 1998 in Bonn, and constitutes the rallying point of federal ministries (BMZ, Bundesministerium für Umwelt, Naturschutz und Reaktorsicherheit (BMU), Bundesministerium für Ernährung, Landwirtschaft und Forsten (BML)), about 150 NGOs, and German representations of UN organizations.

30 'German foreign policy operates in a dual mode. The government's traditional foreign policy is complemented by Germany's societal foreign policy (gesellschaftliche Aussenpolitik). Most major German institutions conduct their own foreign relations' (Katzenstein, 1997a, pp. 24–25).

31 For example M. Wittman, CDU member of the Bundestag, former president of the Bund der Vertriebenen (BdV), is at the same time personally involved in many societal reconstruction projects in CEEC.

32 We believe that the definition of this broad notion was inspired by Americans, and partly taken up by German ordoliberals to build a 'third way' between liberal capitalism and real socialism (Brodersen, 2000, p. 9). At the time of the Marshall Plan, many Germans were educated by British and American experts, and since its creation in the late 1940s, the concept of social market economy has evolved and adopted different definitions. We rather agree with Peter Eichhorn (1995, pp. 388–389), who argues that the so-called 'model' may be defined through three characteristics: *solidarity* (the welfare system), *collectivity* (the corporate system), and *plurality* (the federal system, the multiplicity of autonomous actors). For another reflection on the German 'model,' see Katharina Bluhm's chapter 9 in this volume.

33 Interview at the *Eesti Pank*, April 6, 2000.

34 Bertrand Badie (1992) explains that the expansion of occidental law 'before answering political strategies, reflects the necessity of organising and codifying economic exchange relations, might they be private or public.' We believe that the expansion of European laws and social norms mainly responds to the same needs.

35 On this point, see Katharina Bluhm's chapter 9 in this volume.

36 Interviews at the CDG, the IRZ Stiftung, the KfW, and the GTZ, February 2000.

37 300 million DM in 1995, 110 million DM in 2000. There are many explanations for the decrease of the bilateral financial component: multilateral (EU) financing, cofinancing by the receivers and by private actors.

38 We think with Katzenstein (1987) that one should not speak of a united German power, but rather of the diffusion of power through transnationalized actors.

Bibliography

Adam, Laurent (1995) 'Le concept de micro-Etat: Etats lilliputiens ou parodies d'Etats?,' *Revue Internationale de Politique Comparée*, 2 (3), pp. 577–592.

Badie, Bertrand (1992) *L'Etat importé: L'occidentalisation de l'ordre politique*, Paris: Fayard, Coll. L'Espace du politique.

Bafoil, François (1997) 'Entreprises et territoire,' in François Bafoil (ed.), *Les stratégies allemandes en Europe centrale et orientale: une géopolitique des investissements directs*, Paris: Harmattan, Coll. Pays de l'Est.

Bartsch Sebastian (1998) 'Politische Stiftungen: Grenzgänger zwischen Staaten- und Gesellschaftswelt,' in Karl Kaiser and Wolf-Dieter Eberwein, *Deutschlands Neue Außenpolitik*, Munich: DGAP.

Biagiotti, Isabelle (1996) 'Pour la démocratie et l'économie du marché: la Fondation Konrad-Adenauer,' *Coopération internationale pour la démocratie*, 'Coopération allemande,' April, pp. 115–128.

BMWi (1998) *Die Beratung Mittel- und Osteuropas beim Aufbau von Demokratie und sozialer Marktwirtschaft: Konzept und Beratungsprogramme der Bundesregierung, Fortschreibung 1998*, Bonn, May.

BMZ (1973) *2. Bericht des BMZ für den AWZ: 4.Grundsätze für die entwicklungspolitische Zusammenarbeit zwischen der Bundesregierung und den politischen Stiftungen*, 2nd BMZ Report for the Parliamentary Committee of Economic Cooperation, August.

BMZ (1999) *Die entwicklungspolitische Arbeit der politischen Stiftungen: Informations- vermerk für den Bundestagsausschuss für wirtschaftliche Zusammenarbeit und Entwicklung*, August.

BMZ (2000) *Journalistenhandbuch, Entwicklungspolitik*, Berlin.

Börzel, Tanja (1998) 'Organizing Babylon: on the different conceptions of policy net- works,' *Public Administration*, 76 (2), pp. 253–273.

Börzel, Tanja and Thomas Risse (2000) *When Europe Hits Home: Europeanization and Domestic Change*, European Integration online Papers, (EIoP), 4 (15), www.eiop.or.at/eiop/texte/2000-015a.htm.

Brodersen, Hans (2000) 'L'economie sociale de marché est-elle dépassée?,' *Problèmes économiques*, 2649, January 26, pp. 7–15.

Brühl Tanja (ed.) (2001), *Die Privatisierung der Weltpolitik: Entstaatlichung und Kommerzialisierung im Globalisierungsprozeß*, Bonn: Dietz.

Czempiel, Ernst-Otto and James Rosenau (1989) *Global Changes and Theoretical Challenges: Approaches to World Politics for the 1990s*, Lexington, MA: Lexington Books.

Dakowska, Dorota (2005) 'German political foundations: transnational party go- betweens in the process of EU enlargement,' in Wolfram Kaiser and Peter Starie (eds), *Transnational European Union*, London: Routledge.

Davis, Patricia and Peter Dombrowski (1997) 'Appetite of the wolf: German assistance for Central and Eastern Europe,' *German Politics*, 6 (1), pp. 1–22.

Denece, Eric and Gilles Sohm (1998) 'Les ONG à la conquête des nouveaux marchés,' *Défense nationale*, 12, pp. 86–97.

Eberwein, Wolf-Dieter and Matthias Ecker-Ehrhardt (2001) *Deutschland und Polen: Eine Werte und Interessengemeinschaft? Die Elitenperspektive*, Opladen: Leske & Budrich.

Ecker-Ehrhardt, Matthias (2002) 'Alles nur Rhetorik? Der ideelle Vorder- und Hintergrund der deutschen Debatte über die EU-Osterweiterung,' *Zeitschrift für inter- nationale Beziehungen*, 9 (2), pp. 209–252.

Eichhorn, Peter (1995) 'Les défis du marché unique européen pour l'économie sociale de marché et les entreprises d'action sociale et sanitaire,' *Revue du Marché commun et de l'Union européenne*, 389, pp. 388–395.

Federal Cabinet Decision (1992) 'Gesamtkonzept zur Beratung beim Aufbau von Demokratie und sozialer Marktwirtschaft in den Staaten Mittel-und Osteuropas sowie der GUS,' March 18, unpublished.

Federal Cabinet Decision (1993) 'Änderung des Kabinettbeschlusses vom 18. März 1992 zum Gesamtkonzept zur Beratung beim Aufbau von Demokratie und sozialer Marktwirtschaft in den Staaten Mittel- und Osteuropas (MOE) sowie in den Neuen Unabhängigen Staaten (NUS),' July 13, unpublished.

Glagow, Manfred and Uwe Schimanck (1983) 'Korporatistische Verwaltung: das Beispiel Entwicklungspolitik, ' *Politische Vierteljahresschrift*, 24 (3), pp. 253–274.

Grabendorff, Wolf (1996) 'International support for democracy in contemporary Latin America: the role of the Party Internationals,' in Laurence Whitehead (ed.), *The International Dimension of Democratization: Europe and the Americas*, New York: Oxford University Press.

GTZ (1999) *Privatisierungsberatung und Zusammenarbeit mit der deutschen Wirtschaft*, Eschborn: GTZ.

Haas, Peter M. (1992) 'Introduction: epistemic communities and international policy coordination,' *International Organization*, 46 (1), pp. 1–35.

Hibou, Béatrice (ed.) (1999) *La Privatization des Etats*, Paris: Karthala.

Katzenstein, Peter (1987) *Policy and Politics in West Germany: The Growth of a Semisovereign State*, Philadelphia, PA: Temple University Press.

Katzenstein, Peter (1997a) *Tamed Power: Germany in Europe*, Ithaca, NY: Cornell University Press.

Katzenstein, Peter J. (ed.) (1997b) *Mitteleuropa: Between Europe and Germany*, Oxford: Berghahn.

Keck, Margaret E. and Kathryn Sikkink (1998), *Activists Beyond Borders: Advocacy Networks in International Politics*, Ithaca, NY: Cornell University Press.

Keohane, Robert and J. Nye (1974) 'Transgovernmental relations and international organizations,' *World Politics*, 27, pp. 39–62.

Maull, Hanns W. (1990) 'Germany and Japan: the new civilian powers,' *Foreign Affairs*, 69 (5), pp. 91–105.

Ortuño Anaya, Pilar (2002) *European Socialists and Spain: The Transition to Democracy*, Basingstoke, Palgrave.

Phillips, Ann L. (2000) *Power and Influence after the Cold War: Germany in East-Central Europe*, Lanham, MD: Rowman & Littlefield.

Pinto-Dushinsky, Michael (1996) 'International political finance: The Konrad Adenauer Foundation and Latin America,' in Laurence Whitehead (ed.), *The International Dimension of Democratization: Europe and the Americas*, New York: Oxford University Press.

Pridham, Geoffrey (1994) *Building Democracy: The International Dimension of Democratization in Eastern Europe*, London: Leicester University Press.

Putnam, Robert D. (1988) 'Diplomacy and domestic politics: the logic of two-level games,' *International Organization*, 42, pp. 427–460.

Radaelli, Claudio M. (2000) 'Whither Europeanization? Concept stretching and substantive change,' European Integration Online Papers (EIoP), 4 (8), http://eiop.or.at/eiop/texte/2000-008a.htm.

Reich, Simon and Andrei S. Markovits (1997) *The German Predicament: Memory and Power in the New Europe*, Ithaca, NY: Cornell University Press.

Risse-Kappen, Thomas (1995) *Bringing Transnational Relations Back In: Non-State Actors, Domestic Structures and International Institutions*, Cambridge: Cambridge University Press.

Rosamond, Ben (1999) 'Discourses of globalization and the social construction of European identities,' *Journal of European Public Policy*, 6 (4), Special Issue, pp. 652–669.

Sabatier, Paul A. and Hank C. Jenkins-Smith (eds) (1993) *Policy Change and Learning: An Advocacy Coalition Approach*, Washington, DC: Westview Press.

Schimmelfennig, Frank (1998) 'Liberal norms and the Eastern enlargement of the European Union: a case for sociological institutionalism,' *Austrian Journal of Political Science*, April, pp. 459–472.

Schürmann, Maximilian (1989) *Zwischen Partnerschaft und politischem Auftrag: Fallstudie zur entwicklungspolitischen Tätigkeit der Konrad-Adenauer-Stiftung*, Saarbrücken and Fort Lauderdale: Verlag für Entwicklungspolitik.

Schwarz, Hans-Peter (1994) *Die Zentralmacht Europas: Deutschlands Rückkehr auf die Weltbühne*, Berlin: Siedler.

Strange, Susan (1996) *The Retreat of the State: The Diffusion of Power in the World Economy*, Cambridge: Cambridge University Press.

Tewes, Henning (1997) 'The emergence of a civilian power: Germany and Central Europe,' *German Politics*, 6 (2), pp. 95–116.

Thielemann, Eiko R. (1999) 'Institutional limits of a 'Europe with the Regions': EC state-aid control meets German federalism,' *Journal of European Public Policy*, 6 (3), pp. 399–418.

Vieregge, Henning von (1977) *Parteistiftungen: zur Rolle der Konrad-Adenauer, Friedrich-Ebert, Friedrich-Naumann- und Hans-Seidel-Stiftungen im politischen System der Bundesrepublik Deutschland*, Baden-Baden: Nomos Verlagsgesellschaft.

Whitehead, Laurence (ed.) (1996) *The International Dimension of Democratization: Europe and the Americas*, New York: Oxford University Press.

Gilles Lepesant

4

State and non-state actors in the management of EU external borders

The tools of border management

As is the case with traditional borders, the management of external EU borders involves both local and state actors. It also involves EU actors since the internal unification of its territory through currency, commercial rules, and migratory rules implies that its traditional functions of state borders are taken over by external EU borders. These borders are managed according to migratory and trade rules that are not defined by individual states, but by the EU. The eastern borders of Germany and Poland are a case in which border location have not altered, but their function is changing dramatically in the context of EU enlargement. Rules that used to apply to Germany's eastern borders are progressively taken over in part by Poland's eastern borders. A transfer is taking place. Different issues are involved: migration policy, cooperation policy, and numerous state and non-state actors are involved. Current and future EU external borders work in a systemic way since the way one is managed has an impact on the other. For example, the issue of free movement of goods and persons between Germany and Poland is partly linked to the implementation of the Schengen Accords along the Bug river. Both borders are today causes of concern. The German–Polish border was one of the issues discussed in the enlargement negotiations, since politicians from German frontier regions feared illegal migration, smuggling, terrorism, trafficking of human beings and other forms of organized crime, and massive flows of Polish workers. The Polish eastern border is also a very sensitive issue. Not all member states believe that the issue of illegal migration has been properly addressed, and at the same time Polish elites are willing not to isolate states like Belarus and Ukraine where the market economy and democracy are not well established. Thus, even if a border conflict is no longer a perspective in this part of Europe, the border issue remains a sensitive one. After briefly outlining the common historical background of the German–Polish and the Polish–Ukrainian borders, this chapter analyzes the interaction between state and non-state actors in the management of them. The idea behind this approach is to understand better the way border management tools are transferred from one border to another border located eastwards, in the context of EU enlargement.

THE HISTORICAL BACKGROUND

From the historical point of view, the eastern borders of Germany and Poland have several similarities. Both were drawn by an external actor (Stalin), during a time of war and violence. In Potsdam, the Allies and the Soviet Union decreed a transfer of Polish territory 150 km to the west. The Polish state thus more or less recovered the western part of the territorial seat of the Piast dynasty but lost the regions and cities (most notably Wilno/Vilnius, Lwow/Lviv) that had belonged to Poland under the Jagiellon when the Polish–Lithuanian Commonwealth extended from the Baltic to the Black Sea.

In both cases, huge population transfers took place and these historical experiences were not openly and publicly discussed until the communist regimes fell (Hann, 1998). Until the Second World War, the territories of today's south-east Poland and western Ukraine constituted the Polish–Ukrainian ethnic borderland, an area inhabited by two ethnic groups and characterized by cultural and religious diversity. The pattern of Ukrainian and Polish settlement was so complex that no meaningful line could be drawn between exclusively Polish and Ukrainian zones. Yet in the aftermath of the Second World War, these ethnic borderlands were divided between two political units, Poland and Soviet Ukraine, and soon after, as a result of mass repatriations, the area lost most of its long-standing ethnic diversity. Ethnic Poles from eastern Ukraine came to Poland, while Ukrainians from Poland came to Ukraine or were settled throughout the former German territories in the north and in the west of Poland. As a consequence, ethno-cultural borders between Poles and Ukrainians became largely coextensive with state borders (Snyder, 1997). Nevertheless, some Poles and Ukrainians remained on the 'other' side of the border and now have minority status (as we explain below). One should also mention the Jewish population, which was numerous in this part of Europe, and of which today only empty and often dilapidated synagogues remain.

Lviv and Przemysl became cities divided by the state border; Przemysl found itself on the Polish side and Lviv in Ukraine. As a result of change of the western border of Poland, numerous cities crossed by the Oder–Neisse river were divided, having their center on either the Polish side (Guben/Gubin), or the German one (Görlitz/Zgorzelec, Frankfurt/Oder/Slubice). Lviv and Przemysl are particular since they played an important symbolic role for the nation on the other side of the border. Poles regarded Lviv, the capital of eastern Galicia, as one of the most historically important urban centres in Poland because of its cultural role (Snyder, 1999). For the Ukrainians, Przemysl's importance stems from its historical role as a Greek Catholic diocesan centre (the Uniate Church was abolished in Poland in 1946 and its properties handed over to the Roman Catholic Church). Territories lost by Germany were meaningful from the economic point of view while regions lost by Poland were very important in the Polish collective memory because many writers were born in cities like Wilno (Vilnius) and Lwow (Lviv). Most Germans who were expelled from Poland came to the western part of Germany but some of them settled close to the border, hoping that the new line was not definitive.

The communist legacy did not permit a true dialog between new border regions. Despite, or perhaps because of, their multi-ethnic past, the cities of Lviv and Przemysl were closely integrated into the newly delineated national territories. Direct contacts across the new borders – along the Oder–Neisse and along the Bug – were non-existent or tightly controlled. In spite of the doctrine of 'proletarian internationalism' and certain symbolic decisions (some streets crossing these borders were named 'Friendship street' or 'Peace Street'), ordinary citizens had very few opportunities to meet each other and to open a dialog on sensitive issues. The Polish government resorted to the nationalist myth of homogeneity of the Polish state (the Piast period) in order to strengthen the legitimacy of the new borders. On the Soviet side, the Ukrainians were portrayed as historical victims of ruthless exploitation by Polish landlords, who found liberation in the 're-unification' of eastern Galicia with Soviet Ukraine in 1939. In Poland, Ukrainians were often portrayed as the collective, historically 'guilty party' *vis-à-vis* the Polish nation (Potichnyj, 1980). In particular, the wartime atrocities committed by the Ukrainian Insurgent Army (UPA) were deeply ingrained in Polish historical consciousness. Under communist rule, the minorities in both countries were also subjected to repressive policies.

The border along the Oder–Neisse river was closed for many years between 1945 and 1989. The expulsion of millions of Germans and the redrawing of the border nurtured resentments that the communist period did not ease. The fact that it was easier for Poles than for east Germans to travel abroad, the conflict over territorial waters in the Bay of Szczecin, and the Solidarnosc Movement that led to the closure of the border, are some of the arguments used by propagandists to keep a climate of mistrust alive.

In this context, one should not be surprised if the reaction of the local Polish and Ukrainian actors was rather negative when in the 1990s minorities began to assert their rights. One must thus distinguish between symbolic aspects of transborder cooperation (minorities, churches) and the 'hard' management tools (Euroregions, legal provisions related to migration issues) that are used to overcome the communist and historical legacies and promote common actions within the border regions.

The symbolic dimension of transborder cooperation

The role of minorities

Ukraine houses significant minorities, mainly Russians, situated in the east of the country and often in a majority at the local level: 430,000 Poles live in

Belarus, 270,000 in Lithuania (south of Vilnius), and 270,000 in Ukraine. These minorities often maintain close ties with the Catholic Church. After the proclamation of Ukrainian independence in 1991 and the opening of the border, the cities of Lviv and of Przemysl became the main outposts of their respective nation-states on the Polish–Ukrainian border. By that time, the minorities in both cities were very few, accounting for approximately 2–4% of the cities' populations. Yet even if the overall numbers were low in comparison to the pre-war period, the post-1989 process of democratization inspired their revival. The assertion of rights by the Ukrainian minority in Poland and the Polish minority in Ukraine challenged the myth of exclusive ethnic ownership of the territories.

Around 400,000 Germans live in Poland, especially in the south, and very few live very close to the border. Some of them lived in these territories before the war and could stay in spite of the expulsion of a million of Germans from CEE approved by the Potsdam Conference. Others from regions located further eastwards were also expelled, but stopped before reaching Germany. Many Germans left Poland during the communist era and after 1989–90, but fewer have done so since Germany introduced more restrictive immigration rules.

Are these minorities important actors in transborder cooperation? They certainly try to play a significant role, but one must distinguish two dimensions of their activity. On the one hand, they have recovered from a long period of more or less harsh repression by developing cultural activities with the support of their state of origin. On the other hand, it is difficult to argue that they have been a 'bridge,' strengthening transborder cooperation thanks to their linguistic abilities or their obvious interest in a peaceful neighborhood. They have rather been cause of conflict due to the historical legacy and the mistrust of the host country towards groups suspected of acting as a fifth column of their kin-state across the border. In the case of the Polish minority, this concern has been expressed at the local level in Ukraine and at the state level in Belarus whereas the Orthodox Church has also accused them of proselytism.

In the early and mid-1990s, several clashes occurred in Poland and Ukraine involving minorities. In Przemysl, the city council reluctantly hosted the Festival of Ukrainian Culture organized by the Ukrainian minority in 1995 and 1997; the city authorities agreed to host the festival only at Warsaw's insistence. The Polish minority in Lviv, which comprises some 20,000–30,000 people (3–4% of the city's population) demanded the creation of a Polish Cultural Centre (Dom Polski). After a prolonged delay the city authorities offered the Polish minority a building that in fact had to be entirely renovated at the expense of the Poles themselves. The representatives of the Polish minority also complained of hostility and a lack of support from the city authorities for any cultural and social initiatives by the Polish minority.

German minorities or refugee associations are willing to promote German culture and, above all, their own interest. Although there are some success stories involving the German minority, it is difficult to argue that they are the 'bridge' that they claim to be between Polish and German societies. The historical background, the fact that most of their elites emigrated, and the demands of the representative organizations located in Bavaria (mainly expellees from former Czechoslovakia) or elsewhere in Germany (mainly expellees from other places) have not helped to ease tensions between minorities and the rest of the population. Similar Polish organizations also face negative reactions from host states. These organizations provide Polish minorities with financial help, but also use the fact that they are not government-financed (they receive most of their funds from the diaspora located in Western Europe and the US as well as from the Polish Senate) to advocate positions that are different from those of the central state and sometimes opposite to them.

The role of churches

Along both the German–Polish border and along the Polish–Ukrainian border, churches have played a significant role at different levels. On the German–Polish side, Catholic Churches actively promoted reconciliation in the 1960s between the two countries by 'forgiving and asking for forgiveness' through an exchange of letters. On the Polish–Ukrainian side, close to the line that divides Latin Christendom in Europe and Orthodoxy, one has to take into account three different levels. At the local level, tensions prevail. In the city of Przemysl, the Greek Catholic Cathedral, which was confiscated by the Polish state in 1946 and handed over to the Roman Catholic Order of Carmelites, has always been a bone of contention. Once the Greek Catholic Church was again officially recognized after the collapse of communism in 1991, the Pope ordered the return of the Przemysl Cathedral to be the Uniate community. A group of local Polish nationalists strongly opposed this initiative, and facing such opposition, the Roman Catholic hierarchy gave in and handed over to the Greek Catholics another church (the so-called Garnison Church), which had never belonged to them (Hann, 1996). Even after the ownership issue was settled, the cathedral continued to be a site of controversy. In 1995, a memorial plaque with anti-Ukrainian text and symbolism was put up on the church wall and unveiled by the city mayor. The local nationalist circles also decided to alter the exterior of the Church by removing a unique and distinctive dome (cupola) which had been built in the nineteenth century when the Church served as a Greek Catholic Cathedral. After a prolonged dispute with representatives of the Central state at the local level, the dome was pulled down (officially for safety reasons). In Ukraine, because of the Polish minority, the Catholic Church is strongly represented in the west of the country. Some representatives of the Polish Church support the Vatican policy that aims to set up a real Ukrainian Catholic Church, while others seem to perceive these Eastern European territories as a 'terre de mission' and would appreciate a stronger presence of Polish priests and Polish symbols in churches. This involvement recalls the role which certain writers and Polish nationalist politicians assigned to Poland in previous centuries: that of a country situated on the periphery of Christianity (Rome being at the centre) and having the vocation of 'civilizing' the East.

As a result, the role of the churches in neighborhood management is ambivalent. On the German–Polish side, the first step undertaken by Polish and German Catholic hierarchies in the 1960s is often mentioned in the official political speeches and is recognized as a valuable contribution to the process of reconciliation. On the Polish–Ukrainian side, local tensions have not yet disappeared and state officials have had to intervene to allay nationalistic acts of Ukrainian and Polish actors.

'Hard' management tools

The Euroregions
The eastern border of Germany is entirely networked by Euroregions, which were set up in the 1990s, mostly at the instigation of Germany in order to foster transborder cooperation between local actors. The main instigator of these initiatives was the European Network of border regions, Arbeitsgemeinschaft Europäischer Grenzregionen (AGEG) located in Gronau (Germany) promoting cross-border cooperation (CBC) in Western Europe and also advocating a stronger regionalism. As part of the European system, the concept of a 'Euroregion' enjoyed a certain legitimacy which helped to convince Polish actors that the device was really aimed at fostering regional cooperation and not at challenging existing borders. The prefix 'Euro' in 'Euroregion' referred to the EU, and was identified with the 'return to Europe,' thereby appearing to hold promise of funds from Brussels. Polish actors have accepted the idea, but not without difficulty. The Polish central state has done everything it can not to lose control of transborder cooperation – for example, by playing a significant role within Commissions responsible for allocating European funds. Some German actors presented the Euroregions as a part of the federal system. Polish actors, except for a few, have accepted the concept of a Euroregion without advocating the federal system considered as inappropriate to the Polish historical and administrative context. Some Polish actors have refused to take part in transborder cooperation, for financial or political reasons, and several conflicts have taken place. Before all the Euroregions were decided upon, the 'Stolpe Plan' (prepared by a private firm and endorsed by the Land of Brandenburg) was criticized by the Polish side because Polish interests had not really been taken into account. Later, within Euroregions, local Polish and German actors supported different priorities. While Polish actors systematically considered infrastructures a top priority, the Germans expressed others. In particular, they were more interested in organizing cultural events. Moreover, some Polish actors were reluctant to accept that the German side would get more EU funding than the Polish side (EU regions are eligible for the Interreg Program, the Polish ones for PHARE) and head up cooperation projects. In this respect, the language issue during meetings became sensitive in some Euroregions. More generally, it seems that German proposals have been accepted when the projects were a framework for

cooperation between equal actors, when the stronger German position could be balanced out by the European Commission or a third party (Danes in the Euroregion of Szczecin), and when they had European legitimacy.

Although the concept of a Euroregion was often perceived in Poland or in the Czech Republic as a German idea, there were divergent opinions in Germany concerning it. At the local level, on the German side, some mayors thought that it was not politically savvy to cooperate openly with Poles suspected by local public opinion of developing illegal activities and working covertly in Germany. On the other side, institutions like AGEG strongly advocated these Euroregions and regionalism. As far as the relationship between state and non-state actors is concerned, some NGO activities may differ from state ones. In the case of both Germany and Poland, refugee and minority associations play a role often perceived by the state as counterproductive. Local actors also express different priorities from states' ones. It cannot be said that they have been at the forefront of German–Polish or of Polish–Ukrainian reconciliation.

Often presented in the Brussels rhetoric as 'laboratories of Europe', border regions benefit from various programs aimed at strengthening local cooperation and economic initiatives. Even before joining the EU, most central European countries also enjoyed such programs. They have a political and administrative impact which is not to be underestimated, since one of the conditions of their allocation is that local and regional actors prepare and manage common projects together. The prefix 'Euro' has also contributed to the success of the Euroregions, at least on paper, since it provides the local actors with the impression that the implementation of such structures implies a 'return to Europe'. The EU is not only a source of money for local initiatives; it is a symbolic resource frequently used (for example, the European flag is on every leaflet in every conference room) to add legitimacy to cross-border initiatives. In the name of Europe, local tensions and prejudices have been overcome.

The European factor is nevertheless a paradoxical one since the EU is very much criticized on different issues. One of them is the implementation of the Schengen rules.

Schengen rules and transborder cooperation

Not only the countries divided by the Iron Curtain enjoyed freer cross-border contacts after 1989; several ex-communist countries also did and trade, cooperation, and civic activities have benefited. Moreover in many transborder areas, two or more ethnic groups still live side by side in a shared area – such as, for example, Transcarpathia in Ukraine. Such areas seem to be particularly well positioned to derive benefits from opened borders, as ethnic minorities within those areas may act as intermediaries between the kin- and host-states. While still applicants, the new members of the EU were incorporated into a regime, known as the Schengen Agreement, which became part of the accession *acquis* as a result of the Treaty of Amsterdam in 1997. In essence, applicant countries were presented with the condition that the opening of their state borders with the Schengen countries could take place only if their external, eastern borders were tightened. To meet the Schengen requirements, a number of measures had to be undertaken on the eastern borders of those countries which will become the external frontier of the Union in late 2007. Until then, all countries have to secure their part of the bloc's external borders, while the EU also needs to complete a new version of its database for sharing information on cross-border criminal activities, such as stolen cars or fugitives. From the EU's standpoint, the internal security agenda has plainly taken priority over the objectives of CFSP, at least until the structural funds have been distributed in the new member states and the Commission has submitted additional financial means in the context of the European Neighborhood Policy (ENP) for the 2007–13 programming period. This is clearly visible in the amounts spent on beefing up border infrastructure, as opposed to the amounts targeted on fostering CBC with neighbors to the east – i.e. countries such as Ukraine. For instance, while over 1993–99, the EU invested 50 million Euro in improving the infrastructure of Poland's eastern border, CBC activity was allocated only about 5% of that sum.

In 2005, the EU financial effort remained less focused on the stabilization of Ukraine and of Belarus than on the internal security of the EU. While Poland seeks to promote a good EU neighborhood policy *vis-à-vis* Ukraine that would pave the way for an Association Treaty between Kiev and Brussels, EU member states express the need to secure the Polish eastern border before the full opening of the German–Polish one.

Poland has gradually been modifying its liberal legislation (concerning the entry of citizens of Eastern European countries on Polish territory). At the end of December 1997, the Polish parliament adopted a stricter law governing access to Polish territory for citizens of Russia and Belarus, two countries that had not signed a readmission agreement with Poland. Many Polish leaders see the possible closing of eastern borders as running counter to the policy established towards the East since the beginning of the 1990s. Sealing the borders would not, in this perspective, make a positive contribution to the stability of the countries in question. Readmission agreements for the return to CEE countries of migrants who have illegally entered Western Europe via CEE have to be implemented or negotiated between Poland and its Eastern neighbors. Germany has used similar instruments towards Poland and the Czech Republic. Such agreements aimed to involve neighboring countries in the control of migratory flows coming from Eastern Europe; these countries must accept on their territory migrants arrested while crossing the border illegally and sent back. That means that it is in the interest of transit countries to improve border control at their eastern border and to be, *de facto*, the guardians of EU borders. Germany provided Poland and the Czech Republic with important means in order to improve these controls at the eastern border (120 million DM in 1990 to Poland and 60 million DM to the Czech Republic in 1993). In twinning actions, German civil servants also played a significant role in exporting the Schengen know-how eastwards. It is all the more possible to use the word 'transfer' in this respect since

EU guard teams were proposed by former Italian Prime Minister Giuliano Amato and British Prime Minister Tony Blair in 2001 to control EU external borders. In 2004, some member states (Austria, Estonia, Latvia, and Lithuania) backed the idea of building transit camps for potential immigrants coming into Europe. Similar proposals were put forward by the British and the German governments and the idea was also backed by the Commissioner for Justice and Home Affairs. The idea was, however, flatly rejected by the Kiev authorities.

Along the German–Polish border, the perspective of free movement of persons raises concerns among the local German population already hit by a very high unemployment rate. In the context of enlargement, several member states introduced a transition period ('Two + Three + Two-year arrangement') on the movement of the labor force from the new member states, thus risking giving Poles the feeling that they were second class citizens in the enlarged EU. However, since some member states (Ireland, Denmark, Sweden) have declared their readiness to open their labor market to workers from Central Europe immediately after enlargement, the Polish authorities hope that the scheduled restrictions will prove unnecessary two years after enlargement. In the meantime, Poland hopes to open negotiations with Germany on the system of quotas that exists between the two countries. In these negotiations, one can assume that German state actors will have to take into account the fears of the border regions.

Along the Polish–Ukrainian border, the implementation of the Schengen rules is perceived by local actors as the setting up of a dividing line. EU officials may argue that once these rules are implemented, the waiting time will be reduced, corruption discouraged, and organized crime less tempting; yet local elites hardly believe that Schengen will 'civilize' the border. Like other border regions as such as Transcarpathia, the Lviv oblast enjoys close economic ties with its neighbor to the west. Poland is Ukraine's seventh largest trading partner, but for the Lviv oblast it is the third. Local elites consider that the visa regime will decrease the volume of informal trade between Poland and Ukraine, which is estimated to be equal to the official one. While state initiatives have been necessary to overcome some local prejudices linked to the historical background, the Schengen issue provides a different picture as regards the interplay between local and national actors. In this case, local actors (at least along the Polish–Ukrainian border) want more openness from EU states.

Interaction between local and state actors

In May 1997, Polish President Alexander Kwasniewski's visit to Ukraine enabled an agreement to be signed that helped to keep historical grievances, particularly those dating from after the Second World War, out of the political dialog between the two countries. Some instruments proposed by the German side were later set up between Poland and its eastern neighbors (Commission for Regional Cooperation, parliamentary groups . . .). In the name of Europe, the German and the Polish government pursue an active policy towards their eastern neighborhood aimed at building a large area of stability and re-establishing links with regions under their direct influence in former times. Like Germany, Poland does not want to hover between stability and instability or between prosperity and poverty, and does not wish to see a new 'curtain' along its borders.

Along the German–Polish border and along the Polish–Ukrainian border, state actors have often intervened to foster transborder cooperation that local actors were sometimes reluctant to initiate. Most of the tensions have their roots in the legacy left by history. In the Polish border city of Przemysl, anti-Ukrainian attitudes have been nurtured by prejudices, by Ukrainian claims (on pre-war properties), and by a common belief that the 'Other' is an enemy of the Polish nation. Fear is also widespread along the German–Polish border. Polish fears of a domination of German capital are expressed, as well as German fears of a massive influx of illegal migrants. In these cases, when state borders no longer present a barrier to closer contacts, the neighbor is deemed responsible for all economic and social troubles and for anxieties linked with the collapse of past certainties. On the German side, local actors have sometimes been reluctant to promote active cooperation with the neighbor and have been quick to criticize political instability on the other side of the border, or claim that smuggling activities, go unpunished because of the border's proximity. In Bavaria, regional authorities have developed a myth about refugees by praising their role in the 'success story' of Bavaria and by 'forgetting' how unwelcome they were when they fled from Czechoslovakia. They also tend to underestimate the role of Germany's partition in the economic record of the Land. Strongly influenced by the most active of their representatives, the Land has repeatedly exerted pressure on the federal authorities in the process of reconciliation to obtain compensation for the expulsion decided according to the Benes Decrees more than forty years previously.

Troubles in borderlands often interfere with inter-state relations. When he declared: 'The last thing we want to see is the reappearance of a new Iron Curtain on our Eastern border,' Kwasniewski underlined Poland's desire not to see the enlargement of the EU and NATO as an end in itself. Poland wanted to become an advocate for its eastern neighbors in the institutions of which it would soon become a member. The decline in Russia's influence, the historical attachments of the former Kingdom of Poland, and Poland's entry into the political–military institutions of the West, have all encouraged the Polish leadership to influence the geopolitical recomposition of the isthmus between the Baltic and Black Seas. If Poland's new eastern frontier established in 1945 was considered taboo throughout the communist era (it was drawn approximately along the Curzon Line, which the Polish leaders had rejected in the 1920s), it was the object of serious debate among the intelligentsia in exile. The journal *Kultura* which, before 1989, devoted one article in every issue to a report on Poland's eastern neighbors, was the principal focus of this debate. The idea gradually took hold that the eastern border of Poland should be accepted and that the country's aim should be the establishment of independent states and allies to the east, capable of creating a buffer zone between Russia and itself. To the desire not to break with the historic confines of Poland was added a strategic analysis that aimed at supporting the independence of Ukraine and Belarus, and which has now to be made compatible with Poland's integration into the EU and NATO. Economic considerations have also encouraged a more active Polish eastern policy since trade with the fifteen former member states of the EU accounts for 70% of Polish external trade. For economic and political reasons, the Polish authorities want to diversify the country's economic relations.

In recent years, the debates over the role Poland ought to play *vis-à-vis* Ukraine have intensified between those who advocate a more active role – as underlined by the role Kwasniewski played during the 'Orange Revolution' – and those who tend to be more cautious and consider that democratization and the market economy should be undertaken by Ukraine itself. Polish elites want Poland to undertake to influence the policy of the EU towards its eastern neighbors while demonstrating that EU accession is not a way for Poland to flee them. The two countries cooperate in the fight against organized crime (joint control of common borders), the economy, and culture (a Polish cultural institute was set up in Kiev in 2000). As it is not conducive to friendly relations, the historical legacy has been left to historians and does not tarnish relations between the two countries. The mobilization of economic, social, and political elites (including regular meetings between Ukrainian and Polish parliamentarians) also tends to add substance to the strategic partnership announced at the beginning of the 1990s.

Poland's eastern policy does not come within the remit of a simple diplomatic initiative. It covers cooperation in different aspects of social, political, and economic life. It implies a transfer of expertise: Polish experts from the American Council for Advancement and Support of Education (CASE) Foundation have thus advised the Ukrainian leadership, the Polish model of economic transition being considered appropriate to the Ukrainian case. The Solidarnosc trade union has also advised the Belarusian democratic opposition.

The proclamations from Warsaw on Ukraine's importance in Poland's foreign and security policy has obliged the Polish capital to intervene directly in local affairs in the border region. The creation of Ukrainian classes in 1990–91 in Przemysl raised protests from the city and regional authorities and the vice-minister of National Education had to intervene to allow the school to open. Kwasniewski paid several visits to the Polish–Ukrainian border, just as German chancellors did along the German–Polish border in order to urge local actors to comply with their policy of reconciliation with their neighbor.

In the case of the Polish–Ukrainian border, the late 1990s witnessed a gradual change on the 'Ukrainian question' in Przemysl. Local elites expressed support for tightening Polish–Ukrainian ties, as declared by the Presidents of Poland and Ukraine on many occasions. How can this change be explained? There was undoubtedly a large degree of pressure exerted on Przemysl by

Warsaw to avoid an escalation in anti-Ukrainian acts at certain critical moments (Wolczuk, 2001). Most notably in the run-up to Ukrainian cultural festivals, Warsaw supported the Ukrainian minority and, as we saw above, insisted on holding the event in Przemysl. Undoubtedly, the message of the importance of good relations with Ukraine for Poland, the so-called 'strategic partnership,' also played its role. Another reason, and a more paradoxical one, can also be mentioned. The administrative reform that occurred in Poland in 1999 deprived Przemysl of its status as a Wojewodship (administrative division) (it went to the neighboring city of Rzeszów) and that change paradoxically contributed to easing local tensions. First, Przemysl lost its administrative decision-making power on many issues relative to the rights of the Ukrainian minority – for example, the new regional capital Rzeszów took over administrative investigation into the restitution of property to the Ukrainian minority and the Greek Catholic Church. As a consequence, Polish nationalists had much less influence on decision-makers in Przemysl. Secondly, having lost its status, the city of Przemysl faced the risk of becoming a backwater town lost in the poorer, eastern, provinces of the country. The city set out to capitalize on its location as that of a major urban center on the Polish–Ukrainian border and a gateway to Ukraine. The city has become associated with a civic initiative to foster Polish–Ukrainian reconciliation, the so-called Capitula of Reconciliation (Kapitula Pojednania), which rewards people who have distinguished themselves in this sphere. The presidents of Ukraine and Poland became the honorary patrons of the Kapitula.

In Lviv, the Lyczakowski Cemetery not only evidences the former Polish presence, in the form of numerous tombs and monuments of distinguished Poles; it also contains a delineated section, the so-called 'cemetery of Lwow eaglets,' a necropolis, which was erected in inter-war Poland to commemorate the defense of Lviv by Polish youths against the Ukrainians in November 1918. In Ukrainian public opinion, the cemetery of the Lviv eaglets 'commemorates soldiers who were invaders [of the Western Ukrainian People's Republic].' For this reason, the restoration of the Lwow eaglets cemetery to its pre-1939 appearance, as demanded by the Polish side, provoked the prolonged resistance of the city authorities, despite decisions at the inter-governmental level. In September 2000, the prime minister of Ukraine, Viktor Yushchenko, issued an official letter to the Lviv city council in which he asked it to approve the provisions of the protocol of the Polish–Ukrainian intergovernmental negotiations of August 2000. Yushchenko argued that this approval was necessary 'in light of the national interests and economic security of our state' because 'soon Poland will become a full member of the EU. Wide-ranging cooperation with it [Poland] will facilitate our fostering of effective relations with the EU.'

As in Przemysl, where the change on the 'Ukrainian question' can be explained by the relations with the center, the stance on the 'Polish question' in Lviv has to be considered in conjunction with Lviv's relations with Kiev. In this case, however, interaction is far more complex since Lviv, as the intellectual and political capital of Ukrainian Galicia (which comprises three western Ukrainian oblasts), has aspired to play a special role in Ukraine. Within Austro-Hungary and inter-war Poland, the region was able to develop political, religious, and cultural institutions that distinguished it from the rest of Ukraine, which (apart from Volynia and Transcarpathia) formed part of the autocratic Russian empire from the end of the eighteenth century and hence was deprived of a similar heritage. In the relatively liberal Austro-Hungarian empire which, in marked contrast to the Russian empire, permitted Ukrainian civic institutions, Ukrainian-language education and the Greek Catholic Church, the Galicians developed a strong Ukrainian national identity (Kappeler, 1997).

Galicia, with its intellectual centre in Lviv, developed a sense of mission for Ukraine and turned into a kind of Ukrainian Piedmont, with the intention to build a modern, Ukrainian nation-state. Although Galicians supported the idea of an independent Ukraine, they now feel that they failed to make a breakthrough in 'returning Ukraine to Europe.' The record of years of independence falls way below the expectations of many Galicians, for whom neighboring Poland is a benchmark of what Ukraine could achieve. Galicia finds itself more and more marginalized within Ukraine, especially because the rest of Ukraine remains a stronghold of Russian culture and language: fear of Polish nationalism is no less strong than the fear of russification. When Kiev exerts pressure, the city council opposes it by resorting to the constitutional autonomy of local self-government. Resistance to Polish demands, despite Kiev's wishes, becomes an act of defense of Ukrainian national heritage in the face of Kiev's passivity. The resistance of Lviv local government bodies to the restoration of the Polish heritage in the city is therefore an act against both Poland and Kiev.

To sum up, one can argue that interaction between local and state actors in border management results not only from the relationships between local actors on both sides of the border but also from the pattern of center–periphery relations in each state. To what extent Polish local administrations receive help or benefit from collaboration with their German counterparts is difficult to assess. German Länder and local administrations are transmitting their own experience of adaptation to EU mechanisms to their Polish partners, but the border remains a line between two sets of norms, especially in this case where neither Poland nor Ukraine is willing to import the administrative system of its neighbor. CBC is instrumental in a number of ways: it promotes social and economic development in the regions concerned and complements EU integration. At the same time, CBC is affected or supported by external factors, especially EU policies, norms, and activities. The administrative reform required by EU regional policy in applicant countries should provide local authorities with more room for manueuver unless financial constraints remain severe; the rules according to which EU funds are allocated also allow different actors (associations, NGOs) to express their views. In short, CBC is affected by state actors, and state actors are likely to be affected by such cooperation as a result of EU requirements. The EU can indeed have profound implications for local and regional government development in the Visegrád countries, as well as in other CEE countries. External factors are no less important than domestic ones. It is, however, too early to determine whether such cross-border activities stimulate greater political participation and commitment and enhance the principle of subsidiarity. On the German–Polish side, as well as on the Polish–Ukrainian side, states have played an active role in promoting transborder cooperation in spite of local reluctance. This is a noticeable difference with other cases (in Slovakia or in Romania, for example) where local actors have faced central state mistrust of developing transborder initiatives. In the German as well as in the Polish perception, cooperation with the eastern neighbor aims to overcome the legacy of the past and to prevent resentments at the local level from undermining the reconciliation desired at the national level. Between Germany and Poland and between Poland and Ukraine it is very likely that Franco-German reconciliation, as well as the European process of enlargement, has widely contributed to turning frontiers into areas of cooperation.

Conclusion

Can Polish actors be said to have implemented the German way of managing the EU's eastern border? There are similarities. As far as Euroregions are concerned, in both cases, local actors are asking for more money, more room for maneuver, and are complaining about the constraints of the border between two systems of norms. However, they expect more funds from the state, and local populations do often perceive the border as a protection against the 'Other.' In the case of Euroregions along the Polish–Ukrainian border, the impetus came from local and national initiatives. The Polish Ministry of Foreign Affairs strongly supported the idea. The emphasis was put on economic and commercial factors, development of transport and communications infrastructures, and cooperation in the field of culture, tourism, and environmental protection. Polish actors are promoting their idea by the same means that German actors did along the Oder–Neisse river. For the purposes of their argument, they sometimes refer to the experience of the Oder–Neisse frontier, where Euroregions are said to have helped overcome the burden of history. They explain that other experiences work perfectly well, although Franco-German cooperation sometimes has difficulties and Polish–German cooperation has not yet overcome all prejudices. They also explain that such initiatives are supported by the lessons of Western European experiences in this field. In the post-war period several dozen areas of transfrontier cooperation were designated, mainly along the borders of Alpine and Rhineland countries: Alpen-Adria, the Working Community of the Western Alps, Regio Basilensis, Sar-Lor-Lux, Euregio on the German–Dutch border. The experiences have been positive: there has been no case in their agenda causing problems either internally (conflicts of jurisdiction) or internationally and one may be led to think that there is a kind of myth surrounding the Euroregions. Ukrainian actors are not always convinced by such arguments, and express the same fears as Polish local actors express along the Polish–German border.

In the German–Polish case, as in the Polish–Ukrainian one, the relation of people to the frontier is not a relation to a particular space but a relation to history and to one's neighbor. The more one's neighbor is familiar, the more will the frontier appear as a simple matter of fact, not as a fence or as an injustice. In this respect, the 'success stories' of the Western European borders – even if they underestimate the unsolved problems, and persisting prejudices – pave the way for numerous local, regional, and state actors in CEE.

The German concepts for fostering transborder cooperation are accepted when they have a European legitimacy – i.e. they are perceived as a part of the European system that Polish actors are keen to adopt and they are adapted to Polish interests. Hence, German actors or Polish actors appear as spokesmen of European values and principles *vis-à-vis* their Eastern counterparts. If we look at the issue from a historical point of view, some scholars argue that Central Europe has very often in the past been a field for the diffusion of Western European models. Innovation and modernisation have come from the West, and have been adapted to the specific needs of each country. Such a scenario appears nowadays as one of the characteristics of the transition process started in 1989, but with one important difference: transfers made by the 'West' are part of a European model, still diverse but engaged in a harmonization process – and, as such, can be made in the name of 'Europe.' The point is that EU applicant countries so far seem to be much more receptive than countries deprived of any EU membership perspective.

Bibliography

Anderson, M. and E. Bort (eds) (1997) *Schengen and EU Enlargement: Security and Cooperation at the Eastern Frontier of the European Union*, Edinburgh: ISSI.

Anderson, M. and E. Bort (2001) *The Frontiers of the European Union*, Basingstoke: Palgrave.

Birch, S. and I. Zinko (1996) 'Dilemma of regionalism,' *Transition*, 1.

Davies, N. (1981) *God's Playground: A History of Poland. 1795 to the Present*, vols I and II, Oxford: Clarendon Press.

Geremek, B. (1977) *L'historien et le politique: entretiens avec Juan Carlos Vidal*, Montricher: Les Editions Noir sur Blanc.

Haas, A. Hudseljak, I. (2000) 'Perspektiven und Probleme der neuen polnisch-ukraini-schen Nachbarschaft,' *Europa Regional*, 8 (2).

Hann, C. (1996) 'Ethnic cleansing in Eastern Europe: Poles and Ukrainians beside the Curzon Line,' *Nations and Nationalism*, 2 (3).

Hann, C. (1998) 'Postsocialist nationalism: rediscovering the past in Southeast Poland,' *Slavic Review*, 57 (4), pp. 840–863.

Himka, J.P. (1994) 'Western Ukraine in the interwar period,' *Nationalities Papers*, 22 (2).

Jachtenfuchs, M. (1995) *Regieren im dynamischen Mehrebenensystem*, Mannheim: Mannheimer Zentrum für Europaische Sozialforschung.

Kappeler, A. (1997) *Petite histoire de l'Ukraine: Cultures et Sociétés de l'Est*, 26, Paris: Institut d'Etudes Slaves.

Potichnyj, P.J. (ed.) (1980) *Poland and Ukraine: Past and Present*, Edmonton: The Canadian Institute of Ukrainian Studies.

Ratti, R. (1996) 'Problématique de la frontière et du développement des régions-frontières,' *Sciences de la Société*, 37, pp. 37–48.

Snyder, T. (1999) 'To resolve the Ukrainian question once and for all: the ethnic cleansing of Ukrainians in Poland, 1943–1947,' *Journal of Cold War Studies*, 1 (2).

Wolczuk K. (2000) 'Ukraine and EU enlargement: the potential consequences at the regional level,' Research Note, Centre for Russian and East European Studies, The University of Birmingham.

Wolczuk K. (2001) 'Polish–Ukrainian borderlands: the case of Lviv and Przemysl,' in Kazimierz Krzysztofek and Andrzej Sadowski (eds), *Ethnic Borderlands in Europe: Harmony or Conflicts*, Bialystok: University of Bialystok, pp. 213–230.

Tanja A. Börzel

5

Restructuring or reinforcing the 'state': the German Länder as transnational actors in Europe

Introduction

Most studies of the EU and its member states are concerned with how processes of European integration impact on the member states. The main question is 'how Europe hits home' or the transformation of 'the domestic institutions of the member states' (Börzel, 1999, p. 574). This chapter shifts the emphasis from this 'top-down' towards a more 'bottom-up' approach and asks whether, and how, differences in domestic institutional constellations shape the way of how national non-state actors use the European level of policy-making.

A lively debate has evolved in European studies on whether European integration resulted in a redistribution of power among domestic actors. A growing number of empirical studies show that European integration affected the distribution of power within the member states in different ways. The EU may provide non-state actors with the opportunity to circumvent their national government. But the extent to which they exploit such transnational relations depends, first, on the degree to which non-state actors are affected by European integration and, second, on the amount of their action capacity or resources (Marks *et al.*, 1996; Risse-Kappen, 1996; Jeffery, 1997c; Börzel, 1999). The more non-state actors are affected by European integration and the more resources they have at their disposal, the more likely they are to transnationally mobilize at the European level.

I argue in this chapter that the degree of affectedness and the availability of resources explains when non-state actors mobilize at the European level. Yet, transnational mobilization does not necessarily imply a circumventing or by-passing of the national state level. Whether non-state actors use their transnational relations with European policy-makers 'against' their national government depends on the domestic institutional culture – the collective understandings about appropriate behavior within a given rule structure. An institutional culture which embodies cooperative norms and practices prevents domestic actors using transnational relations to circumvent their national governments.

I demonstrate my argument empirically in a case study on the role of the German Länder as transnational actors (TAs) in European policy-making. The Länder present a critical case for my theoretical argument. First, European integration broadly affects their legislative and administrative competencies. Second, unlike many other regions, the Länder possess the necessary resources to establish direct contacts with European policy-makers. But while they have made extensive use of their transnational relations to the European level, the institutional culture of cooperative federalism prevented the Länder from using them as a means of circumventing the German government. Rather, direct channels of access to the European policy arena serve as a complement to the participation of the Länder in the formulation and representation of the German bargaining position in European negotiations. The Länder rely mainly on their cooperation with the national government to influence European policy-making. As a result, European integration has reinforced the German federal state rather than restructuring it, by strengthening one group of actors over the other(s).

The chapter proceeds in the following steps. First, I develop an institutionalist model of transnational mobilization in European policy-making, which takes into account the influence of domestic institutional culture on the ways in which non-state actors conduct their transnational relations with European policy-makers. Second, I analyze the mobilization of the German Länder at the European level and how they have made use of their direct access to European policy-making. Finally, I will summarize the argument and findings of the chapter, assess their importance outside Germany, and suggest some avenues for future research.

European integration and transnational mobilization: conceptual considerations

In the literature, the impact of European integration on member states is often conceived as a resource-dependent process. It is assumed that the European structure of multi-level governance provides a political opportunity structure, which changes the distribution of power resources within the member states favoring one group of domestic actors over the others. The outcome of such a distribution of power resources, however, is controversial.[1]

One group of scholars suggests that European integration enhances the autonomy of national governments *vis-à-vis* non-state actors. Andrew Moravcsik, for instance, claims that the transfer of national policy competencies to the European level tends to reinforce the control of the national executives over four crucial resources of domestic power, as the national executives can monopolize or 'gate-keep' the access of non-state actors to the European policy-making arena (Moravcsik, 1994, p. 1; cf. Milward, 1992). This 'paradox of weakness' (Grande, 1996; Kohler-Koch, 1996) is challenged by another group of scholars who turn Moravscik's argument around. They suggest that European policy-making provides non-state actors, such as regions, with additional resources through the possibility to gain direct access to the European policy arena. Transnational relations with European policy-makers allow non-state actors to circumvent or by-pass their national governments (Sandholtz and Zysman, 1989; Marks, 1992, 1993; Cameron, 1995; Sandholtz, 1996). Unlike the early 'Europe of the Regions' literature, where the 'weakening-the-state' argument was most developed, many studies no longer claim that European integration equally strengthens the role of regional and local actors in European politics, giving rise to a homogeneous regional level of governance in Europe. It is acknowledged that regions diverge in their capacity to employ the resources offered by the European policy-making system (Keating and Hooghe, 1995; Marks *et al.*, 1996; Jeffery, 1997). But it remains unclear under which conditions regions will be able to exploit transnational relations with European policy-makers so that we can expect a change in the distribution of power within the member states.

Finally, a third group of scholars does not share the 'zero-sum game' conception of the effect of European integration, which strengthens one group of actors at the expense of the other(s). Rather, they argue that non-state and state actors become increasingly dependent on each other's resources in European policy-making. European integration does not strengthen or weaken, but transforms the national state by fostering the emergence of cooperation between the different actors (Kooiman, 1993; Kohler-Koch, 1996, 1997; Rhodes, 1997). Some authors even contest the emergence of a multiplication of extra-national channels for subnational political activity (Hooghe and Marks, 1996).

Despite a general disagreement on the concrete impact of European integration, most studies suggest that there will be some sort of convergence among the member states, leading to a strengthening, weakening, or transformation of the 'state.' Yet, comparative studies on the effect of European integration have so far not found much empirical evidence for convergence (Hooghe and Keating, 1994; Hooghe, 1995; Jones and Keating, 1995; Jeffery, 1997b; Kohler-Koch, 1998). I argue in this chapter that the impact of European integration on the member states is indeed diverse and 'institution-dependent.'

Institutions matter in the following three fundamental ways.

Institutions influence the capacity of non-state actors to establish transnational relations

The EU can be conceived as a political opportunity structure, which offers resources to domestic actors in the member states (Marks and McAdam, 1996). Yet, the ability of non-state actors to explore new opportunities, or avoid additional constraints, depends on their organizational capacities – i.e. the resources which institutions provide them such as access to the public sphere and political decision-making, financial means, information, and legitimacy (Kitschelt, 1986; Marks *et al.*, 1996).

In territorial politics, the constitutional or legal rules and procedures of a member state determine the distribution of power resources between the central state and the regions. As opposed to unitary or weakly decentralized states, the regions in federal or regionalized states have considerable resources in terms of policy competencies, financial revenue, organizational capacity, and political legitimacy. These resources enable the regions to exploit new European opportunities, while regions in non-decentralized or weakly decentralized states often lack the capacity to do so. At the same time, however, strong regions might benefit less from European opportunities, such as direct contacts with European institutions, as they do not provide a substitute for the loss of formal domestic powers which European integration imposes on them as significant 'constraints' on their institutional autonomy. Nevertheless, empirical studies demonstrate that the likelihood of regional mobilization at the European level increases with the amount of the resources the regions have at their disposal (Marks *et al.*, 1996; Kohler-Koch, 1998):

> The higher the degree of decentralization in a member state, the more likely its non-state actors are to establish transnational relations with European policy-makers.

Institutions influence the degree to which European integration affects non-state actors

European integration does not only provide non-state actors with new opportunities. It can also impose significant costs by depriving them of political power. Moreover, the costs of implementing European policies are usually shifted to the domestic level (cf. Börzel, 1998).

For regions of unitary and weakly decentralized states, Europeanization may offer additional opportunities which could strengthen their autonomy *vis-à-vis* the central state, although weak regions often lack the resources to fully exploit these opportunities. In highly decentralized member states, on the contrary, regions suffer a significant loss of their legislative and administrative competencies from Europeanization, resulting in an uneven distribution of 'say and pay' between the central state and the regions. On the one hand, the central state gains access to regional competencies, which it did not have at the domestic level. When regional competencies are transferred to the EU, the central state governments decide on their exercise in the Council of Ministers while the regions are left without any influence, as most of them are not formally represented in the European decision-making process. On the other hand, the regions are in many policy areas the main implementers of European law. They often have to bear the lion's share of implementation costs of policies in whose formulation and decision-making they do not participate:

> The more non-state actors are affected by European integration – losing power or having to bear the costs of EU policies – the more likely they are to establish transnational relations with European policy-makers.

Institutions influence the way in which non-state actors employ their transnational relations with European policy-makers

While the degree to which European integration affects non-state actors, together with the amount of their resources, explains *why* and *when* non-state actors establish transnational relations with European policy-makers, these factors do not tell us anything about the purpose of non-state actors transnationally mobilizing at the European level – i.e. *how* they make use of their transnational relations.

The European structure of multi-level governance provides the regions with three opportunities for transnational mobilization:

- *Direct contacts* with European policy-makers, mainly channeled through the regional information offices in Brussels, which provide individual regions with a lobbying tool at the European level.
- The *Committee of the Regions* (CoR), the official body of collective interest representation of the regions in the EU, which provides the regions with a formal, albeit weak, participation in the European decision-making process.
- *Inter-regional or transregional lobby associations*, such as the Assembly of European Regions (AER) or the Conference 'Europe of the Regions.'

Not only do the regions differ in the extent to which they have made use of these transnational relations (Marks *et al.*, 1996; Keating and Hooghe, 1995; Jeffery, 1997b; Kohler-Koch, 1998). If regions decided to transnationally mobilize at the European level, they have employed their transnational relations for different purposes.

Regions may pursue two basic strategies in employing their transnational relations to the European level:

- A *confrontative strategy* of circumventing or by-passing the state, which aims at using transnational relations to pursue regional interests independently from, and sometimes even against the interests of, their national government.
- A *cooperative strategy* of coordination with the state, which aims at using transnational relations to pursue regional interests in coordination with, or at least not against, the interests of their national government.

The strategy choice is strongly influenced by the informal institutions or the 'institutional culture' in which non-state actors are embedded. Institutions entail informal understandings about appropriate behavior within a given formal rule structure (March and Olsen, 1989).

In states like Spain, Italy, or Belgium, ethnic, religious and socio-economic cleavages gave rise to *competitive regionalism*, where the collective understanding of the regions about their behavior toward the central state is based on competition and confrontation rather than cooperation. The regions tend to protect their institutional autonomy by constitutional litigation and strive to deal with the central state on a bilateral rather than a multilateral level. This institutional culture of confrontation, competition, and bilateralism favors a non-cooperative strategy of circumventing the state. In states like Germany or Austria, on the contrary, where the institutional culture is characterized by cooperative federalism, the behavior of the regions toward the central state is based on a collective understanding that multilateral bargaining and consensus-seeking are the most appropriate way of dealing with intergovernmental problems. Such an institutional culture favors a cooperative strategy of cooperation with, rather than a non-cooperative strategy of circumventing of the state:

> Non-state actors which are embedded in an institutional culture entailing cooperative norms and practices are far less likely to use their transnational relations to the European level for circumventing their national state.

In sum, while formal domestic institutions (distribution of power resources) define the likelihood of non-state actors mobilizing at the European level, the informal institutional culture guides the ways in which non-state actors make use of their transnational relations. Circumventing the state, which might eventually lead to a 'restructuring of the state,' is likely to occur only if non-state actors, first, are broadly affected by European integration, second, have the necessary resources to establish transnational relations with European policy-makers, and, third, are embedded in an institutional culture which is hostile to cooperation. In other words, affectedness and availability of resources are only the necessary cause for transnational activities of non-state actors at the European level.

The following case study on the transnational mobilization of the German Länder at the European level will demonstrate that, even if non-state actors are motivated to establish transnational relations at the European level and possess the necessary resources to do so, they are unlikely to mobilize against the state if they are embedded in an institutional culture which is based on cooperation and consensus-seeking. The German Länder use their transnational relations as a complement to their cooperation with the national government in European policy-making. As a result, the transnational mobilization of the German Länder reinforce the German state with respect to its territorial institutions rather than restructure it. The formal and informal institutions of cooperative federalism remain intact; they are simply transferred from the domestic to the European realm of policy-making.

The transnational mobilization of the German Länder: complement to rather than substitute for the cooperation with the national state

Europeanization and transnational mobilization
From the very beginning of European integration, the Länder have been aware of the potential costs of Europeanization. As early as 1951, the Minister-President of the Land Nordrhein-Westfalen, Karl Arnold, alerted the Länder that European integration could deprive them of their legislative and administrative

competencies, downgrading them to purely administrative units of the central state.[2] And, indeed, the Länder faced a double loss of competencies as a consequence of European integration, which caused a shift in the territorial distribution of power in favor of the central state (cf. Börzel, 1997, 2002).

First, when exclusive Länder competencies were transferred to the European level, the Länder were deprived of any formal influence on the exercise of these competencies. The central state, on the contrary, whose executive represents Germany in the Council of Ministers, was directly involved in policy formulation and decision-making. As a result, the central state gained access to regional competencies at the European level, which the German constitution placed beyond its reach at the domestic level.

Second, when federal or shared competencies were transferred to the European level, the formal input of the Länder was reduced from a codetermination right in formulation and decision-making to the participation in the implementation of European policies. The central state, however, which also lost decision-making power, still had a major influence on policy formulation and decision-making in the Council of Ministers.

This double loss of competencies has affected the Länder in a wide range of policy areas. The EU practically intervenes in all areas which either fall under exclusive Länder responsibility (culture, educational and vocational training, media), or for which the Länder share competencies with the central state (environment, transport, regional development, agriculture, research and technology). The resulting strengthening of the central state provided a powerful incentive for the German Länder to mobilize at the European level in order to redress the territorial balance of power (cf. Große Hüttmann and Knodt, 2000). The German constitution confers on the Länder the necessary institutional, financial, and organizational resources in order to do so. Not only do the Länder possess (most of) the money, the personnel, the expertise and the experience of acting in a multi-level structure of policy-making. The Länder have a veto right in ratifying any revision of the European Treaties, which provides them with a powerful tool to push their demands for a broad participation in European policy-making at both the domestic and the European level. Yet, during the first twenty years of European integration, the Länder almost exclusively relied on the central state in order to influence European policy-making. Their transnational activities were rather limited.

Regional mobilization at the domestic level: pushing for codecision powers
In order to receive compensation for their loss of competencies, the Länder strove to participate as broadly as possible in the formulation and representation of the German bargaining position through cooperating with the national government (cf. Diedrichs, 2004, pp. 171–175). Subsequently, the Länder achieved information, consultation, and participation rights in European policy-making which were all mediated through the central state. These domestic channels of access to the European policy arena, which were constitutionally codified in 1992, are based on:

- the notification to the Bundesrat (Federal Council) of projects, initiatives, and proposals of the European Commission through the German government;
- the provision of informal and formal European documents by the national government;
- the participation of the Länder Observer and other Länder representatives in European decision-making bodies (Commission, Council, COREPER, committees) as members of the German delegation;
- the right of the Bundesrat to make recommendations to which the German government has to give due consideration; if a European issue affects the essential interests or competencies of the Länder, the Bundesrat opinion is binding for the German government;
- the representation of the German bargaining position in the Council of Ministers if exclusive competencies of the Länder are affected.

These participatory rights grant the Länder a veto right in the formulation and representation of German interests at the European level whenever their core competencies are affected (cf. Dette-Koch, 2004). Hence, in Germany the Bundesländer are very successful in influencing German European policy choices, especially since they are equipped with powerful instruments through article 23[3] of the German Grundgesetz (Basic Law) (cf. Große Hüttmann and Knodt, 2000). With Erwin Teufel, former Prime Minister of Baden-Württemberg, the Länder were also represented with formal voting power as members of the German delegation in the constitutional Convention. Even though Teufel formally represented 'only' the second chamber of the German parliament, his position was based on the unanimous resolutions of the Bundesrat, of the Conference of Prime Ministers, and of the Conference of Europe Ministers. These formal and informal institutions of joint decision-making and interlocking politics provide the national government and the Länder with the necessary coordination mechanisms to make the domestic participation of the German Länder in European policy-making work. European issues were simply integrated into the already existing decision-making structure of German cooperative federalism.

The Länder have been present at the European level from the early 1950s. Yet, until the late 1970s their presence was almost exclusively mediated through the national state. Thus, Länder representatives participated in the European decision-making bodies but only as members of the German delegation.

Emerging regional mobilization at the European level: establishing transnational relations

While the Länder had begun to push for intra-state state channels of influence in European policy-making in 1951 (cf. Börzel, 1997), they first started to establish transnational relations to the European level only in the 1970s by establishing unofficial contacts with European policy-makers. Representatives of the

Länder traveled to Brussels for information visits at the European Commission and some Länder maintained a more or less regular correspondence with the European Commission. Länder trips to Brussels have to be communicated to the Foreign Ministry; the Länder must accommodate the interests of the national government in voicing their opinions to European institutions (Morawitz, 1981: 32). But unlike in other member states, neither of these issues has caused problems with the Länder.

The Bundesrat also established some transnational relations with European institutions. Beside frequent contacts between the EC Committee and members of the EP (Morawitz, 1981, p. 35), the Bundesrat created a contact office with the EP for the mutual exchange of information in 1967 (Jaspert, 1988). Moreover, each Land maintains regular contacts with its regional members of the European Parliament (MEP). These contacts mainly serve for the exchange of information. For some Länder, however, their MEPs also play a lobbying function channeling regional interests through the EP into the European decision-making arena. Bayern and Nordrhein-Westfalen have been particularly adept in using their MEPs as transnational channels of access to European policy-making.

Only in the second half of the 1980s did the Länder begin to open their own offices (Länderbüros) in Brussels.[4] Their main task is to inform their respective Land government about all developments at the European level which could be of particular interest for the Land, to help public institutions and private enterprises of the Land to establish contacts with EU institutions, and to conduct public relations for the Land especially with the Commission (Strohmeier 1988; Fastenrath 1990). Despite some reproaches of 'Nebenaußenpolitik' (parallel diplomacy), which the Länder were said to pursue through their offices in Brussels (Nass, 1986; Hellwig, 1987), the offices mainly serve the individual Länder as 'antennae' and instruments of 'fallbezogenes Lobbying' (issue-specific lobbying) (Morass 1992, p. 298) to pursue individual interests. Since 1992, the Länder offices can even claim official status.

Finally, the Länder, together with the regions of the other member states, gained direct representation at the European level through the Council of Regional and Local Territorial Corporations (established by the Commission in 1988) and the AER (1989, replacing the Council of Regions in Europe founded in 1985). The Länder joined these institutions only reluctantly because of the significant heterogeneity of the members with respect to their institutional autonomy: 'The Länder feel closer to regions with proper legislative competences, such as those in Belgium, than with more administrative units, as in France' (Diedrichs, 2004, p. 174). European institutions of regional representation gained importance for the Länder only when they became potential allies in pursuing their claims for a strong regional participation in European policy-making (see below). Together with the Belgian and Spanish regions, the Länder were crucial in pushing through the Committee of the Regions in the negotiations on the Maastricht Treaty. Influencing the EU agenda through the

Committee of the Regions seems to be far less meaningful for the Bundesländer than the cooperation with the federal government in EU matters (cf. Diedrichs, 2004, p. 174).

Despite their broad domestic access to European policy-making, the Länder have been among the most active regions mobilizing at the European level. Thus, they managed to gain support for their demands for a stronger participation of the regions in European policy-making – which they had formulated prior to the Maastricht Treaty negotiations – by the President of the Commission, the EP, the AER, and the Conference 'Europe of the Regions' (cf. Börzel, 2002). And while the Nice Treaty did not address the allocation of competencies between the EU and the member states, the President of the Commission, Romano Prodi, promised the Länder that the issue would be put on the agenda of the European Council in Brussels in June 2004, which was crucial for ensuring the support of the Länder for the ratification of the Nice Treaty. While often being effective, the European mobilization of the German Länder has never been to the detriment of the federal government.

Transnational relations: complement rather than supplement

As we have seen, the Länder have both the motivation and the resources to establish transnational relations at the European level. Yet, in contrast to other member states, such as Spain and Belgium, where the relationship between the central state and the regions is characterized by an institutional culture of competition and conflict, the institutional culture of cooperative federalism has prevented the Länder from using their transnational relations to circumvent the national state level. Unilateral actions or bilateral agreements which by-pass or even challenge the interests of the German government or other Länder are generally considered as inappropriate.

The institutional culture of cooperative federalism is characterized by a strong sense of conflict avoidance and consensus-seeking. The joint decisions of the national government and the Länder, which are necessary in most policy areas to bring about policy outcomes, are often based on informal decision-making rules approaching unanimity even where, by law, majority or unilateral decisions would be possible (Scharpf, 1989). More importantly, even those Länder that would benefit from a particular policy outcome refrain from voting with the national government if there is no nearly unanimous agreement among all the Länder (Scharpf, 1988; Renzsch, 1995; cf. Scharpf *et al.*, 1976). The ability of the national government to play off the interest of some Länder against the others is the exception rather than the rule. The Länder are careful in forming coalitions with the national government against the interests of the other Länder 'because next time, it could be us against whom such a coalition is formed' (interview, August 1996). Rather, by cooperating among themselves at the 'third level' (cf. Scharpf, 1989), the Länder strive to find a common position which accommodates the interests of all and which then is negotiated with the national government. 'Horizontal self-coordination' among the Länder is facilitated by certain rules like that of non-intervention, according to which those Länder whose interests are not directly affected, abstain. A good example of this close interaction of the federal and the European policy of the Bundesländer is the Treaty establishing a Constitution for Europe. The discussions in and about the Convention contributed to increasing the European profile of the Länder – with good results. The main demands have been fulfilled, such as the right to file an action before the European Court of Justice (ECJ) in case of any violation of the principle of subsidiarity and the establishment of the respect for regional self-government as part of the national identity in the Constitutional Treaty (cf. Brok, 2003, p. 318; Teufel, 2003, p. 348; Europäische Kommission, 2004). And even though the strong demand for mentioning God and Christianity in the pre-amble of the Constitutional Treaty, as demanded by the Länder governed by the Christian Democrats and especially by the Christian Social Union (Bayern), has not been successful, the Bundesrat voted overwhelmingly for the Treaty.[5]

Multilateral bargaining and consensus-seeking in German territorial poli-tics is also favored by the general German political culture which is traditionally averse to conflict (Sontheimer, 1990).The incompatibility of unilateral or bilat-eral action with the institutional culture of cooperative federalism became most obvious after German unification. The Western Länder complained about some of the New Länder, which 'simply do not understand the rules of the game' (interview, March 1998). Sachsen in particular repeatedly violated fundamental rules of cooperative federalism – e.g. by striking unilateral deals with the national government, by refusing to facilitate a consensus with the other Länder on controversial issues, by taking a negative position on issues which concerned the interests of other Länder rather than their own, or by officially voting against proposals supported by the majority of the Länder.

Cooperation does not equal harmony, however. The Länder responses to the challenges of Europeanization have shown some elements of conflict. Several times the Länder threatened to veto the ratification of Treaty revisions in the Bundesrat if the German government did not bend to their demands. In the beginning, the Länder invoked the veto threat only to push for more coop-eration, i.e. for a strong participatory rights in European policy-making. Since the conclusion of the Maastricht Treaty, however, the Länder have become increasingly concerned about the protection of their core competencies, which are constitutive of their state quality. Thus, the Länder have opposed the intro-duction of qualified majority voting (QMV) on issues concerning immigra-tion and public services (Daseinsvorsorge) in both the Amsterdam Treaty and the Nice Treaty, and they asked for a clear delimitation of competencies to be defined in the 2004 IGC. While this may be taken as an indication of the Länder turning away from their cooperative approach towards more competition (Knodt, 2000), cooperative federalism largely prevents such a strategy change. First, the demands for a strengthening of Länder competencies are far from being consensual among the Länder themselves. The economically less power-ful Länder, which are the majority, do not share the enthusiasm of Bayern,

Baden-Württemberg, and Hessen for more Wettbewerbsföderalismus (competitive federalism). And unlike the conservatives, social democrats still link subsidiarity to solidarity rather than competition. Second, it is highly questionable whether the Länder would ever actually execute their veto threat. Their first veto threat concerning the ratification of the Single European Act (SEA) in 1986 triggered strong public criticism, at both the domestic and European levels (see below). So did the threat the Länder voiced during the negotiations on the Nice Treaty. In both cases the Länder finally opted for compromise rather than conflict. In 1986, the Länder had been satisfied with only non-binding participatory rights; in 2000, they agreed to postpone the competence issue to the next round of Treaty revisions, on which the member states agreed in Nice – not so much because of Länder pressure but because many of the 'left overs' from Amsterdam still had not been resolved. It remains to be seen to what extent Bayern and its allies will be willing to move beyond symbolic politics and confront both the German government and the majority of the less resourceful Länder and push for some real institutional changes at both the domestic and the European levels. So far, the logic of cooperative federalism has prevailed.

Cooperative federalism has largely determined the way in which the Länder have employed their transnational relations with European policy-makers. The Länder are careful to avoid any impression of a Nebenaußenpolitik. The federal government is usually informed about important regional initiatives at the European level; even Bayern, whose interests are not always consensual at the domestic level, would not push a position which seriously undermined the interests of the national government or (some of) the other Länder. Being the most active Land in the European policy-making arena, Bayern – like the other Länder – usually pursues a strategy of negative coordination (Mayntz and Scharpf, 1975, pp. 145–150), i.e. it takes into account the interests of the other Länder as well as the national government when pursuing its own interests. Moreover, the Länder and the national government often actively coordinate their activities at the European level, jointly lobbying the Commission, the EP, and other member state governments on the German bargaining position. The 'paradigm shift' of the European Commission in European water policy from an exclusively quality-based to a more emission-based approach is one example of the successful interplay between the German government and the Länder in European policy-making. Under the lead of Bayern, the Länder formulated a joint position, which they coordinated with the German government and which was entered as a position at the Environmental Committee of the EP; the German government and the Länder also lobbied the Danish and British governments, which helped to convince the Commission to change its policy approach (Börzel, 2002).

Transnational relations with European policy-makers serve the Länder in two major ways which render them a complement to, rather than a substitute for, domestic channels of access to the European policy process.

First, the individual Länder use their direct contacts with European policy-makers to realize particular matters, which are either not of interest to the other Länder (like programs of transregional cooperation or attracting foreign investments or Community subsidies for specific regional projects), or which are non-consensual among the majority of the Länder (like certain reform initiatives in environmental or structural policy). Nevertheless, as soon as there is an official German position, the Länder are careful to avoid any activity at the European level which could convey the impression that Germany is speaking with more than one voice.

Second, the Länder have instrumentalized their direct contacts with European institutions as well as their cooperation with other regions to push their domestic demands for strong codecision powers in the formulation and representation of the German bargaining position at the European level (intra-state channels of access to EU policy-making). In 1988, the Länder started to promote the idea of a 'Europe of the Regions.' Using their contacts with European and regional actors, such as the President of the Commission, the EP, the AER, and the Conference 'Europe of the Regions,' the Länder mobilized political support inside and outside Germany for their claims for a strong role of the regions in European politics (Börzel, 1997). In 1986, the demands of the Länder for intra-state participation in European policy-making had been largely considered as 'hostile' to European integration (Hrbek, 1986; Nass, 1986; Hellwig, 1987; Meier, 1987). In 1991–92, however, the Länder were able to legitimize their call for strong, constitutional rights of intra-state participation by embedding their demands in the general concept of a 'Europe of the Regions' which was increasingly embraced by national and European politicians as a means to overcome the legitimacy crisis of European integration.

The instrumental character of transnational relations as a resource to strengthen their domestic position *vis-à-vis* the national government became most obvious after 1992. Although they were crucial in pushing the Committee of the Regions, the principle of subsidiarity, and the participation of regional ministers in the Council of Minister onto the agenda of the Maastricht Treaty, in the negotiations on the revision of the Treaty (in the Amsterdam Treaty of 1997), the Länder did not pay 'more than lip-service to the Third Level ambitions trumpeted during the Maastricht process' (Jeffery, 1997a, p. 73). This may be partly due to the sobering experience of the Länder with the newly established Committee of the Regions. The Länder had to realize that they could not simply control this body in the way in which they had initially thought (Kalbfleisch-Kottsieper, 1993). Moreover, the Länder have diverging opinions on the future role of the regions in Europe. The New Länder are initially very skeptical toward enhancing the political weight of the Third Level (Börzel, 1997). But, most importantly, the cooperation with the national government provides the Länder with a powerful source of influence on European policy-making, for which transnational channels of influence cannot substitute.

Reinforcement rather than reconstruction of the state

As we have seen, the Länder have been very successful in establishing both national and transnational channels of access to European policy-making. But while the Länder have extensively used the opportunities offered by the European system of multi-level governance, the institutional culture of cooperative federalism precluded them from turning their transnational relations into an instrument to circumvent or by-pass the national state. The transnational mobilization of the Länder reinforced the German federal state rather than restructured it. In their attempt to gain compensation for their power losses, the German Länder chose a strategy by which European and domestic resources were employed to enhance their participation in European policy-making through cooperation with the national government. The formal and informal institutions of cooperative federalism and joint decision-making were simply externalized from the domestic to the European realm of policy-making. This flexible adjustment has reinforced rather than changed the existing German territorial structures (Goetz, 1995; cf. Börzel, 2002).

Conclusion: the differential effect of European integration on the national state

The findings of this chapter show that the expectation that European integration would fundamentally restructure the national state may be premature – or, at least may need to be qualified.

Contrary to general assumptions that European integration strengthens, weakens, or transforms the national state, this chapter has argued that the effect of European integration on the member states has been diverse and 'institution-dependent.' In principle, the EU offers non-state actors the opportunity to circumvent the national state by directly accessing the European policy arena. But some actors lack the necessary resources to exploit these opportunities, or they simply do not feel the need to invest resources in the establishment of transnational relations to the European level as they have as yet not been sufficiently affected by European integration.

Non-state actors in highly decentralized states are most likely to mobilize at the European level because they are broadly affected by European integration – and, more importantly, they have the necessary resources directly to access the European level. Yet, because actors mobilize at the European level it does not necessarily mean that they use their transnational relations to circumvent or by-pass their national government. The case of the German Länder demonstrates that non-state actors may successfully establish transnational relations to the European level without turning their European resources 'against' the state.

I have argued in this chapter that the way in which domestic actors mobilize at the European level can be explained only by the institutional culture in which the domestic actors are embedded. An institutional culture which embodies cooperative norms and practices, labels 'circumventing' as inappropriate behavior.

The relevance of institutional culture in explaining the way in which domestic actors employ their transnational relations is further supported if we look at member states, such as Spain, Belgium, or Italy, whose territorial structures are also strongly decentralized but which lack the cooperative institutional culture of Germany or Austria. In the former countries, competition and conflict have traditionally characterized the relationship between the central state and the regions. As a consequence, the Spanish, Belgian, and Italian regions have been prone to exploit their transnational relations with European policy-makers to circumvent the national state. By acting as independent TAs in European policy-making, these regions hope to enhance their autonomy *vis-à-vis* the central state at the domestic level. Catalunya and el País Vasco are two prominent examples of regions which try to promote their political and cultural identity by projecting their ambitions for more institutional autonomy, if not independent statehood, into the European policy arena. Only recently have they started to reconsider their strategy of circumventing the state in European policy-making (Börzel, 1999, 2002).

The differing responses of non-state actors to the opportunities and constraints provided by the European system of multi-level governance should direct future research away from the debate on the strengthening versus weakening versus transforming of the national state. Rather than perpetuating this controversy, we should acknowledge the empirical findings, which clearly show that European integration has a differential effect on the domestic structures of the member states. We should start by identifying conditions under which European integration has a particular effect on the domestic structures of the member states. Why, for instance, has German cooperative federalism largely been unaffected by European integration, while we witness a profound transformation of Spanish competitive regionalism (Börzel, 2002)? Why is it that the business–government relations in France have undergone significant change, whereas those in Great Britain have been left largely unchanged (Cowles, 2001)? Why did the British telecommunication sector have less difficulty in adapting to market liberalization than the German and the French (Thatcher, 1998)? Why has British nation-state identity resisted Europeanization while German nation-state identity opened a space for Europe already more than forty years ago (Risse, 2001)? Why has Spain more willingly adapted to EU economic and monetary policy than Greece (Marks, 1997)? These are the questions which should guide the research agenda of those who are interested in the effect of European integration on the domestic structures of the member states (for good overviews of the state of the art see Featherstone and Radaelli, 2003; Bulmer and Lequesne, 2005).

Notes

For comments on earlier versions of this chapter, I am thankful to Michael Kreile, Anne-Marie Le Gloannec, Antje Wiener, Hans-Dieter Klingemann, and Beate Kohler-Koch.

1   For the following see also Börzel (1999, 2002).
2   Proceedings of the session of the Bundesrat, July 27, 1951, p. 445.
3   The revision of this article in 1992 indicated that European policy was no longer
    regarded as traditional foreign policy in terms of article 32 (1) of the Basic Law;
    rather it adopted the ideal concept of a 'European domestic policy' promoted by the
    German Länder (cf. Müller-Terpitz, 1999, p. 367).
4   Only Niedersachsen had already opened an information office at the end of the 1970s.
    Bayern had planned to open a representation in Brussels in 1979 but the federal gov-
    ernment took a negative view and the plan was dropped (Morawitz, 1981, p. 35).
5   Fifteen Länder (out of sixteen) voted for the Treaty, only Mecklenburg-Vorpommern
    abstained because the PDS as coalition partner was against the Constitutional Treaty
    and the government did not want to risk the coalition.

Bibliography

Börzel, Tanja A. (1997) 'Does the European integration really strengthen the state? The
    case of the Federal Republic of Germany,' *Regional and Federal Studies*, 7 (3),
    pp. 87–113.
Börzel, Tanja A. (1998) 'Shifting or sharing the burden: the Europeanisation of environ-
    mental policy in Spain and Germany,' *European Planning Studies*, 6 (5), pp. 537–553.
Börzel, Tanja A. (1999) 'Towards convergence in Europe? Institutional adaptation to
    Europeanisation in Germany and Spain,' *Journal of Common Market Studies*, 37 (4),
    pp. 573–596.
Börzel, Tanja A. (2002) *States and Regions in Europe: Institutional Adaptation in Germany
    and Spain*, Cambridge: Cambridge University Press.
Brok, Elmar (2003) 'Der Konvent als Wegbereiter der Europäischen Verfassung,'
    Zeitschrift für Staats- und Europawissenschaften, 1 (3), pp. 313–323.
Bulmer, Simon and Christian Lequesne (eds) (2005) *Member States and the European
    Union*, Oxford: Oxford University Press.
Cameron, David (1995) 'Transnational relations and the development of European eco-
    nomic and monetary union,' in T. Risse-Kappen (ed.), *Bringing Transnational
    Relations Back In*, Cambridge: Cambridge University Press.
Cowles, Maria Green (2001) 'The TABD and domestic business–government relations:
    challenge and opportunity,' in M. G. Cowles *et al.* (eds), *Transforming Europe:
    Europeanization and Domestic Change*, Ithaca, NY: Cornell University Press.
Dette-Koch, Elisabeth (2004) 'German Länder participation in European policy through
    the Bundesrat,' in A. Gunlicks (ed.), *German Public Policy and Federalism*, Oxford:
    Berghahn, pp. 182–196.
Diedrichs, Udo (2004) 'The German system of EU policymaking and the role of the
    Länder: fragmentation and partnership,' in A. Gunlicks (ed.), *German Public Policy
    and Federalism*, Oxford: Berghahn, pp. 165–181.
Europäische Kommission (2004) 'Länder fit in Europa,' *EU-Nachrichten*, 26, July 8, 2004,
    at www.eu-kommission.de/pdf/eunachrichten/2604_internet.pdf, accessed on June 1,
    2005.
Fastenrath, Ulrich (1990) 'Die Länderbüros in Brüssel,' *Die öffentliche Verwaltung*, 45 (4),
    pp. 125–136.
Featherstone, Kevin and Claudio Radaelli (eds) (2003) *The Politics of Europeanisation*,
    Oxford: Oxford University Press.
Goetz, Klaus H. (1995) 'National governance and European integration: intergovern-
    mental relations in Germany,' *Journal of Common Market Studies*, 33 (1), pp. 91–116.

Grande, Edgar (1996) 'The state and interest groups in a framework of multi-level decision-making: the case of the European Union,' *Journal of European Public Policy*, 3 (3), pp. 318–338.

Große Hüttmann, Martin and Michèle Knodt (2000) 'Die Europäisierung des deutschen Föderalismus,' *Aus Politik und Zeitgeschichte*, B 52–53, pp. 31–38.

Hellwig, Renate (1987) 'Die Rolle der Bundesländer in der Europa-Politik,' *Europa-Archiv*, 42 (10), pp. 297–302.

Hooghe, Liesbet (1995) 'Subnational mobilisation in the European Union,' in J. Hayward (ed.), *The Crisis of Representation in Europe*, London: Frank Cass.

Hooghe, Liesbet and Michael Keating (1994) 'The politics of European regional policy,' *Journal of European Public Policy*, 1 (3), pp. 53–78.

Hooghe, Liesbet and Gary Marks (1996) 'Europe with the regions? Regional representation in the European Union,' *Publius: The Journal of Federalism*, 26 (1), pp. 73–91.

Hrbek, Rudolf (1986) 'Die Bundesländer im Bremserhäuschen?,' *Europäische Zeitung*, 37 (5), p. 2.

Jaspert, Gunter (1988) 'Die Beteiligung des Bundesrates an der europäischen Integration,' in S. Magiera and D. Merten (eds), *Bundesländer und Europäische Gemeinschaft*, Berlin: Duncker & Humblot.

Jeffery, Charlie (1997a) 'Farewell to the third level? The German Länder and the European policy process,' in C. Jeffery (ed.), *The Regional Dimension of the European Union: Towards a Third Level in Europe?*, London: Frank Cass.

Jeffery, Charlie (ed.) (1997b) *The Regional Dimension of the European Union: Towards a Third Level in Europe?*, London: Frank Cass.

Jeffery, Charlie (1997c) 'Sub-national authorities and European integration: moving beyond the nation-state?,' paper presented at the European Community Studies Association Conference, Seattle, May 29–June 1.

Jones, Barry and Michael Keating (eds) (1995) *The European Union and the Regions*, Oxford: Clarendon Press.

Kalbfleisch-Kottsieper, Ulla (1993) 'Fortentwicklungen des Föderalismus in Europa – vom Provinzialismus zur stabilen politischen Perspektive? Ein Beitrag zur Rolle der Länder, Regionen und Autonomen Gemeinschaften bei den EG-Regierungskonferenzen und der Ratifizierung des Maastrichter Vertrags,' *Die Öffentliche Verwaltung*, 46 (13), pp. 541–551.

Keating, Michael and Liesbet Hooghe (1995) 'By-passing the nation-state? Regions and the EU policy process,' in J. J. Richardson (ed.), *Policy Making in the European Union*, London: Routledge.

Kitschelt, Herbert P. (1986) 'Political opportunity structures and political protest: anti-nuclear movements in four democracies,' *British Journal of Political Science*, 16 (1), pp. 57–85.

Knodt, Michèle (2000) 'Europäisierung à la Sinatra: Deutsche Länder im europäischen Mehrebenensystem,' in M. Knodt and B. Kohler-Koch (eds), *Deutschland zwischen Europäisierung und Selbstbehauptung*, Frankfurt am Main and New York: Campus, pp. 237–264.

Kohler-Koch, Beate (1996) 'The strength of weakness: the transformation of governance in the EU,' in S. Gustavsson and L. Lewin (eds), *The Future of the Nation State: Essays on Cultural Pluralism and Political Integration*, Stockholm: Nerenius & Santerus.

Kohler-Koch, Beate (1997) 'Interactive governance: regions in the network of European politics,' paper presented at the European Community Studies Association, Seattle, May 28–June 1.

Kohler-Koch, Beate *et al.* (1998) *Interaktive Politik in Europa: Regionen im Netzwerk der Integration*, Opladen: Leske & Budrich.

Kooiman, Jan (ed.) (1993) *Modern Governance: New Government-Society Interactions,* London: Sage.

March, James G. and Johan P. Olsen (1989) *Rediscovering Institutions,* New York: Free Press.

Marks, Gary (1992) 'Structural policy in the European Community,' in A. Sbragia (ed.), *Europolitics: Institutions and Policymaking in the New European Community,* Washington, DC: Brookings Institution.

Marks, Gary (1993) 'Structural policy and multilevel governance in the European Community,' in A. Cafruny and G. Rosenthal (eds), *The State of the European Community II: Maastricht Debates and Beyond,* Boulder: Lynne Riener.

Marks, Gary and Doug McAdam (1996) 'Social movements and the changing structure of political opportunity in the European Union,' in G. Marks *et al.* (eds), *Governance in the European Union,* London, Thousand Oaks, and New Delhi: Sage.

Marks, Gary *et al.* (1996) 'Competencies, cracks and conflicts: regional mobilization in the European Union,' in G. Marks *et al.* (eds), *Governance in the European Union,* London, Thousand Oaks, and New Delhi: Sage.

Marks, Michael P. (1997) 'Moving at different speed: Spain and Greece in the European Union,' in P. J. Katzenstein (ed.), *Tamed Power: Germany in Europe,* Ithaca, NY and London: Cornell University Press.

Mayntz, Renate, and Fritz W. Scharpf (1975) *Policy-Making in the German Federal Bureaucracy,* Amsterdam: Elsevier.

Milward, Alan (1992) *The European Rescue of the Nation-State,* Berkeley: California University Press.

Meier, Gert (1987) 'Die Beteiligung der Länder an der Gesetzgebung der Europäischen Gemeinschaften – ein Ende der Diskussion?,' *Zeitschrift für Rechtspolitik,* 20 (7), pp. 228–230.

Morass, Michael (1992) 'Die Interessenvertretung regionaler Akteure im Dreiebenensystem der Europäischen Gemeinschaften. Problemaufriß nach 'Maastricht' am Beispiel der deutschen Länder,' *Österreichische Zeitschrift für Politikwissenschaft,* 21 (3), pp. 289–308.

Moravcsik, Andrew (1994) *Why the European Community Strengthens the State: Domestic Politics and International Cooperation,* Cambridge, MA: Harvard University Press.

Morawitz, Rudolf (1981) *Die Zusammenarbeit von Bund und Ländern bei Vorhaben der Europäischen Gemeinschaft,* Bonn: Europa Union.

Müller-Terpitz, Ralf (1999) *Die Beteiligung des Bundesrates am Willensbildungsprozess der Europäischen Union,* Stuttgart: Richard Boorberg Verlag.

Nass, Klaus Otto (1986) 'Nebenaußenpolitik der Bundesländer,' *Europa-Archiv,* 41 (21), pp. 619–629.

Renzsch, Wolfgang (1995) 'Konfliktlösung im parlamentarischen Bundesstaat: Zur Regelung finanzpolitischer Bund-Länder-Konflikte im Spannungsfeld von Administration und Politik – Vorläufige Überlegungen,' in R. Voigt (ed.), *Der kooperative Staat: Krisenbewältigung durch Verhandlung?,* Baden-Baden: Nomos.

Rhodes, R.A.W. (1997) *Understanding Governance: Policy Networks, Governance, Reflexivity and Accountability,* Buckingham and Philadelphia: Open University Press.

Risse, Thomas (2001) 'The Europeanization of nation-state identities?,' in M. G. Cowles *et al.* (eds), *Transforming Europe: Europeanization and Domestic Change,*

Risse-Kappen, Thomas (1996) 'Exploring the nature of the beast: international relations theory and comparative policy analysis meet the European Union,' *Journal of Common Market Studies,* 34 (1), pp. 53–80.

Sandholtz, Wayne (1996) 'Membership matters: limits of the functional approach to European institutions,' *Journal of Common Market Studies,* 34 (3), pp. 403–429.

Sandholtz, Wayne and John Zysman (1989) '1992: recasting the European bargain,' *World Politics*, 42 (1), pp. 95–128.

Scharpf, Fritz W. (1988) 'The joint-decision trap: lessons from German federalism and European integration,' *Public Administration* 66 (3), pp. 239–278.

Scharpf, Fritz W. (1989) 'Der Bundesrat und die Kooperation auf der dritten Ebene,' in Bundesrat (ed.), *Vierzig Jahre Bundesrat: Tagungsband zum wissenschaftlichen Symposium in der Evangelischen Akademie Tübingen, 11–13 April 1989*, Baden-Baden: Nomos.

Scharpf, Fritz W. *et al.* (1976) *Politikverflechtung, Theorie und Empirie des kooperativen Föderalismus in der Bundesrepublik Deutschland*, Kronberg/Ts.: Scriptor.

Sontheimer, Kurt (1990) *Deutschlands politische Kultur*, Munich and Zürich: Piper.

Strohmeier, Rudolf (1988) 'Möglichkeiten der Einflußnahme auf den Entscheidungsprozeß der Europäischen Gemeinschaften durch die deutschen Bundesländer nach Einrichtung von Länderbüros in Brüssel,' *Die Öffentliche Verwaltung*, 41 (15), pp. 633–637.

Teufel, Erwin (2003) 'Europa in neuer Verfassung: Das Ergebnis des Verfassungskonvents aus Sicht der deutschen Länder,' *Zeitschrift für Staats- und Europawissenschaften*, 1 (3), pp. 347–357.

Thatcher, Mark (1998) 'Europe and national regulatory authorities: the impact of the European Community on telecommunications in member states,' paper presented at the Annual Meeting of the American Political Science Association, Boston, September 3–6.

6

Transnational networking as institutional export: the case of Bavaria

Introduction

One of the growth industries of the post-Cold War era has been the study of united Germany's foreign policy. Showing no signs yet of recession (cf. *German Politics*, 2001, 2005; Harnisch and Maull, 2001; Rittberger, 2001), this industry has revealed a persistent preoccupation with the nature of German power after the *Wende* ('the turn,' i.e. the dramatic changes which took place in 1989–90) (Jeffery and Paterson, 2000). Though no-one has yet arrived at a consensus view of what 'German power' is, and what it means for the rest of us, there is at least a broad agreement that the reality of post-unity Germany is not adequately reflected in 'traditional' and in particular realist accounts of power in international relations (e.g. Katzenstein, 1997a; Markovits, and Reich 1997; Banchoff, 1999; Harnisch and Maull, 2001; Rittberger, 2001). Our[1] view is that German power in the new Europe is multi-faceted, at the margins 'realist' and 'possession'-oriented but generally focused on what Wolfers (1962) called 'milieu goals,' on shaping the environment for international cooperation, and exercised indirectly, 'softly,' and at times unintentionally (Bulmer, Jeffery, and Paterson, 2000, Hyde-Price, 2000; Jeffery and Paterson, 2000).

One of the 'soft' faces of power which has attracted growing attention is that of 'institutional' power, or 'export,' the replication of recognizably German institutional models in the institutional frameworks which shape international cooperation and interaction in Europe, in particular as cooperation has now also come to encompass the post-communist east. These frameworks may consist in part of 'hard' legal requirements – for example, in the Bundesbank-inspired rules governing the activity of the ECB (though, ironically, those rules are now perceived as unhelpful constraints by a German economy condemned to sluggishness by the monetary policies of the Eurozone – cf. Jeffery and Paterson, 2003, p. 64). But they may also reside in 'softer-edged' norms, collective understandings of what is an appropriate way of doing things and what is not. Indeed, one of the more prominent themes which has emerged in the study of German European policy since 1990 is that German policy actors are, to an unusual extent, motivated by normative commitments (Hyde-Price and Jeffery, 2001).

Exploration of institutional replication has largely focused hitherto on matters of 'high politics,' in particular in the EU, where the focus has been on the deals struck by national governments in treaty-making IGCs and European Council summits (e.g. Bulmer, Jeffery, and Paterson, 2000). This chapter takes a different approach. It brings transnational relations into the study of institutional replication. It focuses on the extent to which channels for institutional replication may be created through the relations that German European policy actors outside of the German federal government maintain with partners in other states. The argument proceeds in two stages. First, some theoretical reflections are set out on how transnational relations open up possibilities for institutional replication. Second, and building on this, a series of empirical cases is developed which illuminates the role of one policy actor – the Bavarian government – in replicating both 'hard' rules and 'soft' norms in a series of transnational networks focused on key questions of European politics. The conclusion uses the Bavarian example to reflect on Germany and its power in Europe.

Institutional replication and 'systemic empowerment'?

The most prominent example of the replication of German institutional forms in European politics concerns the role of the Bundesbank in constructing European Economic and Monetary Union. (EMU). EMU is not, though, an isolated example of institutional models from the German domestic arena being recast to then set the parameters for policy-making at the European level (Bulmer, Jeffery, and Paterson, 2000, pp. 40–46). The German Länder also left their mark in the treaty amendments they helped secure in the Maastricht negotiations and, in the case of subsidiarity, at Amsterdam in 1997. German firms had earlier played a defining role in standard-setting in the European Single Market program. More generally, through its traditional role as integration deepener, as a long-standing advocate of multilateral solutions, Germany has naturally left much more of an imprint than, say, the UK, in shaping how things are done in the EU. The net result is the extensive congruence Simon Bulmer (1997, pp. 61–72) has noted between the German and the EU systems of governance, with both displaying comparable constitutional foundations, operational norms, and conventions, and, in large part, policy goals. Bulmer identifies here a 'virtuous circle' in which institutional export results in 'systemic empowerment.' As Jeff Anderson and John Goodman (1993, p. 61) put it: 'Institutions are rarely neutral; rather they are shaped by the interests and resources of member states, and consistently privilege some, particularly the more powerful, over others.' Germany has clearly done much to shape a system which, through institutional congruence, then feeds back such 'privilege.'

This is so far a familiar[2] – though not uncontested (cf. Le Gloannec, 2000, pp. 126–131) – argument. Where we want here to take it further is to look beyond the formal operation of the EU and apply it to broader challenges of governance in contemporary Europe, including that of responding to 'globalization,' but in particular that of the opening up the post-communist states to Germany's east and their integration into existing institutions of (west) European cooperation. For all sorts of reasons – moral, security, economic, sheer geographical proximity – Germany has engaged with the states to its east (especially its nearest neighbors in East Central Europe (ECE)) more intensively and across more fields of social and economic interaction than its west European partners. Much of this interaction in and with ECE has been conducted through the formal channels of multilateral organizations, above all NATO and the EU, or of bilateral 'high politics.' Much, though, has not – occurring instead through a vast range of transnational networks focused on exchange of information, expertise, and best practice and/or in developing responses to commonalities of interest.

Thomas Risse led an important project in the early 1990s – *Bringing Transnational Relations Back In* (Risse-Kappen, 1995a) – which sought to get to a better understanding of the impact of such transnational networks in shaping inter-state relations. He identified two key variables. The first concerned 'domestic structures,' with influential transnational networks likely to be built out of countries where the state is institutionally fragmented and ranged alongside a well-organized civil society. Second, transnational networks were likely to exert higher levels of influence in fields which exhibited a high degree of international institutionalization. In these circumstances, state boundaries become 'more permeable' 'for transnational activities' (Risse-Kappen 1995b, pp. 6–7).

These two variables have immediate relevance to Germany and its 'regional milieu' in Europe. Europe – west and now east – has by some way the most strongly institutionalized frameworks for inter-state interaction in the world, including the EU, NATO, countless other multilateral and bilateral international bodies, and a shared adherence to the structures and processes of the market economy. Germany's international engagement in Europe has been remarkable for its high degree of institutional pluralism: the foreign policy-making apparatus of central government is fragmented and, comparatively speaking, poorly coordinated, leaving high degrees of leeway for particular ministries to pursue 'house' policies in Europe (Bulmer, Maurer, and Paterson, 2001, pp. 186–197). Other state or statutory actors also play a prominent external role, including the Länder, the Bundesbank, or the political foundations. And the German private sector – business, unions, other interest groups – is also highly active in transnational partnership-building. All these actors maintain intensive transnational relations across the highly permeable state boundaries of contemporary Europe.

Such transnational relationships also provide channels for German actors to make an active contribution to the replication of German institutional forms, in both the 'hard' sense of binding legal frameworks, but also in a 'softer' ideational sense as the norms propagated by German actors diffuse into *shared*, transnational understandings. As Dorota Dakowska and Elsa Tulmets suggest in chapter 3 in this volume, borrowing from Radaelli, institutional replication may be about rules, but it can also be about the 'export of ideas,' the 'soft' 'transfer of styles, ways of doing [things], beliefs, and norms (p. 72).'[3]

Examples include: the promotion of the German language through the institutions of 'foreign cultural policy'; the political education and influencing activities of the (party)-political foundations; the mass of activities undertaken or sponsored by German state actors – national ministries, the Länder, even some local governments – in interaction with partners outside Germany; and the activities of the private sector in providing 'meshing' between societies and acting as a conduit for the exchange and propagation of 'German' ideas on the market economy and corporate governance. The net effect of all this appears extremely significant when seen in terms of institutional 'power' or 'export' and its counterpart, 'systemic empowerment.' Myriad aspects of Germany's institutional, regulatory, and normative structures are being propagated largely outside of the decision-making arenas where Germany formally interacts with its European partners. The implication we have hypothesised from this – particularly in the context of the opening up of the former communist states to Germany's east – is that institutional penetration stands to 'pay back' asymmetrically in Germany's favour. As Christoph Jessen (1999, p. 168), a senior foreign ministry official, put it in the context of EU enlargement:

> Germany . . . profits ... from the extension of the familiar environment in which common norms, *most of which have been decisively shaped by Germany*, come to be applied. Any adaptation costs arising from this fall to member states which are less strongly able to shape these norms. *In this way benefits accrue to Germany which are numerically scarcely verifiable but nevertheless considerable.*[4]

Two qualifications need to be entered at this point, which should dispel any notion that we are proposing that Germany is embarked on some kind of hegemonic project designed to increase its power at the expense of others. The first concerns the very character of transnational *networks*. These are by definition groups of actors which come together out of shared interest and for mutual gain, and are not (normally) under the control of any one of the actors involved. If they provide channels for institutional replication, then those channels should not be understood as a one-way-street in which German actors propose something and others adopt it. Turning again to the opening up of the east, examples abound of how ECE actors have established *on their own account* institutional patterns – corporate and banking systems, central banking structures, electoral systems, legal and constitutional structures – directly or indirectly drawn from German models, and in most cases facilitated by some transnational network or other (Katzenstein, 1997b, p. 25). To the extent that this is the case, Germany is a *passive* force, a model to be emulated, a resource to be drawn on. To put it another way, transnational interaction produces opportunities also for institutional '*import*.' Such 'imports' may result in institutional congruence and with it systemic empowerment, but this is an empowerment created by the beliefs and decisions of others, not of German actors.

The second qualification, and the one illustrated most directly in the remainder of this chapter, concerns the institutional pluralism of German European policy actors. The notion of 'institutional pluralism' is by no means new, and has pervaded work on Germany's role in EU decision-making in particular. The combination of Ressortprinzip (ministerial autonomy), weak EU policy coordination structures, and non-central government actors like the Bundesbank and the Länder has always meant that hegemonic projects have never been possible for Germany. German EU policy – even in the high politics of treaty-making and summitry – has often been a messy and illogical compromise brokered by federal government actors. There is an important distinction to register here, though, between this kind of formalized, 'high' politics of European integration and the way transnational networks work. The activities of transnational networks, and of the German actors which belong to them (even, at times, those including federal government actors), are not subject to brokerage. Transnational networking exploits the permeability of the contemporary European state – and the institutional fragmentation of German policy-making – to transcend traditional (national or supranational) boundaries of authority; networks in other words largely 'do their own thing.' Outcomes from this may well be messy and illogical, too, but it is a messiness resulting from largely autonomous processes of interaction across (and within) national and supranational structures.

If, therefore, a Europe is being re-shaped 'in Germany's image,' then this is so as a result of highly complex and disorderly processes of institutional replication – whether exported or imported, whether effected through private or public sector channels. If Germany is reshaping Europe through transnational networks, then it is doing so in a disconnected way, as a result of a cacophony of in principle unrelated actions and decisions. There is no single 'German model' in play here, but a multiplicity of different – and, conceivably, competing – German models. This pluralism has important implications for a question raised by Risse in his study of transnational relations and reiterated by Anne-Marie Le Gloannec in her introduction to this volume: what is the impact of transnational relations on state policies and international relations (Risse-Kappen 1995b: 4)? What is the significance for the German state of the activities of German actors in transnational networks? Do they help or hinder? Do they in reality add to German power in the way that hypotheses about 'virtuous circles' of institutional replication and systemic empowerment might suggest (Le Gloannec 2000)? Le Gloannec (2001, p. 128) is skeptical: 'the question of how connections and contacts, the propagation of norms and rules, and institutional transfer and adaptation translate into political power – if they do – still begs explanation.' The remainder of this chapter seeks to offer a contribution to that explanation by turning to one of the louder voices in the cacophony of German transnational engagement: Bavaria.

Bavaria and the reshaping of Europe

Why choose Bavaria, among all the other voices? One reason concerns the consistency and durability of the Bavarian Land government's attempts to shape wider European integration agendas since the early 1990s. Bavarian agenda-setting is intimately associated with Edmund Stoiber, Minister-President from 1993 till 2005. Stoiber announced his EU policy presence in a remarkable interview with the leading Bavarian newspaper, the *Süddeutsche Zeitung*, in November 1993. In the interview Stoiber condemned the vision of European integration represented by the then Chancellor, Helmut Kohl, as 'outdated.' He openly rejected the received wisdom of moving inexorably towards a 'European statehood' on the grounds that it threatened to 'blur and erode' German – and, indeed, Bavarian – sovereignty (*Süddeutsche Zeitung*, November 11, 1993). This initial clarion call has since been fleshed out into a broader agenda for change whose roots are part-ideological and part-pragmatic. Bavaria has Germany's strongest regional identity, based on a history of separate statehood, a resonant tradition of political Catholicism, and a ruralist nostalgia which persists even in the context of one of the EU's highest-tech (and wealthiest) economies. Ideologically, there is a concern to protect this identity as a fixed reference point in a changing European order, and more pragmatically there is a concern to prevent Bavaria's wealth from leaking out to subsidize other parts of the EU, present and future. The result is a distinctive agenda of autonomy-driven regional protectionism which sits happily (if a little illogically!) alongside a commitment to fighting Bavaria's corner in the global economy.

A second reason for the focus on Bavaria concerns the 'reach' of its voice. Few subcentral actors have a political resonance taken note of by central-state actors in other states. Bavaria is one, reflecting the strong investment it has made in establishing an administrative infrastructure capable of projecting European policy concerns beyond the German political arena. This investment means that its views are widely heard. Bavarian positions on the Structural Funds, the Common Agricultural Policy (CAP), Agenda 2000 (Jeffery, 1998), EMU (Proudfoot, 1997), and successive IGCs (Jeffery, 1995; Bulmer, Jeffery, and Paterson, 2000: pp. 76–91; Jeffery and Hyde-Price, 2001) – have been well publicised. In this way an alternative view (not necessarily shared by other German actors) of how member states *should* engage with the EU has been fed into wider European debates and has had some impact on the EU's formal decision-making processes.[5] Less formally, and perhaps more subtly, transnational networks have provided alternative routes for getting similar and related messages across – and in finding allies with shared interests to add weight to the pursuit of Bavarian goals. The discussion now explores three examples of transnational networking where Bavaria has sought to externalize its own, particular solutions to questions of contemporary governance in Europe. These concern globalization, EU enlargement, and internal security. In each case, attention will be given to the aims underlying the transnational activity and how – and whether – transnational networking helps to realize those aims.

'California man': globalization and the innovative regional economy

Probably the core agenda Bavaria pursues in both domestic and EU politics concerns the need for greater regional autonomy and self-responsibility. This is justified in part at least in terms of the challenges of globalization. In order to compete in an economic environment where production and markets increasingly operate transnationally, the imperative is to maintain competitiveness through innovation and flexible responses to technological change. Innovation and flexibility for Bavaria, are, though, hampered by intervention and regulation, either within the nation-state (e.g. the German fiscal equalization system) or supranationally (e.g. an over-interventionist Commission, in particular in the field of competition policy). A lighter interventionist touch and greater incentives for meeting the challenges of globalization and technological change 'on one's own responsibility' are the prescription.[6] A model example, despite the shackles imposed by German federalism and the EU Commission, is Bavaria, which has successfully harnessed the challenges of the globalizing economy by developing modern, high-tech, future-oriented industries.

This vision of regional autonomy unshackling economic dynamism as the right response to globalization and as a precondition for economic success is one which has been propagated by the Bavarian government through a range of initiatives in transnational cooperation with other 'high-tech' regions or organizations focused on exchange of ideas, JVs, and the creation of investment opportunities. Though some of these are European – e.g. with Alsace, Scotland, or Salzburg[7] – the main focus is on the US, and in particular the high-tech (and low-intervention) paradise of California. Over the last few years various structures for Bavarian–Californian cooperation have been established: a Bavarian–Californian Technology-Transfer Partnership, Venture-Capital Congresses, a California Office in Munich, and a 'GotoBavaria Office' in California.[8] These initiatives have clearly had important bottom-line results in boosting economic activity and job creation in Bavaria. Arguably, their purpose is just as much, though, in image-making. The rhetoric invested in establishing virtue by association with the 'world-wide brand concept of Silicon Valley'[9] or with 'California, the 'Mecca of high technology''[10] is intensive and persistent. This form of rhetoric pervades wider economic policy thinking. Bavaria does not limit itself to having an 'economic policy,' but has rather a 'High-Tech Offensive'[11] supported variously by 'Software' and 'Media Offensives.' The 'model is Silicon Valley in Bavaria's American partner-State, California':[12] for example, the new Siemens Centre for Medical Technology in Erlangen has established 'a medical valley of global significance';[13] and a Bavarian government investment in materials research in Fürth means that 'North Bavaria has the potential to become the 'Silicon Valley' of materials research.'[14]

The implication of this concerted effort in image-building – and the attempt at institutional replication – is that everyone else could have the great advantages which 'Zukunftsstandort Bayern' ('Bavaria, the economic location of the future') has, if only everyone else pursued a similar agenda focused on rolling back the interventionist instincts of superordinate public authorities and on promoting regional autonomy and the capacity for innovation which comes with it. The mood music of Bavarian–Californian partnership in this sense provides a subtle reinforcement of wider messages about the need for a more 'competitive federalism' in German domestic politics (Große Hüttmann, 2000) and for a decentralizing recalibration of the relationship of the EU to its member states and their subunits. As the former Bavarian European Minister Reinhold Bocklet (2000) put it in a speech on 'Subsidiarity and Federalism as Elements of European Integration' in November 2000:

> After all Europe needs strong regions amid global economic competition. Economically strong regions today form the backbone of Europe as a location for business. Bavaria is therefore arguing for an effective Europe of nations and regions, a Europe which works, whose building blocks are the nations, but which also recognises the role of regions … as a third level, close to the citizen, and which protects and promotes their autonomy.

How direct an impact this mood music has in realizing Bavaria's decentralist agendas is unclear. But more of the German Länder are moving towards the Bavarian position on 'competitive federalism' (Jeffery, 2002, 2005). The Bavarian government has skillfully constructed linkages between wider issues – not least eastern enlargement of the EU – and its narrower concerns on lessening EU competition policy and ratcheting up regional autonomy (Jeffery and Collins, 1998). It also led the way in placing questions of demarcation of competence – i.e above all a reduction of the role of the European Commission – at the heart of the agenda for the European Convention. Stoiber's performance as 'California man' seems likely, at least at the margins, to have increased the potency of the Bavarian message and helped at least create an opportunity to see it carried through.

EU enlargement and the protected regional economy

Despite the attractions of the Californian Mecca of economic dynamism, unfettered exposure to the global economy does, however, have its limits in Bavaria. Bavarian Standortpolitik is a curious mixture of future orientation and traditional solutions (the cliché of laptops and Lederhosen is highly accurate). And where hard Bavarian economic interests are threatened, then they should rightly be subject to old-fashioned protectionism. This is a prescription readily repeated, in particular in respect of agriculture, which has an identity-confirming resonance in Bavaria whose perpetuation requires subsidy, but more generally there is a view that regions should 'have the right to protect jobs through subsidies' (Stoiber's response to the VW subsidy crisis in Saxony in 1996 in *Münchner Merkur*, August 17, 1996).

Support for this kind of protectionism was expressed especially strongly as EU eastern enlargement approached. Bavaria is an eastern Land, bordering on the Czech Republic, and therefore in the front line of the enlargement process. Until the second half of the 1990s, though, eastern enlargement – for Bavaria and for political opinion in Germany more generally – remained an essentially abstract issue, an inherently positive by-product of the end of the Cold War. But as the concrete details and implications of enlargement began to emerge in the later 1990s, it lost its earlier insulation as an abstractly 'good thing.' For those on the front line at least it became understood increasingly as a problem for the border economy in particular. Support for eastern enlargement as a result became hedged with qualifications (and, in particular, demands for protection of cherished interests). Bavaria took up a position at the forefront of this new 'yes, but ...' politics on enlargement:

> The Bavarian European Minister, Kurt Falthauser, declared that Bayern supports eastern enlargement without reservation. '*But*, precisely because our border regions are interested in harmonious integration we have to make sure that border areas do not suffer disadvantage from the enormous gaps which exist *vis-a-vis* the neighbour countries to the east in terms of economic strength, agricultural structures and also in the question of internal security (January 1998).[15]
>
> Bavaria supports the eastern enlargement of the EU as a means of securing enduring peace in Europe. Eastern enlargement also opens up interesting new markets for the Bavarian economy in particular. *But* enlargement has to be organised in an acceptable way for the current member states through a satisfactory calculation of transitional periods. This is a precondition for EU eastern enlargement being accepted by the people (September 1999).[16]

This 'yes, but ...' position was steadily fleshed out with a definitive statement on enlargement issued in March 2000. This set out reservations concerning the free movement of goods, labor, services and capital, competition policy, agricultural free trade, freight movements, social policy, energy, the environment, and internal security. Specific attention was addressed to 'the particular problems of border areas' whose exposure to lower-wage competition, and the effects of differential environmental and social policy standards was especially high, and which as a result faced the danger of capital and production flight. This danger would then be increased to the extent that European structural funding was set to fall in existing member states at the same time as funding flows commenced in the new member states, creating a widening 'subsidy gap.' The Bavarian prescription was a mixture of lengthy transitional periods prior to free movement, continued EU funding for border regions, and a loosening of EU subsidy controls in the border regions.[17]

These were naturally issues which loomed large in other enlargement border regions elsewhere in Germany, but also in Austria and Italy. Bavaria thus sought to reinforce its message by 'organizing' (western) border region opinion in the form of a network of border regions. Alongside bilateral gatherings, two major 'Eastern Regions Conferences' were held in 1998 which culminated in the publication of a widely circulated twenty-point 'Hof Catalog' on EU enlargement in July 1998.[18] The Hof Catalog was a manifesto, written in a heavy Bavarian accent, for lengthy transitional periods prior to free movement, continued EU funding for border regions, and a loosening of EU subsidy controls in the border regions.

The motivation for developing a new set of transnational relationships in this context was straightforward enough. As the then Bavarian European Minister Kurt Falthauser put it at the Hof meeting: 'We will achieve more if we join forces to draw attention to the particular situation of the border regions.'[19] The precise level of achievement of this transnational joining of forces is again difficult to pinpoint. But without a common statement of all EU regions on the enlargement borderline – representing, as Bavaria rarely failed to stress, 34 million people – it seems unlikely that the Nice Summit of December 2000 would have announced that an Action Program for the border regions was to be published. And even though the eventual Action Program was deemed in Bavaria to be an inadequate 'figleaf,'[20] it nonetheless made available 200 million Euro which probably would not have been distributed without Bavaria taking the border region lead.

Cooperation on internal security

The economic dimension of the border region debate was flanked throughout by concerns about the implications of enlargement for internal security. Bavaria has a record as an internal security 'hawk' which interprets the problems and scale of transnational crime ('drugs and thugs,' people-trafficking and bogus asylum-seeking) perhaps as a more fundamental threat to social order than elsewhere in Germany. This is reflected in the maintenance of extensive 'stop-and-search' patrols even on the Schengen border with Austria, undertaken in the belief that Austrian, but in particular Italian, policing of the EU's external border is insufficient to maintain effective controls on transnational crime.

Eastern enlargement – and the prospect of unregulated flows of people under free movement of labor rules – adds to the problem. EU external borders are with Belarus, Russia, and Ukraine following enlargement – and if the Italians are not up to the challenge of effective border policing, then the Czechs, Poles, and Hungarians cannot be expected to be. Transnational networks have again been mobilized in response in two ways. First, internal security issues were a core concern of the network of border regions and their definitive statement in the Hof Catalog. The Hof statement reflected the Bavarian view that free movement of labor is not just a labor market but also an internal security issue and therefore that it cannot be granted until that point when effective crime-fighting standards have been attained and external borders are secure:

> The fight against organised crime is an important concern of people living in the border regions. The border areas are not just a transit regions, but also a field of activity for organised crime ... The border regions are aware of the fact that considerable efforts in combatting organised crime and in the surveillance of external borders still need to be made in many accession countries. (*Hofer 20-Punkte Katalog*, 1998, pp. 11–12)

The second strand of transnational activity – also flagged as a collective priority at Hof (*Hofer 20-Punkte Katalog*, 1998, p. 11) – was to build up cooperation, and exchange of information and expertise, with police forces in the accession states. The Bavarian Interior Ministry has embarked on a quite extraordinary level of networking with police forces/interior ministries in ECE and beyond as a means, quite explicitly, of 'exporting' Bavarian policing standards – or, as a senior Bavarian police officer put it: 'to maintain rigor' amid the internal security challenges of enlargement.[21] The scale of internal security networking is remarkable, including EU-funded activities such as a Bavarian–Hungarian program on 'Efficiency of Border Management' which ran during 2000; bilateral 'Statements of Intent' with the Czech Republic, Hungary, Russia, Ukraine, Slovenia, Slovakia, Croatia, and Bulgaria; 'training support' for ECE states 'with a view to Bavarian internal security standards'; and a multilateral 'Working Group on Police Cooperation with the States of Central and Eastern Europe' which has provided additional opportunities for building relationships.[22] The aim is 'to bring 'multipliers' from different countries to us, who will then pass on what they learn. The 'multiplication' possibilities are considerable: in 1998 there were fifty-five Bavarian–Czech police cooperation events, twenty-nine with Hungary, and substantial numbers also with Poland, Slovakia, the Czech Republic, Latvia, and Lithuania.[23] If the formal statements arising from bilateral meetings between the Bavarian Interior Minister Günther Beckstein and his counterparts elsewhere have any currency, the effect is considerable. For example, Bavarian–Czech security cooperation in 2000:

> includes direct cooperation at border crossings, joint patrols on the 357km-long German–Czech border in Bavaria, active mutual support in preventative operations, intensified exchange of information and the agreement of common approaches on smuggling. Moreover the Czech Republic intends by the start of 2003 to have met all the core Schengen standards which will be the precondition for the removal of border controls. Beckstein welcomed this emphatically given the criminal–geographical proximity of the Czech Republic, 'since it can only have positive effects on the security situation in Bavaria and also of the EU as a whole.'[24]

Conclusions

The precise 'multiplication' effect of internal security networking, though, is difficult to assess. Equally, the specific and direct effects of Bavaria's protectionist border region network or of the mood music surrounding its high-tech partnership with California cannot easily be tied down. It seems unlikely, though, that they are without effect on institutional replication, either in a 'hard' sense (e.g. on policing structures and techniques in countries situated in 'criminal–geographical proximity' to Bavaria), or in establishing normative frameworks which guide action ('we should limit the competition effects of enlargement' and/or 'we should encourage economic innovation and flexibility through enhanced regional autonomy').

The extent to which institutions are replicated by 'export' or 'import' is similarly difficult to tie down without an extensive program of insider research on network relations. In any case, the dividing line between 'export' and 'import' becomes blurred in the light of the incentive structures which Bavarian agendas would seem to set out. Where do the 'terms of trade' lie in calculations such as the following: 'the sooner we establish Bavarian-style border controls, the quicker we can have free movement of labor'; or 'the sooner we raise our environmental standards to German/Bavarian levels, the quicker we will have free movement of goods?'

What is clear, though, is that a genuine capacity exists for actors outside central governments through transnational engagement to shape the parameters within which social interaction takes place in Europe (and beyond). Bavaria is exceptional in a sense because it has the resources and sense of purpose to leave an imprint across a range of fields. But to differing extents, reflecting their resources and interests, other German actors also leave other German imprints and do so without troubling their federal government – or, indeed, European-level bodies – for the authority to do so.

What does this mean for the German state, its power, and the quality of international relations in Europe? Above all, it focuses attention on the institutional pluralism of Germany's European engagement. One hypothesis would be that though Germany has many powerful institutions, Germany's power is likely to be enhanced only if they all pull broadly in the same direction. Or, to put it another way, Bavaria might at the margins be able to propagate its visions for Europe through transnational activity in opposition to mainstream opinion in Germany, but it would be unlikely to get too far. Some support for this view emerges from the case studies explored above. A more decentralist vision for the EU and a tougher line on internal security have emerged as more broadly German views in the last few years (in part because Bavaria has set agendas and lobbied effectively for their acceptance). In these areas, Bavaria has come some way to meeting its aims. There was less widespread agreement, though, not least among key figures in other Länder,[25] on the level of protection demanded by Bavaria for its border areas. What was for Bavaria a disappointing outcome in the form of the Commission's modest Action Program was perhaps the logical result.

If institutional pluralism provides platforms for competing views, therefore, the collective impact of transnational engagement on and for Germany may not be to enhance German power. As Anne-Marie Le Gloannec (2001, p. 129) put it: 'Is it also not possible that institutional dispersion means incoherence?' But if institutional pluralism is a question of different actors following the same grain – or perhaps of key actors like Bavaria setting out the grains that others follow – then the sheer centrality of Germany to international relations in Europe and the sheer intensity of its transnational networks indeed point to a Europe suffused increasingly by German rules and norms.

Notes

1 This chapter is part of a body of work emerging from a research project on 'Germany and the Reshaping of Europe' in the Economic and Social Research Council's Research Program 'One Europe or Several?' (ref. L213252002). While the chapter is my sole responsibility, it has been much informed by the other colleagues who have made a contribution to the project: Adrian Hyde-Price, Vladimir Handl, Julie Pellegrin, Jonathan Grix, Arthur Hoffmann, Vanda Knowles, Willie Paterson, and Marcin Zaborowski.

2 It is developed most fully in Bulmer, Jeffery, and Paterson (2000), including case studies on the 1996–97 IGC, EMU, and eastern enlargement (chapters 4–6).

3 See Dorota Dakowska and Elsa Tulmets' chapter 3 in this volume.

4 Italics mine.

5 For example, Bavaria played a key role in the German debate about establishing a catalog of competences for the EU and member states which Chancellor Schröder took to the Nice Summit in December 2000 and brought back in the form of the EU's commitment to hold a 'competences' IGC in 2004, which metamorphosed into the European Convention. Since Nice, Bavaria again took the lead in fleshing out what was to be discussed at the Convention and what the German position should be: a careful demarcation of the limits of European competence, including additional competence in some fields like internal security, but most forcefully proposing a rolling back in others like the CAP, structural funding and competition policy. See Jeffery and Hyde-Price (2001); Jeffery and Paterson (2003).

6 Pressemitteilungen der Bayerischen Staatskanzlei, 13. Januar 1998, at www.bayern.de/ Politik/Pressemitteilungen, accessed on November 4, 1999.

7 Pressemitteilungen der Bayerischen Staatskanzlei, 6. Oktober 1997, 5. Oktober 1999, 25.Februar 2000, at www.bayern.de/Politik/Pressemitteilungen, accessed on November 4, 1999 and August 3, 2001.

8 Pressemitteilungen der Bayerischen Staatskanzlei, 28. Januar 1998, 16. März 1999, 12. April 2001, at www.bayern.de/Politik/Pressemitteilungen, accessed on November 4, 1999 and August 3, 2001.

9 Pressemitteilungen der Bayerischen Staatskanzlei, 28. Januar 1998, at www.bayern.de/ Politik/Pressemitteilungen, accessed on November 4, 1999.

10 Pressemitteilungen der Bayerischen Staatskanzlei, 2. Februar 2000, at www. bayern.de/Politik/Pressemitteilungen, accessed on August 3, 2001.

11 Pressemitteilungen der Bayerischen Staatskanzlei, 12. Oktober 1999, at www.bayern.de/Politik/Pressemitteilungen, accessed on November 4, 1999.

12 *Ibid.*

13 Pressemitteilungen der Bayerischen Staatskanzlei, 14. Februar 2000, at www.bayern.de/ Politik/Pressemitteilungen, accessed on August 3, 2001.

14 Pressemitteilungen der Bayerischen Staatskanzlei, 26. Juli 2001, at www.bayern.de/ Politik/Pressemitteilungen, accessed on August 3, 2001.

15 Pressemitteilungen der Bayerischen Staatskanzlei, 29. Januar 1998, at www. bayern.de/Politik/Pressemitteilungen, accessed on November 4, 1999.

16 Pressemitteilungen der Bayerischen Staatskanzlei, 28. September 1999, at www. bayern.de/Politik/Pressemitteilungen, accessed on November 4, 1999.

17 'EU-Osterweiterung. Forderungen Bayerns – Stand: 14. März 2000,' at www. bayern.de/Europa, accessed on August 1, 2001.

18 Pressemitteilungen der Bayerischen Staatskanzlei, 19. Januar 1998, 29. Januar 1998, 25. Juli 1998, at www.bayern.de/Politik/Pressemitteilungen, accessed on November 4, 1999; *Hofer 20-PunkteKatalog* (1998).

19 Pressemitteilungen der Bayerischen Staatskanzlei, 25. Juli 1998, at www.bayern.de/ Politik/Pressemitteilungen, accessed on November 4, 1999.

20 Pressemitteilungen der Bayerischen Staatskanzlei, 24. Juli 2001, 25. Juli 2001, at www.bayern.de/Politik/Pressemitteilungen, accessed on August 1, 2001.

21 Confidential interview with an senior official of the Bavarian Interior Ministry, August 12, 1999.

22 *Ibid.*

23 *Ibid.*

24 Bayerisches Innenministerium PM 580/2000, 6. November 2000, at www.innenministerium.bayern.de/presse, accessed on August 3, 2001.

25 Confidential interview with an official of the Brandenburg Land government, May 17, 1999.

Bibliography

Anderson, Jeffrey J. and John B. Goodman (1993) 'Mars or Minerva? A united Germany in a post-Cold War Europe,' in Robert O. Keohane, Joseph S. Nye, and Stanley Hoffmann (eds), *After the Cold War: International Institutions and State Strategies in Europe, 1989–1991*, Cambridge. MA: Harvard University Press.

Banchoff, Thomas (1999) *The German Problem Transformed*, Ann Arbor: University of Michigan Press.

Bocklet, Reinhold (2000) 'Subsidiarität und Föderalismus als Elemente der europäischen Integration,' Vortrag am 6. November 2000, at www.bayern.de/Presse-Info/Reden, accessed on August 1, 2001.

Bulmer, Simon (1997) 'Shaping the rules: the constitutive politics of the European Union and German power,' in P. Katzenstein (ed.), *Tamed Power: Germany in Europe*, Ithaca. NY: Cornell University Press.

Bulmer, Simon, Charlie Jeffery, and William E. Paterson (2000) *Germany's European Diplomacy*, Manchester: Manchester University Press.

Bulmer, Simon, Andreas Maurer, and William E. Paterson (2001) 'The European policy-making machinery in the Berlin Republic: hindrance or handmaiden?,' *German Politics*, 10.

German Politics, Vol. 10/3 (2001), Special Issue on *New Europe, New Germany, Old Foreign Policy? German Foreign Policy Since Unification*, Douglas Webber (ed.).

German Politics (2005), Special Issue 14 (3) on *From Modell Deutschland to Model Europa: Europe in Germany and Germany in Europe*, Mitchell P. Smith (ed.).

Grosse Hüttmann, Martin (2000) „Die föderale Staatsform in der Krise?,' in Hans-Georg Wehling (ed.), *Die deutschen Länder: Geschichte, Politik, Wirtschaft*, Opladen: Leske & Budrich.

Harnisch, Sebastian and Hanns Maull (eds) (2001) *Germany as a Civilian Power*, Manchester: Manchester University Press.

Hofer 20-Punkte Katalog (1998) *Hofer 20-Punkte Katalog zur EU-Erweiterung. Entschliessung der 2. Konferenz der EU-Grenzregionen am 24.-25. Juli 1998 in Hof,* Munich: Bayerische Staatskanzlei.

Hyde-Price, Adrian (2000) *Germany and European Order,* Manchester: Manchester University Press.

Jeffery, Charlie (1996) 'The German Länder and the 1996 Intergovernmental Conference,' *Regional and Federal Studies,* 5.

Jeffery, Charlie (1998) 'Les Länder allemands et l'Europe: intérêts: stratégies et influence dans les politiques communautaires,' in Emmanuel Négrier and Bernard Jouve (eds), *Qui Gouvernent les Régions d'Europe?,* Paris: L'Harmattan.

Jeffery, Charlie (2002) 'German federalism from cooperation to competition,' in Maiken Umbach (ed.), *German Federalism Past, Present and Future,* London: Palgrave.

Jeffery, Charlie (2005) 'Federalism: the new territorialism,' in Simon Green and William E. Paterson (eds), *Governance in Contemporary Germany,* Cambridge: Cambridge University Press.

Jeffery, Charlie and Stephen Collins (1998) 'The German Länder and EU enlargement: between apple pie and issue linkage,' *German Politics,* 7, pp. 86–101.

Jeffery, Charlie and Adrian Hyde-Price (2001) 'Germany in the European Union: constructing normality,' *Journal of Common Market Studies,* 39.

Jeffery, Charlie and William E. Paterson (2000) 'Germany's power in Europe,' *One Europe or Several? The Birmingham Discussion Papers,* ESRC-IGS2000/10.

Jeffery, Charlie and William E. Paterson (2003) 'Germany and European integration: a shifting of tectonic plates,' *West European Politics,* 26.

Jessen, Christoph (1999) 'Agenda 2000: Das Reformpaket von Berlin, ein Erfolg für Gesamteuropa,' *Integration,* 22.

Katzenstein, Peter (ed.) (1997a) *Tamed Power: Germany in Europe,* Ithaca, NY: Cornell University Press .

Katzenstein, Peter (1997b) 'Germany and Mitteleuropa,' in P. Katzenstein (ed.), *Mitteleuropa: Between Europe and Germany,* Oxford: Berghahn.

Le Gloannec, Anne-Marie (2000) 'Projektbeschreibung,' unpublished paper.

Le Gloannec, Anne-Marie (2001) 'Germany's power and the weakening of states in a globalised world: deconstructing a paradox,' in *German Politics,* 10.

Markovits, Andrei S. and Simon Reich (1997) *The German Predicament: Memory and Power in the New Europe,* Ithaca, NY: Cornell University Press.

Proudfoot, Neill (1997) 'Europeanisation and the new regionalism and the case of Bavaria,' M.Phil dissertation, Cambridge.

Risse-Kappen, Thomas (ed.) (1995a) *Bringing Transnational Relations Back In: Non-State Actors, Domestic Structures and International Institutions,* Cambridge: Cambridge University Press.

Risse-Kappen, Thomas (1995b) 'Bringing transnational relations back in: introduction,' in Thomas Risse-Kappen (ed.), *Bringing Transnational Relations Back In: Non-State Actors, Domestic Structures and International Institutions,* Cambridge: Cambridge University Press.

Rittberger, Volker (ed.) (2001) *German Foreign Policy since Unification,* Manchester: Manchester University Press.

Wolfers, Arnold (1962) *Discord and Collaboration,* Baltimore, MD: Johns Hopkins University Press.

Sabine Saurugger

7

The German nuclear industry and Eastern Europe: the consequences of a paradigm change for state/non-state actors' relationships

The accident which took place at the Chernobyl nuclear power plant in April 1986 was the first event in a long series which showed that the conditions of nuclear power plants in CEE, as well as in the Commonwealth of Independent States (CIS) were a case for concern. Among a considerable number of organizations, governments, and enterprises which attempted to bring these plants up to international safety standards and practices were, prominently, German actors. An analysis of the activities of these actors shows the interaction of state and non-state actors, in this case German utilities[1] and nuclear industries, and underlines that domestic structures of the state as well as the opportunity structures of the EU mediate the policy influence of these non-state actors.

In taking up the question of the interaction between non-state actors and the state rather than focusing on the activities of non-state actors alone, as do pluralist approaches,[2] this chapter will concentrate on the question of whether non-state actors support their 'state' in its international commitments – or, on the contrary, whether they prevent it from doing so. I argue that the answer to this question lies in the relationship that links non-state actors to state actors: if the relationship is characterized by frequent interaction, high cohesion, and shared ideology, non-state actors frequently figure as experts in their specific policy field and thus influence state actors' views on a national and international level. If this relationship deteriorates, non-state actors will seek to strengthen their transnational ties in order to achieve representation of their interests on a transnational level and thus possibly to oppose the interests of governmental actors in a specific policy field.

This chapter explores the variables that lead to the construction and the changes in the relationship between non-state and state actors, as well as the consequences of these changes for the relationship between these actors and the state, by studying the case of German nuclear industries' activities in the field of nuclear safety in Eastern Europe.[3] The decision taken by the new German government in 1998 to abandon the production of nuclear energy in the near future led to a reinforced cooperation among nuclear industries on the European level. The reinforcement was particularly visible in a field where nuclear industries have economic as well as ideological interests: nuclear safety in CEE and in the CIS. The opportunity structure at the European level, produced by the politics of the European Commission services, can be considered a central variable in this process.

The central factor explaining the change in the relationship between non-state actors and state actors is paradigm change in governmental policy. A 'policy paradigm' is defined as the abstract principles, ideas, and perceptions, which define what is possible and feasible in a given society (Kuhn, 1983; Hall, 1993).

This chapter will be divided into three parts. In the first part I shall discuss the representation of German interests in the nuclear field on both the national and the European level. These relationships will be outlined with regard to activities in the field of nuclear safety in Eastern Europe. In the second part, concentrating on the situation in the policy field in the late 1980s and early 1990s, the relationship between German nuclear industries and the German political authorities will be discussed. The German government's and industries' activities in the field of nuclear safety in Eastern Europe will be analyzed in the light of the incremental paradigm change which took place in the field of German nuclear policies. The third part analyzes the Red–Green government's decision to stop the production of nuclear power, and the influence of this decision on the relationship between the German nuclear industry and the political authorities on both the national and the European level.

The nuclear networks at the German and European level

German nuclear energy networks[4]

The relationship between public authorities and industry in Germany is rather consultative in character. Consensus-building is the predominant approach, reflecting the structural features of the German political system, whereby bureaucratic fragmentation, ministerial autonomy, and coalition governments makes interministerial coordination more difficult (Kohler-Koch, 1993). In adding the federal structure of Germany to these factors they contribute to a dispersal of political power, making Germany a 'semi-sovereign state' (Katzenstein, 1987). This includes certain advantages for the government, since by establishing a policy community government can depoliticize a policy area which is thus less likely to be politically dangerous. Furthermore, it makes policy-making predictable and therefore does not present the government with new problems (Hodgwood, 1987). With a policy community, the government agencies know the groups likely to be involved, the demands they will make, and the potential solutions that exist. 'Based on a limited constellation of interests with restricted membership, the communities routinize relationships by incorporating the major interests into a 'closed world.' Policy communities are a means of creating stability and hence they institutionalize the existing distribution of power' (Rhodes, 1988, p. 390).

In the field of nuclear energy, the policy networks have been developed since the 1950s. These networks include the electricity supply industry, the nuclear construction industry, scientific agencies, and the political–administrative system. Contrary to France, where civil nuclear policy was mainly located within governmental agencies since the policy field sprang directly from military technology, private industry played a major role in the development of nuclear policy in Germany. As in the US, it was the nuclear construction industry which monopolized 'nuclear professionalism.' This led to a situation whereby political and administrative actors were very much dependent on the expertise from the nuclear industry to develop a German nuclear policy (Kitschelt, 1980; Radkau, 1983; Lucas, 1985; Müller, 1990). The major utilities were not interested in nuclear power until the end of the 1960s, when they became committed to the nuclear option (Rüdig, 1987; Krug, 1998).[5] Nuclear power principally concerned the major German utility providers, in particular the Rheinisch-Westfälische Elektrizitätswerke (RWE), Bayernwerk, and Preussenelektra, a situation which has not changed until today. For this reason the present chapter will concentrate on the main players in the field. This concerns in the electricity supply industry, as stated, RWE-Energie, Preussenelektra and Bayernwerk,[6] in the nuclear construction industry Siemens KWU (Siemens Power Generation Group), and in the field of scientific agencies the Gesellschaft für Anlagen und Reaktorsicherheit (GRS).

In the context of an existing policy community non-state actors' access to the administration is easy, particularly when there exist long-standing relations and a recognition of common basic principles and rules governing issue areas. Since the creation of the Bundesministerium für Atomfragen (German Federal Ministry of Nuclear Questions) in 1955, the development of nuclear power in Germany has taken place under an agreement reached by the main political parties and trade unions, as well as the scientific community. The networks established in this field were strongly affected by the interests and capabilities of the state institutions. Smith states that: 'If state actors have an interest in a specific policy, they will build a relationship with a group that will provide the capabilities for developing this policy' (Smith, 1993, p. 48).

Further to the relationship that companies and political–administrative actors established, companies, research institutes, and other associations interested in the development of nuclear power joined together to form an association. In 1959, four associations representing the interests of the German nuclear industry founded the Deutsche Atomforum (German Nuclear Forum). The divergence among competing interests in the Forum, which enlarged its membership to nuclear energy utilities in the 1960s, has led to a situation whereby individual firms usually establish ad hoc fora to represent their interests *vis-à-vis* the government and administration, as the present chapter will analyze at a later stage.

In the field of nuclear policy, the cohesion of this cooperation was strong until the mid- 1970s, when the first environmentalist opposition movements began to oppose nuclear power in Germany (Hatch, 1986, 1991). Despite the growing anti-nuclear protest movement, the federal government reaffirmed its commitment to nuclear power, due to the continuing level of instability in the Middle East and the fear of a new oil crisis at the beginning of the 1980s. Advisory committees were established, consisting of high governmental officials from the Ministries of the Interior, Economics, Research, and Technology; executives from the major utilities; reactor manufacturers; and scientific experts. Nuclear orders continued to be placed into the early 1980s, notably by the largest utility, RWE, which permitted a constant development of nuclear policy and power in Germany.

At the European level, the relationship between the nuclear industry and European institutions was of a different nature. In 1960, a European forum of nuclear industries, utilities and scientific organizations was founded. The Forum atomique européen (FORATOM) is an umbrella association of national associations and had very little influence on nuclear questions until the beginning of the 1990s. This was due to the fact that civil nuclear power questions were in the hands of the member states of the European Community.[7] European institutions have very little powers in this field: the European Council decides on development and research programs, the European Commission has a limited role to play in the field of radiation safety.[8] Unipede and Eurelectric, two electricity utilities associations founded at the European level with individual firm membership, both contained working groups on nuclear energy. It is interesting to note that these working groups did not address the question of nuclear safety or energy in Eastern Europe until 1998, however urgent the problem seemed to be.

A particular situation in CEE and the NIS

After the fall of the Berlin Wall, the worrying condition of nuclear power plants in Eastern Europe became known. Given this situation, which deteriorated even more after a serious accident at the Kozloduy power station in Bulgaria in 1991, European, international, and governmental institutions were invited to react (Saurugger, 2003b). The decision to transfer the management of the financial programs supporting economic, democratic, and societal reforms in CEE and the NIS to the European Community – and, more precisely, to the European Commission, had already been taken by the governments of the G-7 during its Paris Summit in 1989.[9] In 1990, the governments of the EC member states requested that the Commission take appropriate measures to improve the nuclear safety of CEE power plants. The Commission mainly used the PHARE and TACIS programs in order to support industrial projects and to assure the interdependence of the nuclear safety authorities. In its need to build these programs from scratch, the Commission depended on external expertise and created a number of loose issue-based networks with European utilities, industries, and nuclear safety institutions.

But the situation was not only relevant on the European level. German operators of nuclear power plants, and the nuclear industry as a whole, were confronted with a crisis of domestic legitimacy after the Chernobyl accident. Chernobyl was the spark for an impressive protest movement. The consequences were seen four years later, when the German operators decided not to modernize the Eastern German reactors in Greifswald and Stendal that had been built according to the Soviet model; the financial cost was considered too high by both the German federal government and the nuclear industry Siemens KWU (Boehmer-Christiansen, 1992). The nuclear power plant in Greifswald was decommissioned and the construction of the reactor in Stendal was brought to an end. The critical situation in Eastern Europe increased the awareness of nuclear operators and industries even more. Siemens, Bayernwerk, and RWE had numerous contacts with the respective administrations in the three relevant ministries: Interior, Economy and Environment, and Nuclear Safety regarding the subject of nuclear safety and nuclear energy in Eastern Europe, and urged them to put the problem on the European agenda.[10]

In its need for competent expertise, the European Commission invited the operators of nuclear power plants to establish the first consortium in 1990. The Twinning Program Engineering Group (TPEG) counted among its members the French electricity producer Electricité de France (EDF), the German RWE, the Belgian and Italian firms TRACTEBEL and ENEL, as well as Spanish, British, and Swedish operators. TPEG played a very important role in the programming of projects. In the sectors of nuclear waste treatment and nuclear fuel, two other consortia were created, followed by others[11] such as the Concertation on European Regulatory Tasks (CONCERT) established in March 1991, which includes the European Nuclear Safety Authorities, the Regulatory Assistance Management Group (RAMG), and the Technical Safety Organization Group (TSOG).

The creation of consortia is in keeping with the objective that encourages operators of Western European nuclear power plants to cooperate rather than to compete in Eastern European markets. This strategy was very much accepted on the national level. The German Minister of Finance warned the nuclear industry not to compete in this market: 'If there is once again a similar catastrophe to that of Chernobyl, nuclear energy will have no more place in Europe and this would have terrible consequences for the European nuclear industry.'[12]

German utilities and nuclear industries were thus present at the European level, by invitation of the European Commission, to participate in the elaboration of different nuclear safety programs. The expertise that these actors could offer was very much appreciated. Nevertheless, the need for this expertise merely led to the creation of very open issue-based networks, with low cohesion. These consortia did, however, allow the firms to be taken seriously and to rebuild their legitimacy in a sector which is in crisis in Western Europe.

The German actors in this field participated in the two associations on the European level, already mentioned: FORATOM and Unipede/Eurelectric. Despite this participation, the issue of CEE nuclear safety was not addressed, and German utilities and nuclear industries preferred to deal with the German or European administrations individually.

Incremental change of policy paradigm and its influence on German nuclear industry representation

A modification of the policy paradigm in the field of nuclear power was clearly visible in Germany after the Chernobyl accident in April 1986.[13] As a result, the SPD in opposition moved quickly to contribute to the debate on the exit strategy for nuclear energy. Elaborating on the decisions taken at the Essener Bundesparteitag of 1984, the SPD decided in August 1986 that, once in power, the German government would abandon nuclear energy in ten years' time.[14] In order to show its support for a more environmentally safe nuclear energy policy, the CDU government created a new Ministry for the Environment and Reactor Safety (BMU). At the same time, the CDU leadership reaffirmed its unwavering support for nuclear power. Despite these affirmations, the option of an exit from nuclear power began to make headway at the grass roots level in the CDU (Hatch 1991, p. 89), without taking the same form of opposition as in the SPD or among Green party activists. One might thus talk about an incremental policy change that took place in the field of nuclear energy policy in Germany from 1986 to 1998. An 'incremental policy change' is a slow change in actors' ideas and perceptions regarding a particular policy field. Peter Hall speaks of first-, second- and third-order changes, whereby first- and second-order changes apply essentially to the modifications of public action's instruments and methods (Hall, 1993). They are seen as improvements in public policy in order to achieve precise objectives. A paradigm breaks down when facts fail to sustain its central propositions. It seems that when faced with new challenges which are not fully comprehensible within the terms of the existing paradigm, policy-makers begin searching for alternative explanations and turn to new sources of advice. However, a paradigm change is not necessarily definitive at first. Over time, supporters of the new paradigm become entrenched in bureaucratic structures and alter standard operating procedures to reflect their ideas. These paradigm changes lead, as we shall see, to a modification of relationships between non-state actors and political and administrative actors.

In the case of the German nuclear industry representation, this was seen in the dissolution of a tightly knit policy community and its reformulation along new lines.[15] Two case studies illustrate the incremental policy change taking place in Germany in a specific context: the German activities regarding the modernization and construction of the nuclear power plants at Mochovce in the Slovak Republic and at Kozloduy in Bulgaria.

The construction of the Mochovce power plant began in 1984, but was suspended in 1991 because of lack of funds. Western experts estimated the cost to complete the plant at 4.5 billion FF (French Francs). In September 1993, with the idea of selling the electricity produced by Mochovce to the West, the French utility provider EDF and Bayernwerk requested a loan from the European Investment Bank (EIB) and the EBRD to finance the completion of the construction of the reactor. For the European Commission as well as for the EBRD, the construction of the Mochovce nuclear reactor was linked to the closing of another Slovakian reactor at Bohunice, that was not considered up to Western nuclear safety standards by the International Atomic Energy Agency (IAEA). Although Slovakia did not make any international commitments to close the two reactors in Bohunice, the Slovakian government adopted a resolution in 1994 which envisaged the closing of the reactors by 2000 at the latest. This, however, was dependent upon the opening of the new reactors in Mochovce. In January 1994, EDF concluded a JV agreement with Slovensky Energeticky Podnik to construct and manage the two Mochovce reactors. The works, which were to be undertaken for the nuclear part of the facilities by the construction companies Framatome (French) and Siemens in the context of the European Consortium Mochovce (EUCOM) consortium, were scheduled to begin in May or June 1995. The first unit was to have been completed by the end of 1997, the second in 1998. Additional expertise would have been provided by RISK-AUDIT (the German Gesellschaft für Reaktorsicherheit – GRS – and the French Institut de protection et de sûreté nucléaire – IPSN). However, on February 16, 1995, despite the support of the German and the French governments for the project, the EP voted to suspend the funding for Mochovce until the safety issues had been resolved. The electricity producer, Bayernwerk, unlike its French partners, wanted to participate in the project only if Western safety criteria were respected and if the EBRD agreed to contribute to the financing of the project. EDF asserted that if the West were to pull out, the reactors would be completed with the assistance of Russian authorities, whose compliance with safety norms would be questionable.[16] Following the refusal of Slovakian officials to meet these conditions, Bayernwerk indeed withdrew,[17] while EDF continued to participate in the project. Given the sensitivity of the nuclear issue, the German government exercised indirect pressure on the nuclear operator, despite the formal independence of the latter from any political influence. Many have raised fears that German producers, prevented from constructing plants in Germany, would delocalize their power production to Eastern Europe. The safety standards of such installations would then come into question.[18] Wishing to avoid domestic and international criticism, the German government as a whole convinced the Bayernwerk executives to abandon the project.[19]

The case of Kozloduy is highly relevant, as it shows how conflicts among different German governmental officials regarding the question of nuclear power made it ever more difficult for German industries to decide on a clear strategy. This underlines the influence of the particular structural features of the

German political system, where bureaucratic fragmentation, ministerial autonomy, and coalition governments make coordination more difficult. The
Kozloduy nuclear power plant consists of six reactors, four of which (1–4) are
operational. According to West European nuclear safety officials, the two
remaining reactors (5–6), which were still under construction, could be mod-
ernised to bring them into line with Western safety standards. In 1991, the
Bulgarian authorities approached the IAEA to request technical assistance. On
the basis of the conclusions of the IAEA experts, the director of the IAEA
demanded the immediate closure of the plant. Following the refusal of Bulgaria
to do so, given its dependence on this source of energy, the World Association of
Nuclear Operators (WANO) decided to undertake the necessary works on the
1–4 reactors in order to ensure the continued, yet limited, functioning of the
plant. Financial assistance was to be provided by the European Commission.
The key actor in WANO is EDF, which supervised the modernization process.
Early on in the project, a consortium between EDF and Siemens was created to
undertake completion of the works. At the European level, the European
Commission continued to pressure the Bulgarian authorities to close the
reactor.[20]

In 1995, however, EDF recalled its experts when an accident in the nuclear
reactor was avoided by the narrowest of margins. The respective reactions of
French and German officials are highly instructive: while the French government, and the Ministry of the Environment, in particular, congratulated EDF
for its efforts to promote nuclear safety at Kozloduy, the German Bundestag, as
well as the EP, called for the closure of the reactor.

The closing of the plant was problematic since both EDF and Siemens considered that the works completed on the four reactors would allow the plant to
continue to operate for a period of time longer than that proposed by the
European Commission. Furthermore, the review of the modernization program
by the nuclear safety organization RISK-AUDIT concluded that the works had
been completed in a satisfactory manner. The German Chancellor Helmut Kohl
supported the functioning of the nuclear power plant during a visit in Bulgaria
in 1998. This was very much influenced by the fact that the only German nuclear
industry, Siemens KWU, led the consortium charged with the modernization of
the nuclear power plant.[21] This support from the highest level of the German
government for the project, initiated during the visit of the German Minister for
Economy in March 1998 in Bulgaria, and for the actions of a German non-state
actor, shows that the German industry can profit from the fragmented nature of
the German political structure if they have sufficient resources to have access to
the highest level of the political hierarchy. It is important to note that the
network existed between high civil servants in the ministries and CDU/CSU
governmental politicians, but not with the delegates in the Bundestag. While the
German parliament asked for an immediate closure of the reactor, the close contacts with the relevant political actors in external commercial affairs – the
executive – benefited the industry. Existing conflicts between the various

government departments and state institutions thus make the problem more political in nature and subject to debate. At the same time, agencies and political actors attempt to attract non-state actors into the arena in order to strengthen their position against other actors and to increase their legitimacy (Smith, 1993, p. 63).

A paradigm change and its consequences

The definite paradigm change with regard to nuclear power in Germany took place in 1998. That same year German nuclear power plants generated 161.7 billion kWh, which represented a decrease compared to 1997 because of reactors being stopped for political reasons. Since 1988, nuclear power has constituted about one-third of the country's overall energy consumption; at the legislative elections on September 27, 1998, the SPD won with 40.9% and installed a coalition government with the Alliance 90/The Greens. Their coalition agreement stated: 'Phasing out the use of nuclear power will be comprehensively and irreversibly regulated by law within this legislative period.'[22] After nearly two years of conflict-laden negotiations, the German nuclear industry and the government came to an agreement in June 2000. The agreement states that nuclear reactors will be shut down after thirty-two years of functioning. This decision makes it clear that a definite paradigm change had taken place in the field of nuclear politics. As a consequence, the policy community created by the utilities, the nuclear industry, and administrative and political actors broke up. Changes in the regulatory environment, state and local government involvement, the financial markets, and public opinion interacted to destroy this tightly controlled policy network (Baumgartner and Jones, 1991).

The main changes took place in the two central ministries that deal with nuclear energy policies: the Ministry of Economy and the Ministry of Environment and Nuclear Safety. However, whereas the new Minister of Economy was a former executive of VEBA, a German electricity utility company of which Preussenelektra was a part, and with whom the nuclear industry as well as the German utilities could hope to continue their collaboration, this was not the case with regard to the new Minister of Environment, Jürgen Trittin. Despite the fact that the new Minister of Economy, Werner Müller, was part of the German government and bound by the coalition declaration to abandon nuclear energy production, the networks between these non-state actors and the administration were not initially much disturbed. The nuclear industry, as well as the main electricity utilities, continued to have access to the administration, and continued to contact more or less the same people.[23] The Minister's positions seemed to be less opposed to nuclear energy than those of his environmental counterpart, Jürgen Trittin. Müller even declared in an interview in 1998: 'No one knows today how we will cover the energy needs in fifty or hundred years if the fossil energy resources like gas or fuel are exhausted. Perhaps, the Greens will then be leading those who demand for the construction of new nuclear power plants . . . No one can contest that the production of nuclear energy does not pollute the air – contrary to . . . coal, gas or fuel.'[24] In the Ministry of Environment, Jürgen Trittin chose another approach. In the early days of the SPD/Greens coalition government, networks continued to exist between high officials and the nuclear industry in their role as experts. Trittin, however, began preparations for amending the Atomic Energy Act, which would effectively abolish nuclear energy in Germany, with two of his closest advisors, State Secretary Baake and Chief of Staff Renneberg, both from the Ministry of Environment in Hesse. This approach lead to an extremely tense atmosphere in the federal ministry. As a consequence, Trittin started to replace high officials, particularly in the field of nuclear safety, an attitude which rather effectively destroyed any existing networks.[25] The Minister of Environment used the same approach at the beginning of his mandate *vis-à-vis* the Reaktorsicherheitskommission (Commission for the Safety of Nuclear Power Plants – RSK) and the Strahlenschutzsicherheitskommission (Commission for Radiation Protection – SSK), which did not include any opponent of nuclear power. In December 1999, Trittin dissolved the two Commissions and appointed different members. In reaction, the Länder governments in Bavaria, Hessen, and Baden-Württemberg appointed their own RSK. Threatened by Trittin's approach, which also included withdrawing certain commitments made with nuclear energy companies,[26] the German nuclear industry turned to the Chancellery to plead its case.[27] Differences between the two ministers led to a number of conflicts over issues related to nuclear power. Supporters of the new paradigm became more and more entrenched in bureaucratic structures, and were able to alter standard operating procedures to reflect their ideas. Established networks – in our case, policy communities – came under fire and were finally dismantled. New networks took their place composed of other actors, which led utilities and constructors in the field of nuclear power to search for support in other administrative sectors, in particular at the Chancellery and the Ministry of Economy.

This also had consequences for the transnational strategies of the industry. With regard to the German nuclear policy in CEE and the CIS, the support of the German government and administration once displayed toward German nuclear industries was at an end. Neither suppliers nor constructors were spared.

This development can be observed in an analysis of the German activities regarding the closure of the Chernobyl nuclear power plant. One of the major nuclear insecurities in the NIS concerns the nuclear power plant in Chernobyl. In 1995, the EU member states agreed to finance the completion of two reactors[28] in Ukraine if the Ukrainian government agreed immediately to close down the last still functioning Chernobyl reactor. The German government agreed to contribute the sum of 900 million DM, which would have been enough for German constructors to get new commissions. The former Minister of Environment, together with high civil servants from his ministry, collaborated very closely with different German companies to develop a concrete project. The new government, however, was extremely skeptical with regard to this agreement. The SPD and Greens in the Bundestag voiced their concerns and decided to oppose the plans for this project. At the same time, the Ukrainian government refused the offer made by the German delegation to finance the construction of gas-powered plants in exchange for ending construction of the two nuclear power plants. The new Chancellor, Gerhard Schröder, was, however, closer to the German industry than some of his colleges would have liked. The debate inside the German government therefore remained open.

A second consequence regarding the international activities of the German nuclear industry is the fact that the German government no longer grants external financial guarantees (Hermesbürgschaften) to companies involved in nuclear safety or power projects in Eastern Europe, companies which need these guarantees for projects abroad. Until 1998, a certain number of projects in the nuclear power and safety field in CEE were made possible only after the awarding of these guarantees. The Minister for Environment has decided that these grants will henceforth no longer be disbursed.[29]

After the dissolution of the policy communities by the ministry, nuclear energy companies lost the possibility to influence the decision-making powers with regard to the siting of nuclear power plants in Eastern Europe. Group/state relations are strongly affected by the interest and capabilities of the state institutions. If political or administrative actors modify their interests or adapt to a new paradigm, non-state actors are constrained to search for other ways to influence policy. The multi-level nature of the European political system offers this possibility.

Our research has shown that the German nuclear industry, while having created relationships with the EU before 1998, reinforced these networks, both in establishing closer cooperation with other European companies and in cooperating in the relevant associations. The issue of nuclear safety in Eastern Europe gained in importance as the enlargement negotiations with the CEE candidate countries started in March 1998. While the nuclear safety standards are not part of the *acquis communautaire*, the body of community legislation the candidates have to transfer in their own political systems, they play a very important political role in the negotiation.[30] The European Commission – and in particular DG IA,[31] the Directorate General responsible for relations with the candidate countries – is very demanding about expertise in the nuclear industry. The German nuclear industry thus had significant opportunities to circumvent their government after the paradigm change in the nuclear field in 1998. The Commission as 'purposeful opportunist' (Cram, 1997, p. 154; Smith 2004) is constantly engaged in attempts to expand the scope of its competences and to get its preferred issues on the policy agenda. As it is the Commission which leads the enlargement negotiations (Saurugger, 2003a), the contact with Commission services is highly relevant for the German industry to represent its interests concerning Eastern Europe. The cooperation with other EU-based nuclear industries reinforces their capacity to influence the agenda set by the Commission (Greenwood and Aspinwall, 1998). Empirical evidence shows that the contacts between the German nuclear industry and DG IA have increased since 1998.[32] CEE, as well as the CIS, is of crucial importance for an industry which has no significant economic prospects in its home country.

Increased activities were also visible in the framework of European associations, Eurelectric, and Foratom. Working groups were established in order to reinforce cooperation between West European nuclear power utilities and industries, in which German industries play a major role. Resources were invested in these working groups[33] in order to reinforce the weight of these associations *vis-à-vis* the European Commission, as well as with member states. In pooling resources, the members of these associations on the one hand gain in expertise, which is central for issues of CEE nuclear policy. This primarily today takes the form of nuclear safety issues. On the other hand, they find their legitimacy reinforced through their membership in these working groups, which is of particular importance for the German nuclear industry. Furthermore, the European Commission prefers to deal with a constituted group of non-state actors, without differentiating between industrial, employers, labor, or civil society groups.[34]

Having earlier analyzed the Commission's attitude at the beginning of its CEE policies, when a number of consortia were created, the hypothesis stating that political and administrative actors are the main incentives in creating policy networks seems to be verified. The cohesion of networks is dependent on two factors: first, the political or administrative actors' need for expertise and the non-state actors' capacity to supply it. The second factor is the need for legitimization with regard to both the political and administrative actors' policies and with the non-state actors' actions in the particular field. These two causal needs do not exist any longer at the German level, but are still partly present at the European level. The fact that the Commission's need for expertise and legitimization is only partial now leads to a situation where the German nuclear industry and utilities cannot create the same form of networks as on the German level.[35]

The main German nuclear power plant constructor, Siemens KWU, chose a third route to circumvent its economically grave situation in the wake of developments in its own country. Siemens KWU and Framatome decided to merge. The joint project for the construction of a new nuclear reactor (European Pressurised Water Reactor – EPR) by Siemens and Framatome prepared the way for the eventual corporate merger, decided in 1999. Thus, Siemens now has the chance to participate in the network Framatome has already established with French political and administrative actors, and it can now hope to increase its legitimacy at both the European and the international levels.

While the new German government expresses suspicion concerning nuclear power in Eastern Europe at the European level,[36] the German industry has reinforced its activities at the European and international levels in order to re-establish networks similar to that which once existed in Germany. This has not yet been realized. However, the time factor is of particular importance when trying to create these networks. Erhard Friedberg's words are of relevance when he speaks of the emergence of relationships of confidence (rapports de confiance) (Friedberg, 1997) in this context.

Conclusion

Do non-state actors support their state in its international commitments or, on the contrary, do they hinder them from doing so? In trying to answer this question, this chapter has suggested that the answer may lie in the relationship that links non-state actors to state actors: if the relationship is characterized by frequent interaction, high cohesion, and shared ideology, non-state actors frequently figure as experts in their specific policy field and thus influence state actors' views at the national and international level. If this relationship deteriorates, non-state actors will search to strengthen their transnational ties in order to achieve representation of their interest at a transnational level and may thus oppose the interests of governmental actors in a specific policy field. This has been shown in analyzing a specific group of non-state actors: the German industry. We have shown in the case of German nuclear policy towards Eastern Europe and the CIS that industry, when confronted with a paradigm change in their country, has sought to create new policy networks at the European and international level. The cohesive relationship, or policy community, which linked the industrial non-state actors to political and administrative agents, was undone by this paradigm change. The position of the German government after 1998 changed with regard to Eastern European nuclear policy issues. Instead of continuing a mutually supportive attitude in this respect, the German government decided to act against German nuclear industry interests. In order to circumvent this situation, the German industry reinforced its European activities.

It thus seems that the initial question should be reformulated. Instead of asking whether non-state actors support their government at the international level – or, conversely, whether they oppose its activities – one must concentrate on the factors which influence attitudes at moment *t* as well as over a longer time period. It is therefore important to analyze the specific institutional contexts.

As this chapter has shown, power structures matter. The overarching structure of any political system – particularly how powers are distributed between different institutions – will set the parameters within which policy networks can operate (Bomberg, 1998, p. 168).

Notes

1 A large number of small and regional German electricity utilities are semi-public enterprises in which public authorities on a community or regional level own parts

of the enterprise (various Stadtwerke). This would make the use of the term 'non-state actors' problematic in the context of this study. However, the three utilities which are at the center of our study, are private enterprises – RWE, Bayernwerk, and Preussenelektra – the last two having since merged into E-ON. They produce nuclear electricity in Germany and have sufficient financial resources to allow them to act independently at the international level.

2 Pluralists, in analyzing the activities of non-state actors (or, more precisely, interest groups) focus on their resources. Truman (1951) suggests that the access the groups have to government depends on the social position of the group, the extent to which it is organized and the skills and organization of the leadership. This, however, does not account for the differences that arise in the state/non-state actors' relationships when resources remain constant.

3 This chapter is based on a hundred semi-directive interviews which were conducted with the relevant political and industrial actors between 1998 and 2000. In this study, the term 'non-state actors' will be applied to industrial companies which play the role of interest groups. Interest groups can be seen as a subgroup of the general term of 'non-state actors.' For the present purposes, 'interest groups' are defined in a broad way as entities which seek to represent the interests of a particular section of society in order to influence policy processes (Jordan and Richardson, 1987; Smith, 1993; Offerlé, 1994)

4 I use the term 'policy network' to describe a relationship between non-state and state actors which may take a variety of forms and require a more nuanced categorization than the strong–weak state or the pluralist–corporatist formulation (Atkinson and Coleman, 1986, p. 66). 'Policy networks' are conceived as a generic term for a continuum of relationships at whose ends can be distinguished policy communities and issue networks. Policy communities are 'networks characterized by the stability of relationships, continuity of a highly restricted membership [and] vertical independence based on shared service delivery responsibilities' (Marsh and Rhodes, 1992, pp. 13–14; Marsh, 1998; Marsh and Smith, 2000). Issue networks, at the other end of the continuum, are much more open, unstable, and include a higher number of participants.

5 Based on a comparative research of American, Canadian, German, French, and British nuclear policies from the 1950s to the 1980s, Rüdig (1987) presents the development from a 'star-like' form of reactor policy networks to a 'triangle network' form. The star-like form of reactor policy networks was composed of four actors, whereby a nuclear energy agency constituted the star's center and had a relationship with three outer actors that were (a) the electricity supply industry, (b) the nuclear construction industry, and (c) the political–administrative system. The triangle, which developed in the 1960s and 1970s, was formed by electricity supply industry, nuclear construction industry, and the political–administrative system.

6 I use the company names as they were before the merger movement which started in 1999, and came into force in 2000. Since June 2000, when the European Commission authorized the merger between VIAG and VEBA, the two electricity groups in which Bayernwerk and Preussenelektra were parts, both electricity producers became parts of the holding company E-ON.

7 I use the term 'European Community' when addressing questions before 1993, and 'EU' when analyzing processes after the ratification of the Maastricht Treaty.

8 Traité instituant la Communauté européenne de l'énergie atomique, Titre II, Chapitre 1, Chapitre II (Elaboration of norms in the field of radiation safety, Article 31).

9 The participating governments transferred the responsibility for the management of financial funds granted in the framework of various bilateral and multilateral

programs in Central Europe. The first program concerned the economic restructuring of the two Central European countries which were the most advanced in their economic transition: Hungary and Poland. The PHARE program was very soon extended to other CEEC. A similar program, the TACIS program, was created for the CIS in 1992.

10 Interview, French Ministry of Foreign Affairs, November 10, 1998.

11 It is important to note that Commission internal competition between different Directorate Generals (DGs) significantly influenced the creation of these consortia. One of our interlocutors from DG XI, responsible for environment and nuclear safety, stated that 'We are in charge of nuclear safety, and not, as is DG XVII [responsible for energy policy], of the promotion of nuclear energy. It is nuclear safety which is in jeopardy in Eastern Europe, but DG XVII does not want to understand.'

12 *Frankfurter Allgemeine Zeitung*, July 8, 1992.

13 For a detailed analysis of the German anti-nuclear movement in this context see Joppke (1990).

14 'Sichere Energieversorgung ohne Atomkraft – Beschluss zur Energiepolitik der SPD, Parteitag in Nürnberg, 25.8–29.8.1986, I, 1,' in *Politik – Informationsdienst der SPD n. 13, September1986.*

15 For an application of this concept see Jordan and Greenaway (1998).

16 Interview, EDF, December 4, 1998.

17 Interview, VIAG/Bayernwerk, February 2, 1999.

18 Interview, RWE, January 27, 1999.

19 During this time, Siemens and Framatome were planning the reactor of the future with Moscow. The idea originated in the G-8 meeting of Energy Ministers on March 30–April 1, 1998 in Moscow. The EPR which was being constructed by Nuclear Power International (NPI), whose common subsidiary was Framatome, and Siemens, was of interest to the Russians who planned to develop their own nuclear industry. In order to test the EPR, it was necessary to build a prototype. This would not be possible in Germany, and difficult even in France. The Russians welcomed the project, but proposed several amendments which run contrary to the Western 'nuclear safety culture.' Negotiations are in progress and Western officials, who keep the Commission, in particular DG XVII (Energy) informed as to the status of the project, do not appear to be willing to compromise on this matter.

20 These negotiations, which took place in the subcommittee created by the Europe Agreements, took on considerable importance following the launching in March 1998 of the pre-accession strategy with Bulgaria. It was agreed that the 1–4 reactors would be shut down once the modernization of reactors 5–6 was completed.

21 The consortium consists of Siemens, Framatome, and the Russian company Atomenergoexport.

22 According to survey results from the Institute for opinion polls, Allensbach (IDF-Umfrage 5151/01, 15.1–21.1.1999), 63% of the German population were in favor of an exit from nuclear energy, 26% were against, and 11% did not have any opinion. Nevertheless, immediate exit seemed to be unrealistic for 70%, whereas 24% desired an immediate stop to nuclear energy. In 2005, however, this radical change was questioned . A high official in the German Ministry of Environment stated that he did not know whether a CDU/CSU government would decide to start constructing new nuclear power plants once again.

23 Interview with RWE, November 5, 1999; Siemens, July 6, 1999 and July 7, 1999; German Ministry of Economy, 11 August, 1999.

24 *Der Spiegel*, 45, 1998; see also *Süddeutsche Zeitung*, February 2, 1999.

25 Interviews with the German Ministry for Environment and Nuclear Safety, November 2, 1999; *Frankfurter Allgemeine Zeitung*, June 30, 1999.

26 Such as a contract the Ministry of Environment concluded with GRS on a study on the safety of pressurized water reactors for 14 million DM.
27 Interview with the German Ministry for Environment and Nuclear Safety, November 2, 1999 and November 4, 1999.
28 Chmelnizki 2 and Rovno 4.
29 Interview in the Ministry of Environment and Nuclear Safety, November 2, 1999.
30 As the frequent veto of the very anti-nuclear Austrian government in the Council with regard to the opening of the negotiations of the energy chapter with the candidate countries possessing working nuclear power plants on their territory shows.
31 I continue to use the term 'DG 1A' instead of 'DG Enlargement,' as the change in appellation took place only in September 1999. My research covers the period from 1989 to 1999.
32 Interviews with DG 1A, April 4, 1999; Siemens, July 12, 1999.
33 Interview, Foratom, June 26, 1999; Eurelectric November 26, 1998. However, this cooperation is at the same time very conflictual as the liberalization of the electricity market in 1997 reinforced competition among European electricity producers. The companies are now in a situation where they have constantly to weigh the profits of cooperation, in the sense that it reinforces their influence in European policies, against the profits of non-cooperation, whereby exchange of information reinforces the information advantage of the competing company.
34 See SEC (92) 2272 Final, *An Open Structured Dialogue between the Commission and Interest Groups.*
35 This was different at the beginning of the Commission's activities in Eastern Europe (see Saurugger, 2003a).
36 Without, however, taking the same anti-nuclear stand as the Austrian government in this field.

Bibliography

Atkinson, Michael and William D. Coleman (1986) 'Strong states and weak states: sectoral policy networks in advanced capitalist economies,' *British Journal of Political Science*, 19.

Baumgartner, Frank and Bryan D. Jones (1991) 'Agenda dynamics and policy subsystems,' *Journal of Politics*, 53 (4), pp. 1044–1074.

Boehmer-Christiansen, S.A. (1992) 'Taken to the cleaners: the fate of the East German energy sector since 1990,' *Environmental Politics*, 1 (2), pp. 196–228.

Bomberg, Elisabeth (1998) 'Issue networks and the environment: explaining European Union environmental policy,' in David Marsh (ed), *Comparing Policy Networks*, Buckingham: Open University Press.

Cram, Laura (1997) *Policy-Making in the EU: Conceptual Lenses and the Integration Process*, London: Routledge.

Friedberg, Erhard (1997) *Le pouvoir et la règle*, Paris: Seuil.

Greenwood, Justin and Mark Aspinwall (1998) *Collective Action in the EU: Interest and the New Politics of Associability*, London: Routledge.

Hall, Peter (1993) 'Policy paradigm, social learning and the state,' *Comparative Politics*, 25 (3) pp. 275–296.

Hatch, Michael T. (1986) *Politics and Nuclear Power: Energy Policy in Western Europe*, Lexington: Kentucky University Press.

Hatch, Michael T. (1991) 'Corporatism, pluralism and post-industrial politics: nuclear energy in West Germany,' *West European Politics*, 14 (1), pp. 73–97.

Hogwoo, B.W. (1987) *From Crisis to Complacency*, Oxford: Oxford University Press.

Joppke, Christian (1990) 'Nuclear power struggles after Chernobyl: the case of West Germany,' *West European Politics*, 13 (2), pp.178–191.

Jordan, Andrew and John Greenaway (1998) 'Shifting agendas, changing regulatory structures and the 'new' politics of environmental pollution: British coastal water policy, 1955–1995,' *Public Administration* 76 (4), pp. 672–673.

Jordan, Andrew and J.J. Richardson (1987) *Government and Pressure Groups in Britain*, Oxford: Clarendon Press.

Katzenstein, Peter J. (1987) *Policy and Politics in West Germany: The Growth of a Semi-Sovereign State*, Philadelphia, PA: Temple University Press.

Kitschelt, Herbert (1980) *Kernenergiepolitik: Arena eines gesellschaftlichen Konfliktes*, Frankfurt: Campus.

Kohler-Koch, Beate (1993) 'Germany: fragmented but strong lobbying,' in M.P.C.M. Van Schendelen (ed.), *National Public and Private EC Lobbying*, Dartmouth: Aldershot, pp. 23–48.

Kuhn, Thomas S. (1983) *Structure des révolutions scientifiques*, Paris: Flammarion.

Krug, Hans-Heinrich (1998) *Siemens und die Kernenergie*, Duisburg: Siemens KWU.

Lucas, Nigel (1985) *West European Energy Policy: A Comparative Study*, Oxford: Clarendon Press.

Marsh, David (ed.) (1998) *Comparing Policy Networks*, Buckingham: Open University Press.

Marsh, David and Rod A.W. Rhodes (eds) (1992) *Policy Networks in British Government*, Oxford: Clarendon Press.

Marsh, David and M. Smith (2000) 'Understanding policy networks: towards a dialectical approach,' *Political Studies*, 48, pp. 4–21.

Müller, Wolfgang D. (1990) *Geschichte der Kernenergie in der Bundesrepublik Deutschland: Anfänge und Weichenstellung*, Stuttgart: Schäffer-Poeschel.

Offerlé, Michel (1994) *Sociologie des groupes d'intérêt*, Paris: Montchrestien.

Radkau, Joachim (1983) *Aufstieg und Krise der deutschen Atomwirtschaft, 1945–75*, Reinbek: Rowohlt.

Rhodes, Rod A.W. (1988) *Beyond Westminster and Whitehall*, London: Unwin Hyman.

Rüdig, Wolfgang (1987) 'Outcomes of nuclear technology policy: do varying political styles make a difference?,' *Journal of Public Policy*, 7 (4), pp. 389–430.

Saurugger, Sabine (2003a) *Européaniser les intérêts? Les groupes d'intérêt économiques et l'élargissement de l'Union européenne*, Paris: L'Harmattan.

Saurugger, Sabine (2003b) 'Governing through networks. Nuclear interest groups and the Eastern enlargement of the European Union,' in Thomas Christiansen and Simona Piattoni (eds), *Informal Networks in the European Union*, Cheltenham: Edward Elgar, pp. 207–225.

SEC (92) 2272 Final (1992) *An Open Structured Dialogue between the Commission and Interest Groups*, Brussels.

Smith, Andy (2004) *Politics and the European Commission: Actors, Interdependence, Legitimacy*, London: Routledge.

Smith, Martin J. (1993) *Pressure, Power and Policy*, Pittsburgh: University of Pittsburgh Press.

Truman, David (1951) *The Governmental Process*, New York: Alfred A. Knopf.

Fabienne Boudier-Bensebaa

8

Non-state actors and transnational relations: the German example

Introduction

A process of economic integration has taken place between Western and Eastern Europe since the opening up of the CEECs in 1989–90. This integration has occurred from both a formal point of view (association and interim agreements, accession of eight CEECs to the EU) and as a *de facto* process via the development of relationships between the two parts of Europe. Germany's influence in the CEE area is long-standing. More specifically, German firms have played a key role in integrating Central European firms into EU corporate structures, by using both external markets (trade) and internal markets (FDI), or by combining the two. Central European enterprises have became increasingly tied into a network of interdependencies with Western European firms, above all German firms. As a result, new regional 'translocal' structures have emerged.

This chapter aims to analyze to what extent German economic presence through trade, FDI, and OPT has been beneficial to growth and development in Central Europe, especially in the three most advanced transition CEECs – i.e. the Czech Republic, Hungary, and Poland. As a result, the second question to be answered in this chapter is what stage of development should be attributed to Central European economies.

The chapter is organized as follows: the next section surveys the theoretical background; the following section stresses the main patterns of the *de facto* integration of Central Europe through German economic presence; the next section aims to assess its effects upon Central Europe's development; and the final section considers whether German firms have implemented a new division of labor in Europe.

Theoretical background: effects of regional integration on the development path of host countries

Integration is a multi-dimensional phenomenon, which means that interactions occur between several fields (economic, political, social, etc.) and at different levels (international, regional, etc.). From an economic point of view, regional integration agreements (RIAs) lead to a reduction of regional trade barriers and investment restrictions. The theory suggests that RIAs generate static effects in the short run through the development of exchanges and investment but also dynamic effects in the long run through various positive externalities (Blomström and Kokko, 1997a). Two main effects can thus be expected from a regional integration process and, more particularly, from the Eastward enlargement of the EU.

Stimulation of intra-regional trade and investment, and access to larger markets

For the integrated country, accession to the EU means access to the Single European Market but also access to international markets in general through the insertion of local firms in MNE networks; consequently, it leads to a higher integration in the world economy. Moreover, the accession to the EU, even its perspective, provides the integrated country with a more credible policy environment and encourages economic reforms, particularly through the obligation of assuming the *acquis communautaire* (Kaminski, 2001).

More efficient resource allocation

First, economic efficiency is improved because openness puts a competitive pressure on endogenous enterprises to adopt efficiency-enhancing strategies. Second, trade, contractual agreements, and FDI promote technological improvement by allowing for the transfer, diffusion, and generation of technology. 'Technology' is conceived in a broad sense (OMC, 1996, p. 66), and includes not only 'hard' technology but also organizational know-how – and, in particular, the corporate governance culture of a market economy. Indeed, technology can be embodied in capital and differentiated intermediate goods (Grossman and Helpman, 1995) but can also be transmitted through arm's-length trade – e.g. via licensing, franchising, OPT, etc. In particular, OPT can be defined as a learning process 'by exporting to knowledgeable buyers, who share product design and production techniques' (Clerides, Lach, and Tybout, 1998). Finally, FDI is considered as the main conduit for technology (Blomström and Kokko, 1997b). In this respect, FDI can be considered as a key element for the restructuring of CEECs, which suffer from a lack of market institutional structure (Dunning, 1993, p. 227).

In the long run, the combination of these effects is supposed to promote growth and a sustained development of the integrated countries. As predicted by Dunning (1981a, 1981b), an investment-development path (IDP) can develop. The main idea of the IDP is that a country's FDI position (outward direct investment stock minus inward direct investment stock) is related to its level of development. A country is expected to go through five stages of development, which can be classified according to its propensity to be a net recipient of FDI or a net exporter of FDI.[1] In particular, at the beginning of the path, inward FDI is motivated by the comparative advantages of a country (especially availability and cost of various production factors). The stronger the location advantages are, the more attractive to FDI the country is. Moreover, a strong export-orientation of inward FDI will favor the recycling of the comparative advantages of a country and support its industrialization. Indeed, MNEs are looking for locational advantages to supply export markets from host countries more profitably than from their home country or to increase their efficiency at the global or regional level. In both cases, to operate across international borders is more efficient for MNEs, because they can better exploit their ownership advantages. It is particularly true when affiliates are vertically organized and specialized according to the comparative advantages of the host country. It increases vertical specialisation and involves an international division of labor at the regional level.

As a result, 'an interactive path' of pro-trade FDI and economic growth may occur, in which a home developed country and host developing countries are involved, as shown in the 'flying-geese paradigm.' Initially conceptualised by Akamatsu (1961), the paradigm was then developed by Kojima (Kojima, 1975; Kojima and Ozawa, 1984, 1985), who introduced the FDI dimension: the graphic representation of this sequential process looks like a flight of geese. A host country 'industrializes and goes through industrial upgrading, step by step, by capitalizing on the learning opportunities made available through its external relations with the more advanced world' (World Bank, 1995, p. 259). As far as Central Europe is concerned, the EU – and more particularly Germany – appear as the 'lead goose.' The mutual interaction between the leading country (i.e. Germany) and the less developed economies (i.e. Central Europe) yields demonstration, learning, and emulation effects in the latter and helps their restructuring and economic growth.

A sign that a developing country has been successful in implementing this catching-up process relying on external relations, and above all on FDI, is the emergence and the development of outward FDI. According to the IDP paradigm, there is a tendency towards downstream investment – i.e. investment in countries which are at earlier stages of their IDP and, therefore, have lower *per capita* GDP. In this respect, the growth of outward FDI, which is a measure of the internalization of a country's domestic firms, can be considered as a positive evolution, although it diminishes the balance between inward FDI and outward FDI. Through outward FDI, countries are benefiting from access to *locational assets* (e.g. cheap inputs, markets), which strengthen the competitiveness of the enterprises involved.

De facto integration of Central European economies into the EU and German economic presence

The data suggest that a *de facto* integration of Central European economies took place before their formal accession to the EU began. The accession process was much longer than that of Greece (1981) or Spain and Portugal (1986). Nevertheless, tariff barriers and non-tariff barriers (NTBs) between the EU–15 and the eight future new EU members from CEE had already been reduced or eliminated in 1998, as a result of the interim and association agreements. Therefore, there was already a dramatic economic integration of Central European countries into the EU, supported by FDI, contractual arrangements, and foreign trade, with German firms playing the leading role.

German economic dominant presence in Central Europe

German firms developed linkages with Central Europe through trade and OPT before 1989, which were the only ways for Western firms to serve CEE markets. But since 1990–91, it has been possible for these trade links to be reinforced, or even replaced, by FDI, since the local settlement of a foreign firm in Central Europe became possible. Indeed, the arm's length relations developed before 1989 allowed German firms to build up closer relations with Central Europe by using them as stepping-stones for the setting up of local affiliates.

At present, Germany remains the first economic partner of CEECs as a whole (Table 8.1); 20% of CEECs' import and 18% of CEECs' export in 2003 were from German firms. German firms were also the first main contractor country for OPT: in 1997, Germany alone represented 60% of the re-import after outward processing from the CEECs in the EU, far more than France (7%) and Italy (13%) (Andreff, Andreff, and Boudier-Bensebaa, 2001). Germany has also become the main investor in the CEECs, with a 15% share in 2003.

Table 8.1 German firms' presence in Central Europe: German share in CEECs' trade, FDI inward stock, and EU re-import after outward processing

	Import, 2003 (%)	*Export, 2003 (%)*	*Re-import after OP, 1997[a] (%)*	*FDI inward stock, 2003 (%)*
World – CEECs	20	18	60	15
World – Central Europe	**26**	**33**	**66**	**25**
World – Czech Republic	33	37	86	31
World – Hungary	25	34	49	26
World – Poland	24	32	66	17
World – Slovakia	26	31	59	36
World – Slovenia	19	23	75	12

Sources: Trade from COMTRADE; OPT from Eurostat; FDI stock from Deutsche Bundesbank and UNCTAD. Own computations.

Note: [a] International subcontracting between EU members and associated CEECs could be assessed through OPT until 1997; once trade barriers were eliminated after 1998–99 the advantages associated with OPT vanished and it was no longer possible to investigate such international subcontracting.

Table 8.2 Importance of Central Europe in German economic relations with CEECs: share of Central Europe in German trade and OPT with CEECs, and FDI into CEECs

	German import from CEECs, 2004 (%)	German export to CEECs, 2004 (%)	German re-import after OP from CEECs, 1997 (%)	German FDI in CEECs, 2003 (%)
Central Europe	67	63	64	84
Balkans	7	11	25	8
Baltic States	2	3	4	2
CIS	24	23	7	6

Sources: Trade from Statistisches Bundesamt; OPT from Eurostat; FDI stock from Deutsche Bundesbank. Own computations.

Table 8.3 Czech Republic, Hungary, Poland: distribution of German FDI stock, by industry, 2003

	Czech Republic (%)	Hungary (%)	Poland (%)
Manufacturing	50	51	53
of which automotive	19	29	11
Trade	10	8	15
Bank and insurance	3	7	14

Source: Deutsche Bundesbank. Own computations.

The bulk of the German economic presence in the CEECs is in Central Europe, which accounted for about two-thirds of German trade and of German OPT with CEECs and for more than 80% of German FDI in CEECs (Table 8.2). German economic presence is much more concentrated on Central Europe than is the case for other home countries. Moreover, the importance of the Czech Republic as a host country for German firms should be noted: more than a third of Czech import from and export to the world in 2003 came from (or went to) Germany; 86% of the EU re-import after outward processing from the Czech Republic in 1997 was from German firms; almost a third of the inward FDI stock attracted by the Czech Republic in 2003 originated in Germany (Table 8.1). This relative preference given to the Czech Republic is specific to Germany. The preferred target of other home countries was Hungary, which gave up the lead to Poland in 1996.

When considering commodity structure, German economic presence in Central Europe is concentrated in the manufacturing sector and more especially in Germany's traditional specialization industries. In particular, a half or more of German FDI attracted by the Czech Republic, Hungary, or Poland in 2003 was in the manufacturing sector; between 11% (Poland) and 30% (Hungary) in the automotive industry (Table 8.3).

Importance of Central Europe for German firms

Central Europe looks very attractive to German firms and even more attractive than other developing or emerging economies (Table 8.4). Compared to Asian, African, or American developing countries, Central Europe has attracted an increasing share of German FDI and has accounted for a growing share of

Table 8.4 Importance of Central Europe in German trade, OPT and outward FDI

	German import, 2004 (%)	German export, 2004 (%)	German re-import after OP, 1997 (%)	German outward FDI stock, 2003 (%)
CEECs	14.5	12.4	61	5.9
Central Europe	**9.8**	**7.8**	**39**	**4.9**
Czech Republic	2.9	2.4	11	1.7
Hungary	2.3	1.7	7	1.5
Poland	2.8	2.6	15	1.2
Slovakia	1.3	0.8	3	0.5
Slovenia	0.4	0.4	2	0.1
Developing and emerging economies				
Asia and the Pacific	14	11	22	4.2
Latin America and the Caribbean	2	2	12	3.1
Africa	2	2	3	0.6

Sources: Trade and OPT from Statistisches Bundesamt; FDI from Deutsche Bundesbank. Own computations.

German trade. Moreover, the dramatic use of OPT by German firms to enter Central European economies should be noted.

German firms resort to OPT much more than EU firms in general, extensively using this non-equity contractual arrangement to enter the CEECs both before and after 1989, focusing on some particular industries and countries and therefore having a dramatic impact (Andreff, Andreff, and Boudier-Bensebaa, 2001). Indeed, German firms, mainly medium-sized enterprises in labor- intensive industries such as clothing, electrical equipment, wooden furniture, etc., make an important use of this non-equity form of international production when expanding eastwards. More generally, German SMEs are more present in CEECs, especially in Central Europe through FDI as well as trade and OPT than other EU SMEs – or, more generally, Western SMEs. This reflects the specificity of the German industrial fabric, dominated by the 'Mittelstand'[2] and explains why supply determinants (especially unit labor costs) are more important for German firms than for other investing firms. German transnational operations in Central Europe correspond more often to relocations than to market-seeking activities, unlike the other home countries.

CEECs have always been the main host countries of German OPT. At the end of the 1990s, their most important partners were the Czech Republic, Hungary, and Poland, to which a Balkan state, Romania, has to be added (Boudier-Bensebaa and Brezinski, 2001). At present, the loss of comparative advantages based on low labor cost in Central Europe ensures a shift of OPT from Central Europe to the Balkan states and CIS members, and to Asian emerging countries. In particular, OPT in clothing is moving from Central Europe (especially Poland) to the Balkan states (especially Romania). Moreover, the share of Germany in EU OPT with CEECs in clothing has decreased, whereas that of Italy has increased (Boudier-Bensebaa and Andreff, 2004).

The dominant role of German firms in integrating Central European firms into EU corporate structures is obvious. When using the term 'domination,' we refer to Perroux's terminology – i.e. asymmetrical economic relations between a developed center and a less developed periphery. Indeed, dynamic changes have appeared in economic relations between Central European countries and the EU, above all Germany, which appears as the core country. These asymmetrical relations lead to the building of regional networks.

German economic presence and Central Europe's development-path

Indeed, by extending their production and commercial networks in Central Europe, German firms have forged tight links with local producers, especially as suppliers. They transfer not only capital resources but also technological and management know-how, and therefore are a key source for the building of competencies in certain industries (automotive industry, electrical products, clothing industry, chemical industry, etc.), the upgrading of local skills, and the insertion of domestic firms in world markets. They therefore strengthen local capabilities.

At present, an important share of the gross domestic product (GDP) of Central European economies derives from activities of enterprises linked to German corporate networks through equity relationships (enterprises partly or fully owned by German investors) or non-equity relationships (OPT, for example) (Table 8.5).

As evidenced by the test of the IDP (Boudier-Bensebaa, 2005), a catching-up scenario is at work in Central Europe, based on spillovers through FDI from Germany, and more generally from the advanced EU-15 members, to these countries, as described by the 'flying geese' pattern of development. Nevertheless, the relationship between FDI and growth in the case of Central Europe does not necessarily match the theory (Mencinger, 2003). Indeed, high

Table 8.5 **Importance of German economic presence for Central European economies: German trade and OPT with CEECs and German outward FDI stock in CEECs as percentage of the GDP of Central European economies**

	Import, 2003 (%)	*Export, 2003 (%)*	*Re-import after OP, 1997 (%)*	*FDI stock, 2003 (%)*
Central Europe	14.4	14.7	12.6	8.4
Czech Republic	21.4	22.4	12.6	14.2
Hungary	18.3	17.1	10.6	13.4
Poland	8.6	10.1	15.8	4.3
Slovakia	26.5	19.4	10.6	11.3
Slovenia	9.6	10.9	8.9	1.8

Sources: Trade and OPT from Statistisches Bundesamt; FDI stock from Deutsche Bundesbank; GDP from World Bank. Own computations.

Table 8.6 GDP *per capita*, outward FDI stock *per capita*, 2002, dollars

	GDP	Outward FDI stock
Czech Republic	6,808	147
Hungary	6,481	213
Poland	4,894	38
Slovakia	4,403	89
Slovenia	11,181	757
Croatia	5,025	407
Estonia	4,792	498
Russia	2,405	331

Sources: GDP and population from World Bank (*World Development Indicators* database); FDI from UNCTAD (2004).

GDP growth went hand in hand with increasing FDI (Poland) or, conversely, FDI increased although GDP was low (Hungary and the Czech Republic in 1995), or even negative (Hungary in 1993). It seems that FDI was stimulated rather than attracted by GDP growth. This result could be explained by the fact that inward FDI had been mainly led by privatization and had mostly taken the form of acquisition.

At present, Central European countries are moving along their IDP towards the latter end of stage 2 – or even towards the beginning of stage 3, in the Slovenian case (Boudier-Bensebaa, 2005). On the one hand, as a larger recipient of the region, Central European has attracted a threshold level of inward FDI which has provided spillover effects: in particular, created assets have developed. On the other hand, since the mid-1990s Central European economies have begun to invest abroad.

Outward FDI from Central Europe showed an almost fourfold increase between 1995 and 2002 to an estimed US$ 7 billion, but far from outward FDI from Russia, which accounted for more than US$ 47 billion (UNCTAD, 2004). In terms of absolute figures, Hungary takes the lead, followed by Croatia, the Czech Republic, Slovenia, and Poland. The underperformance of Poland has to be noted in view of its size, and in particular of its share in region-wide GDP.[3] In relative terms, the picture is somewhat different. Slovenia, whose outward FDI stock *per capita* reached US$ 757 in 2002, has taken the lead, followed by Estonia and Croatia (ᵗABLE 8.6). The exposure to Western markets of Slovenian Wrms in the past thirty years has favored their internationalization (Svetlicic ET AL., 2000). Among the largest twenty-five TNCs in CEECs reported by UNCTAD in 2002 (UNCTAD, 2004), eighteen belong to Central European countries (Table 8.7).

The emergence of Central European countries as investors suggests that outward FDI is related to the level of systemic transformations and, therefore, partly to the level of inward FDI, which has been attracted. It seems that Central European local firms have developed specific ownership advantages, partly through inward FDI. A part of Central European outward FDI is 'indirect' FDI (Altzinger *et al.*, 2003) – i.e. carried out by affiliates of foreign firms. According

Table 8.7 Largest non-financial TNCs from Central Europe, ranked by foreign assets, 2002, million dollars

Corporation	Country	Industry	Foreign assets
Pliva Group	Croatia	Pharmaceuticals	689.1
Gorenje Group	Slovenia	Domestic appliances	312.8
Hrvatska Elektroprivreda d.d.	Croatia	Utilities	272
Mercator d.d., Poslovni sistem	Slovenia	Retail trade	224.6
Krka d.d.	Slovenia	Pharmaceuticals	180.7
Petrol group	Slovenia	Petroleum and natural gas	108.5
Richter Gedeon Ltd	Hungary	Pharmaceuticals	105.6
Malév Hungarian Airlines Ltd	Hungary	Transportation	105.0
Prodavka Group	Croatia	Food and beverages/ pharmaceuticals	102.4
MOL Hungarian Oil and Gas Plc.	Hungary	Petroleum and natural gas	95.9
BLRT Grupp AS	Estonia	Shipbuilding	66.2
Zalakeramia Rt	Hungary	Clay product and refractory	65.0
Intereuropa d.d.	Slovenia	Trade	45.0
Merkur d.d.	Slovenia	Trade	43.3
Budimex Capital Group	Poland	Construction	23.8
Croatia Airlines d.d.	Croatia	Transportation	23.4
Finvest Corp d.d.	Croatia	Forestry	22.2
Iskraemeco d.d.	Slovenia	Electrical machinery	20.7

Source: UNCTAD (2004, p. 317).

to empirical studies (Svetlicic and Rojec, 2003), an important share of outward FDI is made by subsidiaries of foreign firms in Estonia (particularly in the banking sector), in Hungary, and in the Czech Republic, whereas outward FDI is directly done by locally owned firms in Slovenia.

At the same time, Central European economies are losing comparative advantages based on low unit labor cost in labor-intensive industries. This phenomenon can be seen through the decrease of OPT in these industries. At present, Central European outward FDI is still mainly market-seeking (Jaklic and Svetlicic, 2001) and in particular aims at overcoming the profit constraints of small national markets. But rising labor cost is likely to encourage domestic firms to invest in countries at lower stages of development. The influence of the previous links inherited from the past on the present geographical distribution of outward FDI from Central European countries is still obvious (Table 8.8).

Have German firms implemented a new international division of labor in Europe?

The political and economic opening up of CEECs has taken place at a time when the loss of attractiveness of the German economic territory (the problem of the 'Standort Deutschland') was one of the Germany's main preoccupations. It has

Table 8.8 Geographical distribution of outward FDI from Central European countries, 2001, percentage

To From	Croatia	Czech	Hungary	Poland	Slovakia	Slovenia	Baltic states	Balkans	CIS
Croatia[a]				47		10		34	
Czech Rep.			4	5	24				2
Estonia							95		3
Poland		3					2	1	3
Slovakia		41	6	7					11
Slovenia[a]	58			9				25	3

Source: OECD. Own computations.
Note: [a] 2000.

led to a certain complementarity between the needs of the Central Europe and those of Germany. The latter has benefited from a sort of constellation of favorable conditions in the area, since the double proximity of the locational advantages of Central European countries and of Western consumption markets offered German firms the possibility of recovering their lost competitiveness through delocalization.

The loss of attractiveness of German economic territory in the 1990s was the cumulative result of a number of factors. First of all, the price competitiveness of German products on foreign as well as domestic markets was questioned, all the more so as the activity concerned is labor- intensive, because of labor costs among the highest in the world, and the appreciation of the DM/Euro along with the depreciation of the dollar. Faced with such a situation, German firms have been pushed to make structural adjustments, for the whole of their production or just for those segments which are intensive in unskilled labor and which are losing their comparative advantages. They have either substituted capital- and knowledge-intensive technologies for labor, or delocalized, through subcontracting and/or FDI, thus profiting from the localization advantages of the host countries, among which is Central Europe. Forced to transfer their specific advantages, threatened by the structural changes in their country, to a country displaying localization advantages, FDI has sometimes been the only option, since a contractual relationship such as subcontracting does not permit the internalization of transaction costs on markets, especially in the case of intangible assets.

Furthermore, since the globalization of German firms mainly took the form of exports (preference for internationalization to the detriment of multinationalization) before the 1990s, the relative insufficiency of German FDI compared to US FDI, and of German OPT in low labor cost countries compared to Japanese OPT, have undermined German competitiveness compared to the two principal world economies, and generated a need for catching-up. This need has led to an increase in the foreign production capacities of German firms through FDI or OPT, and this seems to have benefited Central European countries.

Finally, German reunification worsened the problem. Since no wage gap compensated the productivity gap between East and West Germany, the comparative advantages of East Germany in terms of labor cost vanished and the profitability of certain investment projects disappeared, whereas the relative attractivity of Central European economies increased. The progressive alignment of Eastern wages to the high Western level, although logical from the perspective of the constitution of a unified economic space (especially to avoid massive migration flows from Eastern to Western Germany), may however seem questionable. The attractiveness of the Central European countries, two of which (Poland and the Czech Republic) have common borders with Germany, seems to be such that it caused an 'eviction effect' to the detriment of the new Bundesländer.

Central European countries have displayed a good unit labor cost (labor cost/productivity) and particularly the acknowledged abilities of their work force, some R&D facilities, and, until a few years ago, preferential treatments granted to foreign investors on matters of taxes and tariffs. Not only has the lower level of labor costs to be taken into account but also the qualitative characteristics of the labor force: its flexibility, efficiency, and ability to carry out tasks. Thus with a highly skilled labor force able to use the latest technologies and, in some industries, with their technical culture similar to Germany's,[4] Central European countries have been very attractive for German firms.

Germany's geographical, historical, and cultural proximity with Central Europe is no doubt also an important reason for the German presence in these countries. It has allowed Germany to build up privileged trade relations which after the fall of the Berlin Wall were used to create new forms of economic presence.

By benefiting in Central Europe from lower production cost than in Germany, and/or from more dynamic markets than the flagging Western ones, German firms have matched the capacities of the host Central European countries with their own advantages and managed to maintain their cost competitiveness and to 're-establish a concordance between their comparative and their competitive advantages.'[5] In certain branches such as the automotive industry, electrical equipment, and consumer goods, Central European countries are considered by German firms as extensions of Western Europe. They have set up production units in these countries that aim to satisfy the entire European market, even the world market.

Different types of integrated strategies are possible: the firm may supply the German market with foreign-made products, to increase its competitiveness on its domestic market; it may also resort to intra-firm trade as a form of cross-subsidization between costly production and low-cost semi-finished product imports; it may finally aim to supply the local market in which it has established itself, especially if the firm is the first mover and if entry costs are high on this market.

The emergence of new regional structures close to Germany's borders provides an excellent illustration of the regionalization of European economies faced with the globalization of the world economy, with Germany playing the key role. The integration of two groups of European countries at different levels of development is to the advantage of German firms, which have developed an international division of labor at the regional level in Europe. On the whole, German firms are the main firms to benefit from the cluster effects[6] of the integration of Central Europe into an economic European space centered on the EU. Moreover, effects of the formal accession of Central European countries to the EU, particularly the effects on the state, could be expected to be mild. Many foreign investors, above all German investors, entered the Central European markets and exploited their locational advantages during the 1990s so that there will be little additional investment from the accession to the EU. Brenton and Di Mauro (1998, p. 10), using a gravity model, showed that the accession of CEECs to the EU may have little impact on FDI from Germany, because 'the intensity of [German] FDI flows to the CEECs was greater than that to EU partners.' Indeed, the time dimension is very important. The influence of RIAs depends on the pre-existing situation: the patterns of trade and FDI, the level of integration between the integrating country(ies) and the integrated country(ies), the complementarity between the economies, etc. (Blomström and Kokko, 1997a). This *ex ante* structure determines the importance of the necessary adjustment after the agreement. Therefore, changes are expected to be smaller after formal agreement in countries which were already closely linked to the incumbent states than in countries with weakened linkages with their RIA partners. That is the case for the Central European countries, above all through their links to Germany. Then, from a strictly economic viewpoint, the formal accession of the Central European countries to the EU may not have a great impact on the relationships between Central Europe and Germany.

Methodological note

Geographical breakdown
Central Europe: Czech Republic, Hungary, Poland, Slovakia, Slovenia.
Balkans: Albania, Bosnia and Herzegovina, Bulgaria, Croatia, Macedonia, Romania, Yugoslavia.
Baltic states: Estonia, Latvia, Lithuania.
CIS: Armenia, Azerbaijan, Belarus, Georgia, Kazakhstan, Kyrgyzstan, Moldova, Russia, Tajikistan, Turkmenistan, Ukraine, Uzbekistan.

Data on OPT
OPT data on a world scale are not available. Moreover, data on OPT between the EU (and therefore Germany) and Central Europe are no longer relevant after 1998. The complete elimination of tariffs and quotas in 1998 between EU members and the ten associated CEECs has eliminated the specific advantages associated with OPT, so that it is no longer possible to investigate OPT between the EU and the ten associated CEECs after 1997 (for more details, see Andreff, Andreff, and Boudier-Bensebaa, 2001).

Notes

1   For a summary of the IDP, see UNCTAD (1995, pp. 237–238).
2   An untranslatable German term, reflecting the fact that the German economy is dominated by the most substantial pool of SMEs in Europe, which form a very dense and very stable industrial fabric.
3   18% of CEECs' GDP in 2003, 47% of Central Europe's GDP (World Bank and own computations).
4   On the other hand, the skills of the labor force were purely technical and did not include management abilities, which made it difficult to find executives.
5   This refers to the synthetical theory of Mucchielli (1985).
6   A 'cluster' is a group of enterprises, situated in the same geographic area, linked by common characteristics (the same industry) or by complementarities (suppliers and producers of the same final product). Its area could extend to neighboring countries. This geographic proximity produces intra- and inter-industry external economies.

Bibliography

Akamatsu, K. (1961) 'A theory of unbalanced growth in the world economy,' *Weltwirtschaftliches Archiv*, 86, pp. 196–217.

Altzinger, W., C. Bellak, A. Jaklic, and M. Rojec (2003) 'Direct versus indirect foreign investment from transition economies: is there a difference in parent company/home country impact?,' in M. Svetlicic and M. Rojec (eds), *Facilitating Transition by Internationalization*, Aldershot: Ashgate, pp. 91–108.

Andreff, M., W. Andreff, and F. Boudier-Bensebaa (2001) 'Sous-traitance internationale de façonnage et trafic de perfectionnement passif entre les pays de l'Union Européenne et de l'Europe de l'Est,' *Revue d'Etudes Comparatives Est-Ouest*, 2, pp. 5–34.

Blomström, M. and A. Kokko (1997a) 'Regional integration and foreign direct investment,' Policy Research Working Paper, 1750, Washington, DC: World Bank.

Blomström, M. and A. Kokko (1997b) 'How foreign investment affects host countries,' Policy Research Working Paper, 1745, Washington, DC: World Bank.

Boudier-Bensebaa, F. (2005) 'FDI-assisted development in the light of the investment development path: evidence from Central and Eastern European countries,' *Journées de l'AFSE*, CERDI, Clermont-Ferrand, May 19–20.

Boudier-Bensebaa, F. and M. Andreff (2004) 'La subcontratación en la industria textil-confección entre la UE y los países de Europa del Este,' *Boletin de Información Comercial Española*, 2797, pp. 105–118.

Boudier-Bensebaa, F. and H. Brezinski (2001) 'La sous-traitance de façonnage entre l'Allemagne et les pays est-européens,' *Revue d'Etudes Comparatives Est-Ouest*, 2, pp. 35–50.

Brenton, P. and F. Di Mauro (1998) 'The potential magnitude and impact of FDI flows to CEECs,' Working Document, 116, Brussels: Center for European Policy Studies.

Clerides, S., S. Lach, and J.R. Tybout (1998) 'Is learning by exporting important? Micro-dynamic from Colombia, Mexico, and Morocco,' *Quarterly Journal of Economics*, 3, pp. 903–948.

Dunning, J.H. (1981a) 'Explaining outward direct investment of developing countries: in support of the eclectic theory of international production,' in K. Kumar and M.G. McLeod (eds), *Multinationals from Developing Countries*, Lexington: Lexington Books.

Dunning, J.H. (1981b) 'Explaining the international direct investment position of countries: towards a dynamic and development approach,' *Weltwirtschaftliches Archiv*, 117, pp. 30–64.

Dunning, J.H. (1993) 'The prospects for foreign direct investment in Central and Eastern Europe,' in J.H. Dunning (ed.), *The Globalization of Business: The Challenge of the 1990s*, London and New York: Routledge.

Grossman, G.M. and E. Helpman (1995) 'Technology and trade,' CEPR International Trade Discussion Paper, 1134.

Jaklic, A. and M. Svetlicic, M. (2001) 'Does transition matter? FDI from the Czech Republic, Hungary and Slovenia,' *Transnational Corporations*, 2, pp. 67–105.

Kaminski, B. (2001) 'How accession to the European Union has affected external trade and foreign direct investment in Central European Economies,' International Economics Working Papers, 2578, Washington, DC: World Bank.

Kojima, K. (1975) 'International trade and foreign investment: substitutes or complements,' *Hitotsubashi Journal of Economics*, 16, pp. 1–12.

Kojima, K. and T. Ozawa (1984) 'Micro- and macro-economic models of direct foreign investment: towards a synthesis,' *Hitotsubashi Journal of Economics*, 25, pp. 1–20.

Kojima, K. and T. Ozawa (1985) 'Toward a theory of industrial restructuring and dynamic comparative advantage,' *Hitotsubashi Journal of Economics*, 26, pp. 135–145.

Mencinger, J. (2003) 'Does foreign investment always enhance economic growth?,' *Kyklos*, 4, pp. 491–508.

Mucchielli, J.-L. (1985) *Les firmes multinationales: mutations et perspectives*, Paris: Economica.

OMC (1996) 'Commerce et investissement direct étranger,' *OMC, Rapport Annuel 1996*, pp. 51–95.

Svetlicic, Marjan and Matija Rojec (eds) (2003) *Facilitating Transition by Internationalization: Outward Direct Investment from Central European Economies in Transition*, Aldershot: Ashgate.

Svetlicic, Marjan, Matija Rojec, and Andreja Trtnik (2000) 'The reconstructing role of outward foreign direct investment by Central European firms: the case of Slovenia,' *Advances in International Marketing*, 10, pp. 53–88.

UNCTAD (1995) *World Investment Report*, New York and Geneva: United Nations.

UNCTAD (2004) *World Investment Report: The Shift towards Services*, New York and Geneva: United Nations.

KATHARINA BLUHM

9

Dealing with the regulation gap. German multinationals and the institutionalization of labor relations in East Central Europe

Introduction

In the continuing debate surrounding the erosion of the 'German model,' ECE is perceived primarily as a cause for 'concession bargaining' and regime competition that downscales social and labor regulation standards. Yet, how German and other western European companies actually behave when they invest in ECE is largely unknown. The debate on globalization and capitalism models provides two major approaches to the issue.

On the one hand, scholars suggest that companies coming from a highly regulated environment would rather prevent institutionalization of collective workforce representation in the weakly regulated host countries, using the production shift as the opportunity for a radical move toward an individual–flexible model of labor relations that permits smooth adjustment to the ups and downs of volatile markets. Parallels are drawn with the documented hostility of western investors towards unions in the maquiladora industries of northern Mexico (Altvater and Mahnkopf, 1993; Ellingstad, 1997). Some authors even see MNEs experimenting with new arrangements in ECE, which are then 're-imported,' contributing to the 'Americanization' of labor relations in continental Europe (Meardi, 2002, p. 79).

Institutionalists, on the other hand, challenge this concept of convergence. There are two competing institutional concepts. The 'varieties of capitalism approach' (Hall and Soskice, 2001) says that companies from different models of capitalism want to keep their institutional advantages at home in shaping their strategies abroad. German companies relying on a dense institutional infrastructure and a high-quality production system might be less inclined to shift production abroad – at least just for cost-cutting, as British or American companies do. Interested in exploiting institutional differences, they may also show little interest in cross-border concession bargaining. The alternative institutional approach, linked to the concept of business systems (Whitley, 1994), in contrast, predicts that companies from a coherent and strong 'national business system' at home are inclined to transfer key elements of the system when they move abroad. In the German case, this would imply a cooperative labor relations approach based as far as possible on collective labor relations.

The empirical findings presented in this chapter will reveal that convergence as well the institutionalist approaches fail to explain the highly divergent behavior of German companies. Large German-based MNCs in ECE have established collective–cooperative labor relations at plant level, while German family-owned companies (Mittelständler) behave much more heterogeneously. The subsidiaries of those companies are much more inclined towards an individual–flexible model of labor relations and show hostility towards unions – although most of them are covered by collective agreements at home.

This chapter aims to examine the patterns of companies' behavior concerning labor relations policy, for which neither approach mentioned above seems to provide a sufficient explanation. I begin with a brief sketch of the sample and methodology adopted for the empirical study and then present in more detail the patterns of companies' labor policy in the ECE subsidiaries studied.

A major focus of the chapter will lie in testing three different hypotheses that may explain the finding that large German-based MNCs in ECE do not dismantle the collective–cooperative model in labor relations at plant level, while family-owned companies are inclined to do so, accepting workforce representatives in its weakest form at best.

First, I shall test whether the investment strategy is associated with variation in the companies' behavior in labor relations. Second, I shall investigate whether coordinated (as opposed to non-coordinated) human resource management (HRM) makes a difference in labor relations' behavior. Third, I shall discuss the role of management transfer – i.e. the hypothesis that expatriates of MNCs have stronger normative bonds to the 'German model' of industrial relations and are therefore more inclined to act in this way even under more permissive circumstances than their counterparts in family-owned companies.

Based on this analysis, I shall show that not one single factor is decisive for explaining the adherence of MNCs to a collective–cooperative model of labor relations at plant level; more important, rather, is the implicit cross-border collaboration of different actors that constrains management choice and supports the institutionalization of collective–cooperative labor relations in Polish and Czech subsidiaries of German-based MNCs. The preconditions for such cross-border collaboration are much less developed for family-owned companies, even if they are large. And even in the MNCs the success in institutionalizing the collective–cooperative labor model is clearly limited, as a closer look reveals.

Methodology

The research is based on case studies (interviews, plant tours, document analysis) of twenty Polish and Czech production sites of large MNEs of German origin, each employing more than 1,000 people.[1] The subsidiaries, located in the western regions of Poland and the Czech Republic, were founded (or acquired) mainly in the 1992–95 period. The companies studied were chosen from various industries; criteria for selection were variation in product and investment strategy and the importance of the industries as direct investors in the countries chosen (see Table 9.1).

The sample is divided equally into subsidiaries belonging to MNCs, whose shares are listed on stock markets or are held by other companies, and operations of large German companies controlled by private entrepreneurs. The entrepreneurial type of MNE is usually called 'family-owned,' although there is not always a family behind it. I label it 'large middle-sized private enterprise' (LMPE). The precise composition of the study sample is given by size, type, and location in Table 9.2.

For the purposes of this study, contact was made with managing directors (mostly expatriates) and personnel managers (mostly natives) of the subsidiaries, and in case of LMPEs with the owners running the business themselves. In selected cases of production shifts, works council members in Germany were also interviewed. The interview phase took place over two periods: the first from late 1998 to summer 1999, the second from 2002 to 2003.[2] Fifty-five in-depth interviews were conducted, which in eighteen cases were followed up with plant tours.

Table 9.1 Classification according to sector of the companies studied, 2003

Sector	No. of firms	Firms in Czech Rep.	Firms in Poland
Transportation vehicles (incl. suppliers)	11	6	5
Metalworking and electrical equipment	4	2	2
Luxury-food industry	2	–	2
Mass-consumption goods	3	1	2
Total	**20**	**10**	**10**

Table 9.2 Composition of the study sample, 1999–2003

Size of MNE	No. of subsidiaries	MNCs	LMPEs	Location of subsidiary	
				Poland	Czech Rep.
1,000–5,000	7	2	5	3	4
5,001–10,000	5	1	4	4	1
10,001–20,000	4	3	1	1	3
>20,000	4	4	–	2	2
Total	**20**	**10**	**10**	**10**	**10**

The institutionalization of collective workforce representation in CEE

The Polish and Czech systems of labor relations differ widely from those of Germany. After 1989 the legislatures in both countries – in contrast to Hungary and Slovenia – decided against the introduction of the dual-pillar system of workforce representation established in Germany and in other continental European countries. Until EC accession, the trade unions in Poland and the Czech Republic successfully resisted an institutionalization of works councils because they feared an undermining of their overall position at the plant level (Pumberger, 1998; Vickerstaff and Thirkell, 2000). In Poland, works councils were also a reminder of the 'workers councils' of the 1980s and their 'active involvement in the agony of the failing system' (Kohl, Lecher, and Platzer, 2000, p. 4).[3]

Collective agreements can be concluded in Poland, as in the Czech Republic, on two levels:

- on a *plant level* by the enterprise union organizations – i.e. their boards/ committees; the requirements for establishing a union organization are minimal and, as in many European countries, different trade unions are possible in one company;
- on a *sectoral level*, 'higher-order collective agreements' (multi-employer agreements) can be made; these, however, establish only minimum wage and working-condition standards (Pollert, 1999; Myant and Smith, 1999, pp. 270–273).

In neither country has the unions succeeded in overcoming political and employers' resistance to a binding sectoral bargaining level (Carley, 2002).[4] In addition, the union density relative to the size of the countries' workforce is, with an estimated 15% in Poland and 30% in the Czech Republic, relatively low. These facts together explain why the number of employees covered by collective agreements is also low, estimated for the Czech Republic at 25–30% and for Poland at 30–40%. Yet the Polish coverage rate refers mainly to the remaining state enterprises – the private sector is almost completely non-unionized (Janicki, 2000; Carley, 2002, p. 12; Ladó, 2002).[5]

In the light of these institutional handicaps on multi-employer collective bargaining in both countries, union organization and rules for plant-level bargaining are well established in German-based MNCs. As Table 9.3 shows, among the ten MNC production sites, no operation was without union organizations. In all ten companies, formal collective agreements had to be concluded and renegotiated either at regular intervals or as needed. Nine subsidiaries negotiated annually, at least formally, on wages and salaries with the union boards. Further, during the study period in six subsidiaries there were regular meetings between business management and union board members to inform them about the economic and market situation of the subsidiary. In six cases, companies left board members to do union work, in some cases the full-time union job was paid by the company, as with works councils in Germany.[6]

Table 9.3 Institutionalization of workforce representation in MNC subsidiaries ($n = 10$)

Code	MNE total	Employees in Germany	Employees in subsidiary	Presence of unions (no.)	Collective agreements
PL-1	1,000–5,000	1,000–5,000	470 (470)	Yes (2) – (2)	Yes
CZ-1	1,000–5,000	<1,000	1,500 (sec. round)	Yes (1) – (1)	Yes
CZ-2	>5,000	1,000–5,000	580	Yes (2)	Yes
PL-2	>5,000	1,000–5,000	2,500	Yes (1)	Yes
PL-3	>10,000	>5,000	480 (400)	Yes (2) – (1)	Yes
PL-4	>10,000	1,000–5,000	1,500 (800)	Yes (2) – (3)	Yes
CZ-3	>20,000	>20,000	530 (sec. round)[a, b]	Yes (1) – (2)	Yes
CZ-4	>20,000	>10,000	640 (sec. round)	Yes (1) – (1)	Yes
PL-5	>20,000	>20,000	300 (680)[a]	Yes (1) – (2)	Yes
PL-6	>20,000	>20,000	2,400 (<6,000)	Yes (1) – (1)	Yes

Notes: Data refer to the first and second round of investigation. [a] The investor controls several legally independent subsidiaries in the host country. [b] CZ–3 and CZ–4 got separated in the second round.

Table 9.4 Workforce representation in subsidiaries of LMPEs, 1999 and 2002–03 ($n = 10$)

Code	MNE total	Employees in Germany	Employees in subsidiary	Workforce representation	Collective agreements
PL-7	1,100	600	150	Yes (1)	Yes
CZ-5	1,200	340	800[a]	(Informal WC/yes (1)	–
CZ-6	1,000–5,000	1,000–5,000	300	Yes (1)	Yes
PL-8	1,000–5,000	1,000–5,000	390	Informal WC	–
CZ-7	1,000–5,000	1,000–5,000	700[a]	–	–
CZ-8	>5,000	1,000–5,000	650 (1,500)[a]	–	–
CZ-9	>5,000	1,000–5,000	420 (<500)	– (Formal WC)	–
PL-9	>5,000	>5,000	200	Yes (1)	–
PL-10	>10,000	1,000–5,000	920[b]	Yes (2)	Yes
CZ-10	>10,000	>5,000	300 (530)[a]	Yes (1)	Yes

Notes: [a] Same subsidiary is distributed over several locations. [b] The investor controls several legally independent subsidiaries in the host country.

While the German-based MNCs established collective–cooperative labor relations at plant level without much conflict, the LMPEs studied displayed a much greater aversion to union representation and collective bargaining in their Polish and Czech operations. They were more inclined to lean toward an individual–flexible model. Only four of ten LMPE subsidiaries during the study period had union boards *and* collective agreements (Table 9.4). In three cases, informal or formal works councils (WC) were created instead of union boards, which were introduced 'top-down' in order to facilitate the communication between management and employees. In two LMPE operations, workers founded a union organization despite the opposition of managers, who refused to recognize its board as legitimate workforce representation.

Differences in strategy

When companies opt for greenfield investment, they often wish to circumvent the risks of structural inertia which an existing organization usually presents. Former state-owned enterprises (SOEs) in ECE were high-risk investments in this respect, especially for family-owned companies. Moreover, trade unions were widely present in those enterprises, so that potential private investors were often obliged to come to an agreement with them. A first hypothesis for explaining the differences in labor relation models between German MNCs and LMPEs can, therefore, be posited:

> **H1**: *Different preferences in the investment strategy are more important than the type of company. While MNCs acquired SOEs, LMPEs set up new production sites that would easily be kept union-free.*

The data (Table 9.5) fail to corroborate this hypothesis. Among the ten LMPEs, seven opted for a greenfield investment (which can also mean buying or subletting an existing factory building). However, three of seven greenfield sites accepted union organization. Two of three companies acquired by LMPEs were non-unionized. Looking at the MNCs, the unions succeeded in organizing all of the newly established production sites. Thus, the investment strategy is less important than was hypothesized.

Equally unconvincing as an explanation for the difference is the assumption that investors who focus on offshore production behave more rigidly towards unions and collective bargaining than those who entered the host country mainly for the new market. The cost-cutting motive was certainly decisive for six MNCs and five LMPEs, but essentially these companies do not behave differently in their approach to the institutionalization of workforce representation than those with a primary interest in new markets.

Human resource management

The capability of companies to opt intentionally for certain labor practices company-wide, to transfer or not to transfer models, and experiment with new

Table 9.5 Investment strategies and institutionalization of labor representation in subsidiaries of German-based MNEs ($n = 20$)

Type of MNE	Investment strategy (with union boards accepted by the management)		Total
	Brownfield	*Greenfield*	
LMPE	3 (1)	7 (3)	**10**
MNC	6 (6)	4 (4)	**10**
Total	**9 (7)**	**11 (7)**	**20**

practices across borders, is closely related to the question of whether, and how far, headquarters coordinate HRM in general and labor relation policy in particular. Here a second hypothesis comes into play:

> **H2**: *The relatively uniform behavior of German-based MNCs in contrast to LMPEs is related to the coordination of the HRM exercised by firms' headquarters, which includes norms of the collective–cooperative model. The more HRM is centrally coordinated, the more foreign subsidiaries adopt a collective–cooperative model in labor relations.*

For testing this hypothesis the management literature offers four control mechanisms in foreign subsidiaries by which headquarters try to establish uniform rules and standards:

- establishing *formal, company-wide rules and standards* for subsidiaries;
- *social integration* by horizontal project groups, meetings, and training in personnel management areas, by which 'best practices' diffuse through an organization;
- control over *personnel policy* by means of centralized decision-making (administrative control), budget-setting, and reporting (output control);
- control by *management transfer* – i.e. by parent company staff who present headquarters' expectations and exert certain socializing influences over subsidiary employees, thus shaping rules and practices (see Harzing, 1999).

Formal rules and standards

At the outset, it should be understood that none of the firms studied had a production transfer model combining a standardized manufacturing system with a predetermined set of 'best practices' in work organization and HRM, as did some well-known Japanese 'transplants' in the US (Abo, 1994). Of course, most of the large companies have a standardized factory layout, determine technological processes and transfer procedures in quality management (not least through such international norms and techniques as ISO and total quality management (TQM)). In many cases, methods of improvement management were also transferred, though already with adoptions by the local management. However, they rarely combined these systems with models of work organization such as teamwork and specific remuneration and appraisal systems, etc. Only one subsidiary referred the introduction of teamwork at shop floor level to the company-wide HR policy of headquarters.

The formation of company-wide personnel policy rules and guidelines mandatory for all subsidiaries – beyond just international assignment regulations for central staff members – is a new development for German firms. This development results from rapidly growing internationalization in the 1990s and the increasing shareholder value orientation (see Ferner and Varul, 1999, 2000; MPIfG, 2002). During the study period, in only six MNCs did managers report standardization processes in HRM. In one further case, managers were planning company-wide HR standards when the company was taken over by an Anglo-American firm just before my second visit.

Company-wide implementation of uniform HRM standards can be observed in three areas. First, the firms introduced codified general 'codes of conduct' mainly for top management, a decision linked to the 'good governance' movement on stock markets. Those codes also explained the general attitude towards legal, health, and environmental norms, etc. in host countries. However 'codes of conduct' for labor relations were rare. Up to now only one firm under investigation has concluded a company-wide 'code of conduct' for labor relations with the works councils that stipulates association rights, anti-discrimination rules, and a minimum set of labor standards which should correspond at least to the respective national standards.

Secondly, company-wide 'management by objectives' (MBO) has been introduced (or at least recommended internally as 'best practice'). In this system, first developed in the US, subordinates have to negotiate their objectives with superiors (target agreements); this is usually combined with schemes for appraisal and variable pay. In the cases studied, MBO was the most common practice introduced at the top management level of subsidiaries (managing board) by the central or business unit management. It was also found at lower managerial levels and for non-managerial employees, though in a simpler form. The staff members involved varied considerably, and the use and range of performance-related pay was less widespread, and left to the local management. Moreover, there was little evidence that German companies applied world-wide uniform policies on variable pay.

Thirdly, some MNCs were implementing company-wide 'job evaluation systems' standardizing the grading structures in all their locations following Anglo-American examples. In three cases the job evaluation system used was introduced by the consultant firm Hay; in two other cases, central management was developing its own grading structures which were nevertheless patterned after models of international consulting firms. With one exception, the new system in the Polish and Czech subsidiaries applied equally to manual, clerical, and administrative employees, while in Germany it was used only for so-called 'exempted persons' – i.e. personnel who were not covered by firms' collective agreement. The purpose of the company-wide grading systems is to increase the transparency of job remuneration and appraisal systems, which serve not only cost control, but should also facilitate the international rotation of managers and specialists.

Social integration

A 'softer' form of influencing the personnel policy in subsidiaries by the parent company involved training programs and personnel manager meetings for best-practices' sharing. The institutionalization of such procedures corresponds, again, to the commitment to company-wide HRM methods and standards; among the MNCs studied, only six of ten held international personnel manager meetings on a regular basis with the aim of best-practices' sharing. (Only one LMPE conducted regular meetings of its international personnel managers, which was more for information exchange than for developing best practices.) The frequency of the meetings was biennial or annual (usually before sessions of the European Works Councils – EWCs); in a few cases additional in-house training was held two or three times a year. Only in two companies to date were personnel managers from Czech or Polish subsidiaries involved in cross-border HRM projects; these were intended to develop a company-wide system of MBO.

Further, the six MNCs referred to established or expanded management development programs during the 1990s, and with the advent of intranet systems introduced in-house online job marketplaces for 'high potentials,' qualified executives, and specialists. To date, however, only two Polish or Czech subsidiaries of the MNCs studied were linked to such systems – i.e. had newly appointed managers in development programs or were supplying data to in-house job marketplaces. In sum, the social integration taking place in HRM in large German-based companies is currently (still) rather limited.

Administrative and output control

A form of direct control of personnel and labor policy is the centralization of decision-making. In large firms, however, centralized approval procedures exist mostly only for subsidiaries' top management (managing board). German parent-firm headquarters usually decide on the staffing of managing and supervisory boards. In only five cases were other personnel decisions centralized. One LMPE required approval of all new administrative employees, while another, having experienced abuse, made bonus payment rules in the subsidiary dependent on prior headquarters' assent. Highly centralized decision-making was found in one MNC, but only as a temporary response to a sharp decline in orders and prices, after which an acute fall in share value forced the headquarters into a company-wide cost-reduction program requiring prior approval for every new employee and collective agreement. The most rigid form of control was reported from two subsidiaries close to the German border; they were in fact little more than outsourced production departments.

More important than administrative control is output control, in which the central management checks overall cost development and performance rather than single decisions. In all the companies studied, output control rested on an annual 'business plan,' setting targets and budgets, for which subsidiary management had to get approval from the business unit or directly from the headquarters, as well as a monthly report. The extensive monthly reporting, however, usually included only a few personnel data such as headcount and overhead costs, and sometimes information on absenteeism, fluctuation rate, overtime, and training measures (Table 9.6). Within the framework of the annual business plans, however, the subsidiaries enjoyed extensive freedom of action. A major difference between LMPEs and MNCs in this respect was that LMPEs often combined impersonal reporting techniques with intensive personnel reporting

Table 9.6 Control of HRM, by headquarters

Type of MNE	Annual business plan and monthly report	Extra report to HQ personnel dept.	Required HQ approval of single personnel policy measures
LMPE	10	–	3
MNC	10	3	2
Total	**20**	**3**	**5**

though the subsidiary chief executive to the central management (sometimes in weekly meetings at headquarters); some MNCs also demanded extra reporting by the subsidiaries' personnel department.

To sum up so far, standardization of HRM is a new strategy in large German-based MNCs but is far from being an aggressively adopted one. It remains highly selective: standardization is limited to those very large and highly internationalized MNCs which try to steer their organizational cultures towards more transnationality. Even then, business units and foreign subsidiaries have various opportunities for adaptation. The formation of company-wide personnel policy rules and guidelines mandatory for all subsidiaries, and beyond just international-assignment regulations for central staff members, could not be observed in any of the LMPEs.

Standardization in HRM focuses on upper management, transparency, and comparability in the remuneration and appraisal systems, and a greater internal staff mobility. The 'best practices' adopted for the purpose are taken from the wider organizational field of companies (from consultants and competitors) rather than from typical practices of the 'country of origin.' However, there are still few explicit 'best practices' on how to deal with labor relations except the generic rule to respect the labor codes of host countries.

Management transfer

In the management literature, sending expatriates is considered the most important way of transferring rules, norms, and standards (see Edström and Galbraith, 1977; Welge, 1980; Harzing, 1999). Especially in companies of German origin, 'management transfer,' a non-formalized way of transplanting practices, plays a crucial role (see Welge, 1980; Negandhi and Welge, 1984; Harzing, 1999, p. 365). From this, a third hypothesis can be derived:

> **H3**: *Expatriates of MNCs feel stronger normative bonds to the cooperative–collective model of labor relations than managers from LMPEs. Thus they are inclined to pursue this approach when institutional constraints are fewer.*

Similar to observations in other studies (Harzing, 1999), the twenty German-based MNEs under investigation relied heavily on expatriates when they established a new foreign subsidiary. In 1999, just two LMPEs and one

Table 9.7 Parent-company expatriates in German-based subsidiaries, 1999 ($n = 20$)

Type of MNE	In top management	In directive positions:					Total
		Chief executive, chairperson	Head of finance/ controlling	Head of the technical and production department	Head of quality control and logistics	Person. manager	
LMPE	17	5	4	6	1	1	19
MNC	38	9	9	12	7	1	70
Total	**55**	**14**	**13**	**18**	**8**	**2**	**89**

MNC staffed the subsidiaries' top management exclusively with 'locals.' Among all the subsidiaries there were a total of eighty-nine expatriates; of these, fifty-five (62%) were in the highest executive positions.[7]

Here we have to distinguish between expatriates who are delegated to fill management positions full-time, and central managers occupying senior executive positions at the subsidiary and the headquarters at the same time. They commute often weekly between subsidiary and headquarters, leaving the daily business to local managers. In general, this kind of 'personal union' is common in smaller companies. Four of the LMPEs studied staffed the executive manager position of their Czech or Polish production sites in this way.

Table 9.7 indicates that beyond the subsidiary chief executive, the areas of financing, production, and technology have the most positions occupied by expatriates; in the German system the chairperson on the managing board does not act as general manager but is in charge of either finance and accounting or operations and technology.

Management transfer in production and technology is justified by market demand for high quality and technology transfer. Yet the finding also stresses the typical German production and technology focus in management policy, as various other studies in recent decades have emphasized (see Child and Kieser, 1979; Welge, 1980; Welge and Negandhi, 1984; Gergs and Schmidt, 2002). LMPEs invested less in management transfer than MNCs.

In both types of companies, the great majority of executives in top management positions were of German origin. The reason that even highly internationalized MNCs adopted an 'ethnocentric' staffing approach might simply be that the production sites were quite near to Germany. In no subsidiary was a third-country business unit involved in know-how and technology transfer, nor in administrative control. Thus it was not surprising that of the total of fifty-five expatriates in top management, only eight were not of German origin, and of these five were ECE natives, most of whom had spent a long period in Germany.

With respect to the model of labor relations, the interviews revealed that in fact more of the expatriates in MNCs displayed a cooperative attitude towards collective labor representation and unions in particular, while the managers in LMPEs often perceived unions as intruders, disturbing the good relationships

Table 9.8 Workforce representation and cross-border contacts, by company type ($n = 20$)

Type of MNE	Number of companies with:				
	Works councils in Germany	CWCs in Germany	EWCs	Union boards in host county	Regular cross-border contacts
LMPEs	10	4	–	5	–
MNCs	10	10	5	10	5
Total	**20**	**13**	**5**	**15**	**5**

with the employees based on direct individual contacts. The aversion of LMPE managers towards unions is also underlined by the fact that the German system of labor relations provides a formal separation of trade union and workplace representation (works council), giving unions no direct access to the company. In addition, many indigenous managers share this aversion for different reasons, considering unions, from past experience, to be part more of the problem than of the solution.

However, there is no clear correlation between the attitude of the managers and the type of company. Some expatriates from MNCs, too, expressed a strong critique of the unions' role and collective bargaining at any level; in the interviews they openly declared a preference for individual–flexible labor relations as being more in line with the demands of market and new management practices. Yet with respect to the formal institutions of unions and collective bargaining they showed little difference to MNCs in which the recent expatriates in charge displayed a cooperative attitude.

Institutional effects of cross-border collaboration

We have seen that the reason why the German-based MNCs studied are bound to the collective–cooperative model of labor relations lies neither in the acquisition of unionized state enterprises, nor in their HRM coordination and the individual attitude of managers (at least not individually). There is no single-factor explanation. Decisive for MNC behavior is what can be termed the 'institutional effect' of cross-border collaboration of different groups of actors, which supports the institutionalization of a collective–cooperative model in the Polish and Czech subsidiaries, and which is much less developed in LMPEs. Three groups of actors are relevant.

First, at the MNCs' home base, the system of works councils comprises many more layers than in the LMPEs, and this provides workforce representatives with time, equipment, and financial resources for activities. It is also easier for workforce representatives in foreign subsidiaries to address themselves to the central managers if there are conflicts with the local management. All MNCs studied had established *Gesamt-* or *Konzernbetriebsräte* (Central Works Councils – CWC); five provided EWCs, while just six LMPEs had a CWC, and none of them had an EWC (Table 9.8). Hence, both types of companies differ in terms of institutional 'richness' and power of workforce representation, although LMPEs and MNCs provided similar basic institutions (i.e. works councils engaged in unions and coverage by collective agreements).

Table 9.8 indicates that the more developed the system of workforce representation at company level (above plant level) is, the more likely it is that cross-border collaboration between workforce representatives will take place. EWCs have been crucial here but do not guarantee cross-border contacts with ECE subsidiaries. In some companies, Polish and Czech representatives were invited at least informally (if sporadically), but in others no such arrangement existed. In one case cross-border relationships were established by the CWC of the parent company, in which host country representatives were informally included; in another case the unions in Germany and Poland mediated the contacts. The IG Metall union is the most active German union in this respect: its offices in Munich and Berlin have cross-border partnerships with KOVO, the Czech metalworkers' union and Solidarnosc and have been trying to establish and mediate cross-border contracts since the early 1990s. By contrast, in none of the LMPEs studied was there regular cross-border contact between workforce representatives, even when the parent company and subsidiary were closer than 100 km to each other.

A second important actor reinforcing the institutionalizion of the collective–cooperation model in the MNC subsidiaries is the trade unions in host countries. Facing scarce resources and little acceptance among the indigenous private companies, host countries' trade unions focus their organizational efforts on activities with the greatest payoff. Foreign MNCs are attractive in this respect since they usually provide, also in subsidiaries, a high number of potential members. In addition, union action and industrial conflicts enjoy much more public attention in large foreign companies. Thus, for production sites of well-known MNCs, the institutional context might be less permissive than for smaller, private corporations (foreign LMPEs and indigenous companies).

The public media are a third actor channeling attention and turning conflicts into public fora affecting companies' public reputation. Such things happen only with well-known foreign MNCs. Especially for European companies with well-established collective–cooperative labor relations elsewhere, anti-union behavior in ECE appears less tolerable and can create a public scandal.

It would be too much to say that the cross-border collaboration constituted by these three groups of actors established a systematic cooperation; substantially it is communication that takes place. No actual coordination of unions' collective bargaining policy at sectoral level nor among companies' workforce representation could be observed. The most important effect of the cross-border collaboration so far has in fact been an institutional one: it supports the institutionalization of the cooperative–collective model in subsidiaries of German-based MNCs by constraining manager choice and strengthening local workforce representatives (a learning process might also occur). How the cross-border collaboration constrains managers' choice is illustrated by the following example. A long-simmering conflict between the German chief executive of a Czech production site and the union board broke out when he refused the participation – in internal talks with the union board about changes in the break-time rules – of external trade union leaders from KOVO, even though this participation was legally guaranteed. The Czech press then publicized the incident and it was promptly taken up in the German press. Simultaneously, IG Metall and CWC communicated the expatriate's decision to the top management echelons. In the first instance, this resulted in an announcement for talks between KOVO, the subsidiary, and the regional representation of the MNC in the Czech Republic. In the next step a 'code of conduct' for all Czech subsidiaries of the company was concluded stipulating basic obligations for cooperative relationships, information, and consultation procedures.

Yet the example also reveals the limits of this influence – a short time later the subsidiary was sold by the headquarters because the entire business was earning too little profit in spite of the production shifts towards the Czech republic, and some of the managers of other locations declared in interviews that they were not familiar with the agreement.

Limits of the collective–cooperative model in German-based MNCs

Even more important are the limits that the successfully institutionalized cooperative–collective model has set for itself:

First, Polish and Czech subsidiaries of German MNCs have not shown any support for the establishment of efficient institutions of collective agreements at the sectoral level. Only two subsidiaries were formal members of a trade association purporting to represent employers' interests, but they joined the association only because of internal pressures, which the local managers *de facto* combated through passivity. A single LMPE was strongly oriented to the existing framework agreement in its sector; however, this means that there, in practice, only minimum wages were paid.

Secondly, the content of plant-level cooperation is also limited. Negotiation of wages and salaries does not automatically mean that uniform pay increases for employees (workers and non-executive staff), or indeed regular pay increases at all, are agreed. In three cases, the annually negotiated increase was even limited to the determination of an additional minimum pay, which left considerable room for performance-related differentiation. The power asymmetry was also apparent in the fact that no inflation equalizer provision was guaranteed every year. The clear predominance of management resulted from, for one thing, high unemployment (above all in Poland), but also the fact that subsidiaries of MNCs in particular offered good work conditions and pay (compared to other companies in the regions where the production sites were located), so that union demands could be scaled down by employers with relative ease. In fact, the plant-level unions exerted little capacity to win wage–salary concessions above what subsidiary managers were ready to pay.

In addition, there are hardly any signs from either side of cooperation about workplace issues and plant reorganization, to which the management in Germany is bound by the codetermination rights of works councils. Czech and Polish union boards are also ill prepared for such tasks, lacking the professionalism and expert support provided by trade unions in Germany.

The unions' potential for resistance grows most visible around the issues of work hours and overtime. Attempts, for example, by German expatriates to introduce the new flexible forms of time organization used in Germany, and so to reduce the amount of paid overtime, failed in several cases, or could be established only after repeated negotiations with the union board. No resistance at all, on the other hand, was encountered from an effort to lengthen paid overtime, which often exceeded the legal upper limit, as this apparently was seen by employees, as well as union boards, as the main way to improve their incomes.

Thirdly, and finally, it should not be forgotten that only a few of the subsidiaries studied had workforce representation structures on different company levels. A presence on multiple levels is legally permitted, however, in both countries, though in different ways. Czech law, similar to German and Austrian law, demands the election of workforce representatives to supervisory boards if the subsidiary is a joint-stock company.[8] This law applied to only two subsidiaries, both acquisitions. Publicly held Polish companies must, by contrast, have employee representatives on the board only if they are privatized on the basis of the Law on Commercialization and Privatization, and if the state still owns shares in them.[9] Three subsidiaries in the study sample initially fell under this law; two of these have continued the arrangement, although in the meantime the state share of ownership is so marginal that this would not really be any longer necessary. One further subsidiary has a supervisory board without being a joint-stock company; it is however purely a surveillance instrument of headquarters. A blanket statement that German investors avoid the establishment of representation on supervisory boards if at all possible would be less than fully justified, for the findings are too heterogeneous, and the number of companies too small. It can, however, be safely maintained that board-level workforce representation in the subsidiaries studied plays only a marginal role.

Conclusion

The analyses of central control mechanism revealed that MNEs of German origin still do little about explicit coordination of their human resource practices in spite of increasing internationalization in the 1990s. Implementation of company-wide standards represents a relatively new development, limited to the most internationalized MNCs, which are driven by the idea of creating a truly international management and corporate culture. Standardization affects only a few issues relevant to labor regulation (e.g. MBO for non-executive staff members and company-wide grading structures). Beyond this, there was little sign of explicit guidelines on how to manage the relationships with workforce representatives.

What, then, makes German-based MNCs hold to the collective–cooperative model in labor relations, and not shift to an individual–flexible model, as many others in ECE have done, and why are LMPEs more inclined to use the opportunity for a shift? To explain these different patterns of behavior, the chapter referred to cross-border collaboration of different groups of actors constraining management autonomy:

- Although MNCs and LMPEs studied have similar basic institutions, MNCs provide much greater institutional infrastructure and resources for cross-border activities of workforce representatives (professional actors, time, and financial resources).
- In addition, host country unions concentrate their scarce organizational capacities on MNCs; thus plant-level union organizations are more likely in MNCs and obstructive management behavior against them gains publicity more easily.
- MNCs are under more media scrutiny in any case, a fact that helps to highlight management failures, especially when a company breaks its own rules.

While the new concepts of HRM often stem from the wider organizational field of the MNCs and show a strong Anglo-Saxon influence, in terms of labor relations there is obviously a 'country-of-origin' effect that reflects the institutional strengths of the German system of labor relations. But the course of analysis revealed that it would be a misapprehension to identify this with a direct institutional transfer from the home base towards the ECE countries. Nor is it just the unquestioned normative bond that compels individual managers to cooperate with workforce representatives and trade unions. Rather, that which can be described as a normative and institutional bond of the company as a whole constrains the actions of local managers in this respect, even when they prefer another type of labor relationship.

Yet, the institutionalization of collective–cooperative relationships in both countries has significant limits: the collective bargaining, established at plant level, is essentially a flexible, competition-oriented pact that rests exclusively on contractual voluntarism and in wage-setting. Little interest could be observed in supporting the institution-building of a sectoral level of collective bargaining that could establish industry-wide norms and standards in the host countries.

Notes

1   The research was granted by the Volkswagen Foundation.

2   The later study sample was changed slightly: firms examined in 1999 that experi-
    enced unsuccessful operations shifts were omitted and one new subsidiary was
    included; two subsidiaries in the meantime had split up and from 2002 had different
    parent firms at least partly owned by the same MNC.
3   Only with the harmonization with the *acquis communautaire* in preparation for EU
    membership at the end of the 1990s could the proponents of works councils in the Czech
    Republic legally anchor this type of body in the case that, if a company had no union
    committee at plant level, the employees would not remain without delegated represen-
    tation to pursue their information and consultation rights. But there are now codeter-
    mination rights and little legal protection for the new 'works councils.' See Seibold
    (2000, p. 152; Czech Labor Code, Nr. 65/1965 Coll., www.mpsv.cz/files/clanky/
    1126/No_65_1965.pdf; Directive on information and consultation of employees,
    December 17, 2001 (EU110206F). In Poland, political actors including unions and the
    employers' association could not agree to one model until 2006.
4   This applies to all EU candidate countries in CEE except for Slovenia and Slovakia
    (Carley, 2002).
5   The higher rate of collective agreement coverage in Poland is probably due to the
    remaining large state-owned steel, mining, and energy industries. Facing the uncer-
    tainties in data on the coverage rate in Poland, Ladó is especially hesitant in giving an
    estimation for Poland (see Ladó, 2002).
6   By law, the union board members have to be paid for by union membership fees.
7   In most of the companies a further reduction of expatriates was planned in 1999, and
    this was actually carried out during the later part of the study in 2002.
8   If the joint-stock company at the time of board election has more than fifty full-time
    employees, Czech commercial law demands that at least one-third of board members
    be from the ranks of the employees (HGB §200 [1]); if the company statutes do not
    provide otherwise, persons not employed there may also be on the board as employee
    representatives (HGB §200 [1]).
9   As in the Czech Republic these workforce representatives are elected from among the
    employees and have little to do with unions, which makes this corporate law clearly
    different from the Mitbestimmungsrecht applied to large German joint-stock com-
    panies.

Bibliography

Abo, T. (1994) *Hybrid Factory: The Japanese Production System in the United States*,
    Oxford: Oxford University Press
Altvater, E. and B. Mahnkopf (1993) *Gewerkschaften vor der europäischen
    Herausforderung: Tarifpolitik nach Mauer und Maastricht*, Münster: Westfälisches
    Dampfboot.
Bluhm, K. (2001) 'Exporting or abandoning the 'German Model'? Labor policies of
    German manufacturing firms in Central Europe,' *European Journal for Industrial
    Relations*, 7 (2), pp. 153–173.
Carley, M. (2002) *Industrial Relations in the EU Member States and Candidate Coun-
    tries*, European Foundation for Improvement of Living and Working Condi-
    tions, www.eiro.eurofound.ie/about/2002/07/featrue/tn0207104f.html, accessed on
    November 18, 2002.
Child, J. and A. Kieser (1979) 'Organization and managerial roles in British and West
    German companies: an examination of the culture thesis,' in C.J. Jammers and D.J.
    Hickson (eds), *Organization Alike and Unlike*, London: Routledge, pp. 107–138.

Czech Labor Code, Nr. 65/1965 Coll., www.mpsv.cz/files/clanky/1126/No_65_1965.pdf; Directive on information and consulation of employees, December 17, 2001 (EU110206F).

Edström, A.E. and J.R. Galbraith (1977) 'Transfer of managers as a coordination and control strategy in multinational organizations,' *Administrative Science Quarterly*, 22, pp. 248–263.

Ellingstad, M. (1997) 'The maquiladora syndrome: Central European prospects,' *Europe-Asia Studies*, 49 (1), pp. 7–21.

Ferner, A. and M.Z. Varul (1999) *The German Way: German Multinationals and Human Resource Management*, London: Anglo-German Foundation for Study of Industrial Society.

Ferner, A. and M.Z. Varul (2000) "Vanguard' subsidiaries and the diffusion of new practices: a case study of German multinationals,' *British Journal of Industrial Relations*, 38 (1), pp. 115–140.

Gergs, H.-J. and R. Schmidt (2002) 'Generationswechsel im Management ost- und westdeutscher Unternehmer: Kommt es zu einer Amerikanisierung des deutschen Managementsmodells?,' *Kölner Zeitschrift für Soziologie und Sozialpsychologie*, 54 (3), pp. 553–578.

Hall, A.P. and D. Soskice (2001) 'Introduction to varieties of capitalism,' in A.P. Hall and D. Soskice (eds), *Varieties of Capitalism: The Institutional Foundations of Comparative Advantage*, Oxford: Oxford University Press, pp. 1–70.

Harzing, A.-W. (1999) *Managing the Multinationals: An International Study of Control Mechanisms*. Cheltenham and Northampton, VT: Edward Elgar.

Janicki, M. (2000) 'Nowa Walka Klas,' *Polityka*, 47, www.polityka.onet,pl162,1012807, druk.html.

Kohl, H., W. Lecher, and H.-W. Platzer (2000) *Arbeitsbeziehungen in Ostmitteleuropa zwischen Transformation und EU-Beitritt*, Friedrich Ebert Stiftung, Abteilung Internationaler Dialog (ed.), *Internationale Politik*, H. 85.

Ladó, M. (2002) *Industrial Relations in the Candidate Countries*, European Foundation for Improvement of Living and Working Conditions, www.eiro.eurofound.ie/about/2002/07/feature/TN0207102F.html, accessed on November 18, 2002.

Meardi, G. (2002) 'The Trojan horses for the Americanization of Europe? Polish industrial relations towards the EU,' *European Journal for Industrial Relations*, 8 (1), pp. 77–99.

MPIfG (2002) *Arbeitsbeziehungen in Deutschland: Wandel durch Internationalisierung*, Cologne: Bericht über die Forschung am Max-Planck-Institut für Gesellschaftsforschung.

Myant, M. and S. Smith (1999) 'Czech trade unions in comparative perspective,' *European Journal for Industrial Relations*, 5 (3), pp. 265–285.

Negandhi, A. R. and M. Welge (1984) *Advances in International Comparative Management. A Research Annual. Beyond Theory Z: Global Rationalization Strategies of American, German and Japanese Multinational Companies*, Greenwich and London: JAI Press.

Plumberger, K. (1998) *'Rohrstock'-Kapitalismus oder soziale Partnerschaft? Anmerkungen zu Gewerkschaften, Management, Arbeitgeberverbände und Arbeitsbeziehungen in der Tschechischen Republik*, Prague: Friedrich Ebert Stiftung.

Pollert, A. (1999) 'Trade unionism in transition in Central and Eastern Europe,' *European Journal of Industrial Relations*, 5 (2), pp. 209–234.

Seibold, R. (2001) *Osterweiterung der Europäischen Union und das Arbeitsrecht der Tschechischen Republik: Eine Kompatibilitätsuntersuchung*, Frankfurt am Main: Lang

Vickerstaff, S.A. and J. E.M. Thirkell (2000) 'Instrumental rationality and European integration: transfer or avoidance of industrial relations in Central and Eastern Europe,' *European Journal for Industrial Relations*, 6 (2), pp. 237–251.

Welge, M.K. (1980) *Management in deutschen multinationalen Unternehmungen: Ergebnisse einer empirischen Untersuchung*, Stuttgart: Poeschel Verlag.
Whitley, R. (1994) 'The internationalization of firms and markets: its significance and institutional structuring,' *Organization*, 1 (1), pp. 101–124.

Anne-Marie Le Gloannec

Conclusion

An increasing body of literature has been devoted to the study of non-state actors – transnational actors (TNAs), as they are most often known. While focusing on global TNAs with national affiliates or again on TNAs which are trying to modify or challenge a particular state's policy, students of world politics have often failed to look at certain categories of non-state actors and their behavior: those which are firmly rooted in a given national framework and which entertain with 'their' state a complex and nuanced relationship which more often than not is not one of competition.

Germany is the state we have chosen to analyze, for very good reasons. As Lily Gardner Feldman points out in chapter 1, recalling Walter Brühl's statement, Germany surpasses most other nations in its degree of transnational (and multilateral) connections. In his seminal work on TNAs, Thomas Risse had actually identified two key variables, as Charlie Jeffery reminds us in chapter 4: domestic structures, with influential transnational networks likely to be built out of countries where the state is institutionally fragmented alongside a well-organized civil society; and the degree of internationalization. Transnational networks were likely to exert higher levels of influence in fields that exhibited a high degree of international institutionalization. Peter Katzenstein underlined the fragmented nature of the German state and the centralization of its society, and this particular complexion favors the development of a variety of non-state actors. Moreover Germany is enmeshed in a network of organizations and institutions, the EU first and foremost, like most other European states – or even more than other European states, at least from the point of view of ideas, norms, and behaviors. To this extent, Germany and German TNAs offer an interesting case – which does not necessarily qualify as an example but still provides the analyst with useful perspectives on TNAs' relations to the state in which they are rooted, the host country, and the relations between both states and societies.

Germany is rich indeed in non-state actors, some of which are particularly characteristic of the country. Though some non-state actors – such as minorities, enterprises, or lobbies – exist in other countries, others hardly do – i.e. the Länder (due to the fact that Germany is a federal state) and political foundations. A number of contributors to this volume delve into the nature, aim, and role of German political foundations in Latin America or Central and Eastern Europe. Soledad Loaeza in chapter 2 differentiates political foundations from think-tanks – though political foundations also play the role of think-tanks, providing the party they are close to with political analyses. Yet the goal of political foundations is institution-building, Loaeza shrewdly remarks, and they engage in networking with local actors, targeting economic, academic and political elites, while think-tanks have more restricted contacts and human right organizations a broader public. Most of all, political foundations entertain a symbiotic relationship with the political party to which they are close (even with their state), and they perform a particular function in the states and societies where they are physically present. The closest they might be compared to are American political foundations as well as NGOs, often American in origin, working in foreign countries where they promote democracy and human rights.

As Lily Gardner Feldman notes in chapter 1, previous works on TNAs do not take into account the physical presence of non-state actors on the territory of another country – be it minorities, enterprises, or political foundations. Yet this physical presence allows for specific actions that are described in this volume as having several components. At face value, this involves collecting information, agenda-setting, providing ideological references as well as material and moral resources, building contact networks and durable relations through the work of political foundations and similar institutions, outsourcing production, a 'parallel foreign policy' of the Länder, etc. In so doing, non-state actors act in different ways in relation to the state in which they are embedded. In chapter 1, Gardner Feldman distinguishes between four roles that non-state actors may perform: they may compete with their state as competitors, but they may also work with it as catalysts, complements, or conduits. Catalysts stimulate official activity, complements act in parallel to it, while conduits serve as official cover while the government plays a hidden role. These distinctions prove to be fruitful. The Länder that Tanja Börzel and Charlie Jeffery study in chapter 5 and 6 do support state policy but also decisively 'shape the parameters within which social interaction takes place in Europe' (see Jeffery's chapter 6 in this book). As to private economic actors, they certainly circumvent the state – such as in the case of the nuclear industry – but in so doing they influence governmental policy and together with other economic agents, such as the SMEs which invested in CEEC before enlargement, they may have acted as catalysts of governmental policy, supporting early EU enlargement. The political foundations studied by Loaeza in chapter 2 and Dorota Dakowska and Elsa Tulmets in chapter 3 also serve as complements – in Mexico, in particular, where they certainly have been more effective in shaping Mexican policies than a foreign government would have been; but they are not catalysts though they may be looked upon as conduits, channeling information and building networks which sustain government policy. The actions of minorities and local authorities that Gilles Lepesant analyzes in chapter 4 often compete with state policy and undermine it: on the whole, the state is more of a catalyst or a prime mover while local actors have, more often than not, tried to prevent transborder cooperation.

Beyond these various modes of action, non-state actors are the conduits or the vehicles of the *transfers* that Dakowska and Tulmets in chapter 3, echoed by Charlie Jeffery in chapter 6, describe as either the transfer of 'hard' norms, the so-called 'German model' that Peter Eichhorn defines as three-pronged – solidarity, collectivity, and plurality, or legal requirements such as the rule of the Stability Pact – or again the transfer of 'soft' norms, ideas, and beliefs, styles, a collective understanding of what is an appropriate way of doing things . . . The next question, of course, is: what accrues from this transfer, what do both parties gain from it? The receiver obtains information, learns practices, and borrows ideas, beliefs, norms, and institutions in the broader sense of the word. As Loaeza analyzes it in chapter 2, the KAS helped to modernize the party program and the identity of the PAN in the context of a weakened authoritarian state and a greater openness to TNAs. Or as Lepesant shows in chapter 4, the rules that used to apply to the eastern borders of Germany are progressively being taken over by the Poles and Ukrainians managing the eastern border of Poland. Dakowska and Tulmets show in chapter 3 that both content and institutional practice are being transferred: the specificity of German expertise is to be sought both in structural features of assistance (the relationship between public and private actors) and in its ideal components (the diffusion of elements of German political culture such as the social market economy and the experience of unification). Yet none of these transfers under scrutiny point to an isomorphic replication of German institutions. What is taking place is a phenomenon of 'hybridization,' well described by those studying transfers. Here *adoption* means *adaptation*.

At this point, one may wonder whether a German model is being exported. Emphasis needs to be placed on both 'German' and 'model': is what is being exported German, or European, or international? And is it a model that is being exported? The very notion of 'hybridization,' of adoption through adaptation points at the lack of a model. It is not a model which can be transplanted as whole; it is more bits and pieces of 'hard' or 'soft' norms which are being adapted to various situations. Are these bits and pieces of institutional, regulatory and normative structure, then, still specifically German? As Loaeza puts it in chapter 2, 'what is international and what is specifically German?'. Dakowska and Tulmets in chapter 3 categorically state that 'there are no German solutions anymore, there are European solutions,' while Jeffery in chapter 6 makes the opposite claim – namely that there is a lot of Germany in Europe: 'the sheer centrality of Germany to international relations in Europe and the sheer intensity of its transnational networks indeed point to a Europe suffused increasingly by

German norms and rules (p. 142).' By implanting bits and pieces of institutional, regulatory, and normative structures, Germany pervades Europe. Bluhm in chapter 9, however, points to a paradox: the most internationalized firms, the large MNCs, appear to be at the same time the most tightly embedded in the German institutional system of labor relations. In other words, the more internationalized, the more German . . .

Ideological consensus and cohesion may account for this, or again the close relationship which a number of non-state actors entertain with the German state. Not all TNAs seek to challenge their state, as was previously often assumed. Certainly they may challenge the central state; as Lepesant recalls in chapter 4, local actors and the states – in this case, Poland and Ukraine – have often been at loggerheads and troubles in borderlands often interfered with inter-state relations. Or, again, the state may end the relations they entertained with certain non-state actors. Sabine Saurugger in chapter 7 thus states that 'if the relationship is characterized by frequent interaction, high cohesion, and shared ideology, non-state actors frequently figure as experts in their specific policy field and thus influence state actors' views on a national and international level. If this relationship deteriorates, non-state actors will seek to strengthen their transnational ties' (p. 157). In that case, the Red–Green government rescinded its privileged partnership with the nuclear lobby as it ceased to rely on nuclear energy. Gardner Feldman in chapter 1 also underlines the fact that some non-state actors may oppose their state's policy. But protest is certainly not the only prevailing pattern: non-state actors may act as catalysts, complements, and conduits, provoking their own government to act, shaping their behavior and acting as surrogates. 'As catalyst, conduit, or competitor, it is the TNA that dictates the terms of reference, with the German government performing in a more reactive mode. When TNAs are complements, the government sets the overall tone. The role of catalyst or competitor involves relations of tension with the government, whereas activity as complement or conduit by TNAs suggests harmonious relations' (p. 17). The Länder, as non state-actors or as non-centralized state actors, do not necessarily act in opposition to the central government, as is sometimes assumed. In agreement with other contributors in this volume, Börzel in chapter 5 asserts that the transnational mobilization of Länder does not necessarily mean circumventing or bypassing the national-state level: 'whether non-state actors use their transnational relations with European policy-makers 'against' their national governments depends on the domestic institutional culture' (p. 111). Whereas Gardner Feldman in chapter 1 considers that some TNAs may supplement the state, Börzel in chapter 5 sees a complement rather than a supplement in the examples she studies – and so does Jeffery in chapter 6.

Considering the intricate pattern of relations between the state and non-state actors, the question of what is accruing to the state in which the non-state actors are embedded begs further examination. Some authors resort to similar formulation: Fabienne Boudier-Bensebaa in chapter 8 looks at German firms in Central Europe as having anticipated enlargement, as do Dakowska and Tulmets in chapter 3. To go one step further, some non-state actors are seen as political 'facilitators,' permitting the establishment of trust between two countries. Loaeza thus stresses that 'Political foundations are perceived as . . . political 'facilitators' that are not seeking immediate economic or political gains . . . They have built trust . . . Their link to the German state lends them authority and legitimacy in the region.' The authors attempt to define the political returns that Germany may obtain from its non-state actors. Jeffery in chapter 6 goes as far as to think that institutional replication fosters *systemic empowerment*, a concept borrowed from Simon Bulmer, though this has been challenged in the past. The advantages that accrue to Germany may actually be more subtle. Dakowska and Tulmets in chapter 3 understand that with enlargement German decision-makers cease to be the privileged interlocutors of central European partners. Yet discussion habits and communication channels last, and political credit is being accumulated. And political credit may indeed be the most important gain, the most important resource for non-state actors in Germany, a resource on which the country may draw if official foreign policy or bilateral relations undergo a period of apnoea.